Paternalism and Protest

Contributions in Economics and Economic History

Paternalism and Protest

Southern Cotton Mill Workers and Organized Labor, 1875–1905

Melton Alonza McLaurin

CONTRIBUTIONS IN
ECONOMICS AND ECONOMIC HISTORY
NUMBER 3

A Negro Universities Press Publication

*Greenwood Publishing Corporation
Westport, Connecticut*

Library of Congress Catalog Card Number: 70-111261
SBN:8371-4662-3

A Negro Universities Press Publication
Greenwood Publishing Corporation
51 Riverside Avenue, Westport, Connecticut 06880

Printed in the United States of America

*This book is dedicated
to my grandmother and great-aunt,
who gave me my appreciation of history;
to my parents, who made possible my education;
and to my wife, who understood and tolerated
a husband engaged in research and writing.*

Contents

List of Tables

Acknowledgments

Grateful acknowledgment is made to Dr. Tom E. Terrill, University of South Carolina, and Dr. Gustavus G. Williamson, Jr., Virginia Polytechnic Institute, whose encouragement and constructive suggestions contributed significantly to the completion of this study. Special thanks are also due Mr. Moreau Chambers, Department of Archives and Manuscripts, Catholic University Library, and Mrs. Mary E. Goolsby, Research Assistant, McKissick Library, University of South Carolina, for their wonderful cooperation. Sincere appreciation is extended to the staffs of the following institutions: Caroliniana Library, University of South Carolina; Southern Historical Collection and North Carolina Room, University of North Carolina Library; Duke University Library; North Carolina State Department of Archives and History; Alabama Room, University of Alabama Library; and the management of Graniteville Manufacturing Company and South Carolina Electric and Gas Company. Additionally, the financial assistance granted by the University of South Alabama's Research Committee, which made possible much of the research on the Knights of Labor, is gratefully acknowledged.

Introduction

The image of the Southern cotton textile worker as a docile and tractable laborer, an image which still clings to Southern mill hands, was created and carefully cultivated by promoters of the New South, by state government agencies, and by mill owners and mill presidents of the era from 1875 to 1905—a quarter of a century during which the South's cotton textile industry developed and grew. Labor historians also share some responsibility for the durability of the docile mill hand image. The Southern operatives' agrarian origins, the hours they labored, the wages they received, and the paternalism of the mill villages in which they lived have received considerable attention from scholars and interested observers since the late 1890s. However, these historians have largely neglected detailed study of the Southern cotton mill workers' organizational activities prior to World War I and, thus, have inadvertently perpetuated an inaccurate portrait.[1]

Aside from the inaccurate image of the Southern cotton mill laborer as docile, there is the belief that organized labor made no serious attempt to organize the South's mill operatives until well into the twentieth century. This interpretation of the past was also carefully nourished by the era's mill owners and their spokesmen, and historians writing before 1930 have generally accepted this thesis. A good example of this attitude is found in August Kohn's study of South Carolina mills, written just after the turn of the century. Kohn blithely ignored union activity in the mills of the Columbia area, including a major strike in 1901.[2] In his survey of the industrial development of the New South, Philip A. Bruce mentioned the Augusta, Georgia, strike of 1902, but asserted that no serious labor disputes occurred in either North Carolina or South Carolina.[3] Norman J. Ware failed to mention the activities of the Noble Order of the Knights of Labor in Southern textiles in his study of the nineteenth-century labor movement.[4] In *The Rise of Cotton Mills in the South,* Broadus Mitchell suggested that "the first concerted union attention to the South as an unorganized field" came only after World War I.[5]

In the only major study of Southern textile unionism, *Textile Unionism and the South,* George Sinclair Mitchell, Broadus' brother, began to draw the vague outlines of early union activity. His interest in the subject, however, had been sparked by the renewal of labor-management struggles during World War I and the late 1920s. As a result, Mitchell devoted scant attention to and seriously underestimated the pervasiveness of textile unions in the South prior to these events. In their "feeble attempt to organize the Southern mills," the Knights of Labor made no effort "to unionize the mill people as a separate group," and with the demise of the Knights, "agitation disappeared completely" during the 1890s. He reported the growth of the National Union of Textile Workers (NUTW) near the turn of the century, but was in error as to both the time and manner of the union's establishment in the South. He was also unaware of the union politics involved in the development of Southern locals.[6]

Because G. S. Mitchell's work is considered to be a basic

study of Southern textile unionism, its inaccurate account of early labor organization in the cotton mills is accepted, with slight revisions, by later historians. Selig Perlman and Philip Taft relied almost completely on the Mitchell account in *Labor Movements*.[7] This same tendency is seen in *Labor and Textiles* by Robert Dunn and Jack Hardy. Like Mitchell's work, *Labor and Textiles* was primarily concerned with the operatives of the post–World War I era.[8] In *The Cotton Mill Worker,* which also concentrates heavily on events after 1914, Herbert J. Lahne continues to rely on Mitchell. He did engage in additional primary research, which resulted in a more accurate presentation of the role of the Knights of Labor in Southern mills. Yet, he failed to comment on the significance of this organization in shaping the resistance methods later used by mill management to combat unionism. Unfortunately, he also accepted Mitchell's basic account of the NUTW, although he did add some very pertinent information concerning the strength of that union.[9]

In *Origins of the New South,* C. Vann Woodward adopted Mitchell's discussion of the development of the NUTW in the South, while contributing additional insights into the relationships between the NUTW and the American Federation of Labor (AFL). He explicitly questioned the validity of the thesis concerning the docility of Southern labor in view of the activity of the Knights and the NUTW in Southern mills and noted the need for further, more detailed studies of organized labor in the South.[10] F. Ray Marshall's recent study of Southern labor, which devoted only one chapter to the years prior to 1932, ignored the efforts of the Knights in the region's mills. Marshall accepted Mitchell's account of the NUTW, although he did note that interest in organization among operatives began some two years before the NUTW came South.[11] In short, everyone writing on the Southern mill operatives since the publication of Mitchell's *Textile Unionism* has relied heavily on that work, especially on its description of the role of the NUTW in the

South. Thus, in the absence of further studies based on primary material, Mitchell's errors have been perpetuated.

Actually, neither the Southern cotton mill workers' response to unionism nor organized labor's attempts to unionize the workers before 1905 were negligible. Indeed, considering the obstacles to labor organization in the Southern cotton mills—intransigent management, the constant economic and social threat of the Negro laborer to the operative, the operative's illiteracy, his lack of an industrial tradition, and his inclination to accept the traditional Southern agrarian values, class structure, and thought patterns—it is remarkable that any response to unionism developed among the South's mill hands in the early stages of the industry's development. Yet even before the coming of the Knights of Labor, in isolated cases, mill hands had voiced their dissatisfaction with existing conditions by engaging in strikes. And though the efforts of the Knights among the Southern mill hands were secondary to that organization's attempt to organize the artisan laborer and the farmer, they were far from feeble. By introducing the concept of organized labor to the Southern mill operative and establishing textile unions throughout the Piedmont of North Carolina, South Carolina, and Georgia, the Knights struck hard at the concept of the docile, anti-union Southern mill hand and, for the first time, caused mill management to fear the economic power of their operatives, even to talk of socialistic revolution. The Knights' efforts proved that the Southern mill hand, especially in urban areas, would respond to an organization which he felt would improve his condition. Reacting to this threat, management forged the weapons with which it successfully resisted unionization until well into the twentieth century.

The weapons which management employed against the Knights—the lockout, the blacklist, eviction, the threat of employing Negro labor, the blatant intimidation—were used again against the NUTW and its successor, the United Textile Workers of America (UTWA). The NUTW–UTWA, in the years from 1896 to 1905, provided management with an even stronger challenge than the Knights. With better financing, professional organizers, financial aid from the AFL, and second-generation operatives to organize, these unions made a serious effort to penetrate the mills of the Southern Piedmont. Concentrating on the larger mills in the South's urban and traditional textile centers, the NUTW established locals throughout the South from Virginia to Alabama. Again, management rose to the challenge and defeated the unionization drive, but only after crushing bitterly fought strikes in four of the leading textile states of the South. Thus, all attempts to organize Southern mill hands prior to 1905 eventually failed. Despite their organizational efforts, the operatives never gained enough solidarity within their own ranks or support from the public to challenge management successfully. Management's economic, political, and social power simply overwhelmed the organized operatives and cowed those who sympathized with them. Yet significant attempts to organize were made, eliciting substantial responses from the Southern cotton mill worker. It is the history of those attempts and responses, their initial successes and eventual failures, and management's reactions to them, heretofore largely ignored by historians, with which this study is primarily concerned.

The simple narrative history of the involvement of the Knights and the NUTW with Southern mill operatives does not reveal the entire story, however. For this reason, an attempt is also made to examine the thought patterns of both owner and operative to determine the influence of the South on them and, in turn, to determine their influence on both the textile labor movement and the South. In many respects, the history of the unions in the mills is actually a history of the New South, since the cotton mill brought about Southern industrialization. The cotton manufacturer, more than any other figure, personified the South's acceptance of a modern mechanized society. The operative, on the other hand, symbolized the reluctance of the South to repudiate its agrarian tradition, although that tradition clearly had been outmoded in a society dedicated to the industrial concept of material progress. Forced into the mills by economic necessity, the operative slowly began to adjust to industrialization and to attempt to improve his newly acquired position. By playing on the operative's old fear of the Negro, exploiting his xenophobia, and using his individualism while ruthlessly applying the concepts of Social Darwinism through the paternalistic mill village system, management defeated all such attempts.

Thus, in the New South as in the Old South, the worker that produced its wealth had no voice in the determination of its distribution. Shackled by ignorance, poverty, and racial prejudice and faced with laissez-faire economic dogma as rigid as any slave code, the operatives were no match for the aristocracy of the New South.

Paternalism and Protest

1

The Rise of the
Southern Textile Industry

The surge of industrial development after 1880 that created the
modern textile industry in the South changed both the face of
the land and the life pattern of much of the white population
of the Piedmont. In towns, villages, and open fields, cotton mills
sprang up in a traditionally agricultural land until it became
impossible for one to escape the physical evidence of the mills'
dominance of the area—"by the time the water tower of one
[mill] has disappeared over one's shoulder, another has loomed
up in the foreground."[1] Two- or three-storied, red brick, with
rows of multi-paned windows and, often, towers or turrets
placed either at each end or squarely in the middle of the building, the factory buildings left little doubt that the industrial
revolution had finally come to the South. The mills' constantly
expanding looms and spindles demanded an ever-increasing
labor force. Like some gigantic, insatiable being, the mushroom-
ing cotton mills of the South lured through their gates thousands
from their cotton and corn farms in the area's red clay soils.
Yeoman farmers, tenants, and poor whites all came to the mills.

Simple, independent, poor, uneducated, and culturally homogeneous, the people of the Piedmont willingly abandoned the land in droves to seek the more affluent life which the mills promised, and often delivered.

Although the rise of the Southern cotton textile industry did not begin to attract much national attention until the year 1880, the dramatic growth of the industry after that date had firm foundations in the antebellum and immediate post–Civil War years. In each of the three leading Southern cotton textile states, North Carolina, South Carolina, and Georgia, many antebellum factories were directly linked with the cotton industry's period of rapid growth in the 1880s and 1890s. The achievements of three men who created textile fortunes in their respective states and whose careers spanned the antebellum and postwar years clearly demonstrate these connections.

Two of these three early cotton textile entrepreneurs, one a Southerner and the other a Yankee, began their careers in the 1830s, ironically the decade in which the Old South irrevocably cast its lot with the political economy of slavery. George Parker Swift, a Boston dry goods merchant who emigrated to Georgia in 1832, established a small cotton mill at Waymanville soon after his arrival. Primarily by catering to the local market, the factory prospered until the Civil War, after which Swift moved to Columbus. There, with his sons and son-in-law, he built a textile fortune, beginning with the founding of Muscogee Mills in 1869.[2] Edwin Michael Holt, another founder of a textile dynasty and a native of North Carolina, built his first mill in that state in Alamance County in 1837. During the 1850s, his mills were manufacturing plaid goods which gained acceptance in the national market under the name of "Alamance Plaids." After the war, Holt's sons expanded their father's mills into one of the South's largest textile empires, making Alamance County one of the nation's leading cotton manufacturing centers.[3]

Towering above all other early cotton manufacturers of the

South was William Gregg, who, more than any other, directly influenced the development of the postwar industry. Undoubtedly, the antebellum South's preeminent spokesman for industrialization, Gregg, after 1840, spent much of his time urging the agrarian South to turn to the manufacture of cotton. Gregg had been connected with the Southern textile industry from boyhood when he aided an uncle in an unsuccessful attempt to establish a cotton factory in Georgia before the War of 1812. After his uncle abandoned the project, Gregg moved to South Carolina and became a jewelry merchant, establishing a thriving business in Columbia and Charleston during the 1820s and 1830s. By 1837, he had accumulated enough capital to invest in a cotton mill at Vaucluse, South Carolina. When the factory was threatened by bankruptcy proceedings in the summer of the same year, Gregg took personal control and, in eight months, liquidated the mill's $6,000 deficit and turned the company into a profitable concern. His experience at Vaucluse convinced him of the feasibility of establishing cotton factories in the South. By applying liberal amounts of enthusiasm and persuasiveness, Gregg in 1845 convinced the South Carolina legislature to charter what was to become the South's best-known antebellum cotton mill, the Graniteville Manufacturing Company. From that time until his death in 1867, the names of Gregg and Graniteville were synonymous.[4] Using local cotton and local white labor and selling through several Charleston commission merchants, he created a profitable concern that was able to compete in the national market with the mills of New England. After Gregg's death, his treasurer, H. H. Hickman of Augusta, Georgia, succeeded him as president. Hickman was extremely successful in the 1870s, continually expanding the company and making it the major industry of South Carolina's Horse Creek Valley cotton textile manufacturing complex.[5]

While the endeavors of such men as Swift, Holt, and Gregg established significant precedents, they failed to turn the antebellum South from its fascination with the cotton plantation.

These men were pioneers in the use of both native white labor and water power provided by the streams of the Piedmont. They also proved that Southern textile manufacturers could make considerable profits. But the growth of the cotton textile industry proved to be painfully slow. Gregg's plea for Southern industrialization went almost unheeded. Most of the South's antebellum mills remained small spinning establishments, restricted to a limited local market and employing only a handful of operatives. Capital investments in the industry were minute. Georgia outstripped by far her sister states, but the growth of her mills was less than spectacular, as Table 1 demonstrates.

Although the charge that "Union raiders destroyed every mill or factory they could possibly reach" was unfounded, the mills of the South failed to escape completely the destruction caused by the Civil War.[6] Among the Georgia factories destroyed were the Columbus mills which were burned along with 60,000 bales of cotton.[7] In North Carolina, five mills were burned at Fayetteville, as were mills at Rocky Mount and in Caldwell County.[8] Mills escaping destruction, such as Graniteville, had dilapidated machinery, because the extremely effective Union blockade had made it impossible to obtain replacements during the war. Many of the smaller factories were forced to close in the economic chaos that followed the war; others were sold at auction and reorganized.[9] The census figures of 1870 starkly revealed the severity of the blow dealt the cotton mills of the South by the war. After five years of rebuilding, the South had only slightly more spindles and fewer looms than it possessed in 1860.[10] Yet, in an area almost devoid of capital, in a state of economic turmoil, and engrossed in a powerful social struggle, this represented a rapid recuperation, which augured well for the future of the Southern cotton textile industry.

The decade from 1870 to 1880 saw a quickening of mill development, definitely presaging the South's highly successful cotton mill campaign of 1880–1900. During the decade, Georgia continued to set the pace for the South. Her spindles

Table 1

Growth of the Southern Cotton Industry, 1840–1860

State	Year	Mills	Dollars Capital	Average No. Workers	Spindles	Looms
N.C.	1860	39	1,272,750	1,755	41,884	761
	1850	28	1,058,800	1,619	—	—
	1840	25	995,300	1,219	47,934	—
S.C.	1860	17	801,825	891	30,890	525
	1850	18	857,200	1,019	—	—
	1840	15	617,450	570	16,355	—
Ga.	1860	33	2,126,103	2,813	85,186	2,041
	1850	35	1,736,156	2,272	—	—
	1840	19	573,835	779	42,589	—

Source: U.S. Bureau of the Census, *Twelfth Census of the United States: 1900. Manufacturing*, vol. 9, *Special Reports on Selected Industries* (Washington, D. C.: Government Printing Office, 1902), 56–57 (hereafter cited as *U.S. Census, 1900, Manufacturing*).

increased from 85,602 to 198,656; her looms from 1,887 to
4,483; her workers from 2,846 to 6,349; and her capital investments from $3,433,265 to $6,348,657. North Carolina's
increases were equally dramatic, as she continued to hold second place in the South. Her capital investments rose from
$1,030,900 to $2,855,800; her spindles from 39,897 to 92,-
383; her looms from 618 to 1,770; and her work force from
1,453 to 3,343. South Carolina's statistics revealed the same
upward trend, her spindles increasing from 85,602 to 198,656;
her looms from 745 to 1,676; her operatives from 1,123 to
2,053; and her invested capital from $1,337,000 to $2,776,100.
The total number of establishments in the three states rose
from 79 to 101, with Georgia and North Carolina showing the
largest increases as South Carolina began a marked tendency
to develop larger, though less numerous, mills.[11]

Southern mills earned lucrative profits during the 1870s, as
is amply demonstrated by the experience of cotton manufacturers in South Carolina. Henry P. Hammett, whose Piedmont
factory began operating in 1876, was convinced by 1880 that
any "well-managed" mill should yield a return of from 15 percent to 20 percent on invested capital.[12] The Reedy River Mill
in 1879 paid 8 percent on capital investments of $47,000, in-
vested $2,000 in new machinery, and put another $2,000 in
reserves. The Red Bank Manufacturing Company in the same
year paid 12 percent dividends while investing heavily in new
spinning machinery. Dexter Edgar Converse, a Vermont native
who established the Glendale factory in 1866, also reported
"handsome profits," as did numerous others.[13] Few, however,
could match the record of H. H. Hickman, who took control of
the Graniteville mills in 1867 when that firm was producing
240,000 yards of goods per fortnight. Early in 1880, Hickman
revealed his company's fantastic growth:

From the time I took charge up to the present I have spent on
this mill [Graniteville] and the property on this place $200,000 at

least. I have doubled the production of the mill. I purchased 1,160 shares of stock, for which I paid $150,000, and cancelled it, reducing the capital stock to $600,000 from $716,000. I have built the Vaucluse property out of the earnings of the Graniteville Mill. That property is worth $350,000, and during all this time, in addition to these outlays, I have paid dividends averaging 9½ per cent on the capital stock.[14]

Such generous returns on invested capital naturally enticed an increasing number of investors into the field, and, building upon the foundations laid in the immediate postwar years, the South developed a modern textile industry between the years 1880 and 1900. By 1900 the South had captured the dominant position from New England in the manufacture of coarse goods for both the domestic and foreign markets, and was beginning to challenge seriously New England manufacturers in the production of fine yarns.[15] Again, the 1900 census figures (Table 2) mutely, but cogently, attest to the industry's incredible growth in the South during these two decades.

This growth continued after the turn of the century. From 1900 to 1905, spindles in the South's three leading textile states increased from 3,382,126 to 6,060,615. The number of looms in the South rose from 110,015 to 179,752 in the same five-year span, with by far the greatest percentage of the increase occurring in Georgia and the Carolinas. During this period, the Southern textile firms continued to improve the quality as well as the quantity of their products and to place additional emphasis on the production of woven cloth.[16]

A striking feature of this development was the dominance of the Carolinas during the 1890s. In each of the Carolinas, however, the industry developed in a particular pattern. In North Carolina, the mills continued to be rural and small, as is indicated by the large number of factories in the state by 1900, although large establishments also did become more numerous. But in South Carolina the construction of large cotton factories

Table 2
Growth of the Southern Cotton Industry, 1880–1900

State	Year	Mills	Dollars Capital	Average No. Workers	Spindles	Looms
N.C.	1900	177	33,011,516	30,273	1,133,432	25,469
	1890	91	10,775,134	8,515	337,786	7,254
	1880	49	2,855,800	3,343	92,385	1,790
S.C.	1900	80	39,258,946	30,201	1,431,349	42,663
	1890	84	11,141,833	8,071	332,784	8,546
	1880	14	2,776,100	2,053	82,334	1,676
Ga.	1900	68	24,222,169	18,348	817,345	19,398
	1890	53	17,664,675	10,314	444,452	10,459
	1880	40	6,348,657	6,349	198,656	4,493

Source: U.S. Census, 1900, Manufacturing, 56–57.

during the decade gave to that state the leadership in the Southern textile industry. Georgia also showed a tendency to build large mills and an even more marked inclination to cluster these large mills in urban areas such as Columbus, Atlanta, and Augusta. Among the growing ranks of manufacturers who, after 1880, began to build larger, more modern mills were such giants of the industry as Robert L. McCaughrin, John Henry Montgomery, Ellison Adger Smyth, James L. Orr, Jr., and W. B. Smith Whaley of South Carolina; Moses and Caesar Cone, Daniel A. Tompkins, and William Allen Erwin of North Carolina; and Gunby Jordan, Eugene and James Verdery, Stuart Phinizy, and Jacob Elsas of Georgia.

Earlier historians have portrayed the rise of the Southern cotton mills as an epic folk movement.[17] After the rigors of Reconstruction were over and General Winfield Hancock's defeat in 1880 had proven politics an unlikely answer to the South's problems, all classes allegedly responded en masse to the call to industrialize. Southerners naturally turned to the manufacture of raw cotton, their most abundant resource, thus bringing the cotton mill to the cotton field. In this interpretation, the entrepreneurs appeared as benevolent leaders who entered into cotton manufacturing for the sake of the prosperity of their communities. The people called them forth to lead the South's drive to rebuild its economy along industrial lines. Profits were only secondary. Indeed some students of the South have maintained that "any profit that might accrue to the originators of the mill was but incidental; the main thing was the salvation of the decaying community, and especially the poor whites."[18] Such an interpretation, quite naturally, reflects the early entrepreneurs' view of themselves. Much of the supporting evidence for this belief actually comes from interviews with mill presidents and other management personnel.[19] The operatives who came to the mills also probably held this view, at least in part; certainly, they were constantly reminded of it by their employers.[20]

Although the folk movement interpretation holds a considerable amount of truth, it greatly underestimates the complexity of the economic factors that triggered the development of the South's textile industry. Acknowledging the fact that the rise of the mills was partially a social movement, later historians have correctly stressed such economic causal factors as the development of adequate Southern railway systems to provide national markets, the desire of the lowland commercial class to find new outlets for capital investments, and the need to create a large white laboring class as a safeguard against the political possibilities of the large Negro population.[21] The industry's steady expansion and high profits during the 1870s were influential not only in obtaining capital from coastal Southern cities such as Charleston, but in persuading Northern commission merchants and textile machinery manufacturers to invest as well, although Northern firms did not begin to move South until later, toward the turn of the century. Machinery manufacturers often extended long credits and accepted stock for payment, usually selling such shares back to the mill promoters as soon as they were financially stable.[22]

Still other factors contributed significantly to the development of the industry. The federal government's dominant high tariff policy, which was supported by some Southern textile spokesmen, especially near the turn of the century, protected the industry from European competition in the domestic market.[23] Asia's limitless market for coarse cotton goods proved to be a bonanza in the 1890s, furnishing a market for the products of the South's rapidly proliferating mills. It was this trade that enabled the South's mills to weather the depressions of the 1890s more easily than did their Northern competitors. Thus, Southern manufacturers became ardent champions of the open door policy and expansion into the Far East.[24] Declining prices of textile machinery after 1880, the development of hydroelectric power near the turn of the century, and an increase of native capital from Southern industrialists in other fields, such as the Dukes of the American Tobacco Company, all combined to accelerate the industry's growth.[25]

One factor never overlooked by historians of the industry, although emphasized to varying degrees, is the availability of cheap labor. Melvin T. Copeland, a knowledgeable contemporary observer, concluded that "the corner stone of the structure [of southern cotton manufacturing] has been the supply of cheap and tractable labor."[26] That judgement adequately reflected the thought of mill men during the era and has been confirmed by later scholars.[27] During the two decades following 1880, farm tenancy and technology combined to allow the manufacturer to utilize to the fullest the seemingly inexhaustible supply of cheap, white labor in the Southern Piedmont.

Tenancy came to the Piedmont in the form of the crop-lien system as a result of the Civil War. Faced with a serious shortage of cash, the Piedmont farmer turned to the small town banker and merchant for loans or for credit for supplies. Since cotton was still king in the Southern mind, merchants and bankers advanced money only on the promise to plant cotton, and to guarantee their investment, demanded a lien on the crop. The natural results of such a system were continually increasing cotton crops and continually falling cotton prices. Unable to break this cycle, the farmer soon became so indebted that foreclosure became inevitable, and farm after farm passed over to the lien holder. The yeoman farmer slipped into tenancy, cultivating on shares land that had once been his own. As early as 1880, in five South Carolina Piedmont counties, the number of crop liens equaled the number of farming units. Throughout the South, this situation worsened with each decade.[28] Thus, the people of the Piedmont, chained to the treadmill of the crop-lien system, welcomed the avenue of escape provided by the mills.

Three major technological advances allowed this vast pool of willing, but unskilled and illiterate laborers to be tapped as never before. The first was the invention in 1871 of the Sawyer ring spindle, and the invention of the Rabbeth double spinning ring spindle soon afterward. The ring spindle doubled the spinning speeds of the machinery to 10,000 revolutions per minute. The device also permitted simultaneous spinning and winding, whereas, in the old process of mule spinning, these two operations were alternated.[29] The ring spindle also vastly reduced the skills needed by spinners, whose major task then became merely that of piecing broken threads, a task easily performed by women and young girls. Also, the invention allowed a single operative to man an increased number of "sides" of spindles. Thus, one unskilled operative could produce more yarn than a more skilled mule spinner.[30] The second advance—the development of the humidifier and temperature regulators—permitted the controlling of the moisture content of the air and reduced the breakage of the yarn that would have otherwise occurred on such high-speed spindles.

The third major technological advance was the invention of the automatic loom after 1880. By allowing the operative to produce much longer cuts of cloth in the same amount of time, for which the operative received an adjusted piece wage, keeping his salary at previous levels, the automatic loom greatly reduced the per unit cost of production.[31] Coupled with the ring spindle and humidifier, the automatic loom placed an even greater premium on unskilled labor, although weavers continued to be among the most skilled of the Southern operatives.[32] Thus, the Southern manufacturer was able to combine the technological advances within the industry with the immense supply of unskilled labor in the Piedmont, resulting in considerable production-cost advantages for the South.[33] As one student of the industrial South has observed, "unless the South was to shut its eyes to the reality of the times and settle into permanent stagnation, the development of manufacturing was both obvious and imperative."[34]

Given the industry's foundation in the antebellum and immediate postwar years, the collapse of the region's traditionally agrarian economy, and the technological developments that made possible the utilization of the Piedmont's unskilled labor, the development of a major Southern cotton textile industry was also almost inevitable. The spectacular rapidity of the industry's growth, however, resulted from a veritable crusade to industrialize the South that actually began in the 1870s. Everywhere, newspaper editors and politicians, with the fervor of camp-meeting evangelists, urged Southerners to turn to the manufacture of cotton. Industrial expositions at Atlanta, Charleston, and Raleigh in the early 1880s extolled the benefits the region could reap through the manufacture of its native cotton. High profits made by the early postwar mills attracted new entrepreneurs, eager to share in the wealth the industry promised. In addition to wealth, such investors could also expect increased social status, for no longer was the Southern manufacturer regarded as suspect. Rather, he came to be hailed as the savior of the South.

Throughout the South, communities sought to establish mills to boost their local economies. In several such communities, funds were gathered for the construction of mills by community subscriptions. Hundreds of citizens paid their dollar per week until enough capital for the proposed mill was raised. Determined to break their dependence as a completely agrarian society on the industrial North, the South plunged into a frenzy of mill construction.[35] Within two decades, its people built a modern cotton textile industry, thus laying the foundation that enabled the region eventually to become the center of the national textile industry.

2

The Industrial Plantation

The Southern factory, according to Wilbur J. Cash, was almost invariably "a plantation, essentially indistinguishable in organization from the familiar plantation of the cotton field."[1] C. Vann Woodward echoed this judgment when he asserted that "mill village paternalism was cut from the same pattern of poverty and makeshift necessity that had served for the plantation and crop-lien system."[2] The mill president replaced the plantation owner; the mill village replaced the slave quarters and the tenant's weatherbeaten shack. The company store replaced the peck of meal and pound of meat rationed the slave and the country merchant who "carried" the tenant. Like the planter, the entrepreneur looked after the social and moral, as well as economic, well-being of his work force.

However, there was an essential difference between the plantation and the factory, between the slave or tenant farmer and the mill operative. Physical force, not paternalism, kept the Negro on the plantation. The crop-lien system, produced by the economics of Reconstruction, bound the tenant to land that was not his own and kept the yeoman farmer continually in debt. As long as the South maintained its completely agrarian economy, the indebted farmer had little choice but to remain on the farm and hope for better prices or an increased harvest. The coming of the cotton mills introduced an element of choice into the economic lives of the Piedmont farmers. Limited though it was, the choice between the farm and the factory presented an alternative which neither the slave nor the tenant had possessed. The mill was their only avenue of escape from the drudgery and disappointment of the farm, and the Southern Piedmont whites took advantage of it. But, once in the mill, the operatives found themselves bound almost as fast to the factory as the tenant and slave had been bound to the farm and the plantation. Most, seeing no alternative, accepted their lot. But a substantial minority chose to defy the economic and social dicta of the South in an effort to continue to improve their condition as members of an industrial community.

The Labor Force

Nearly the entire work force that watched the whirling spindles and manned the clicking looms of the mills of the New South had lived their whole lives within a few miles of their birthplaces in the rolling red hills of the Southern Piedmont. Only the very skilled employees, such as the superintendents and, perhaps, a few foremen were imported, primarily from New England.[3] These native Piedmont workers were the progeny of the same Anglo-Saxon Protestant stock that populated the rest of the almost completely ethnically homogeneous white South. Well before the American Revolution, their forefathers had settled the region, and their descendants had tilled its soils ever since.

Although postwar economics had reduced to poverty nearly all who moved from the land to the mills, at least three different social groupings were represented in this hastily created work force. A few were land-owning yeoman farmers, seeking to escape indebtedness incurred through the crop-lien system.[4] Most were tenants, many of whom had owned land before the war, but had been forced into tenancy during Reconstruction.[5] Neither of these groups, despite their poverty, should be considered "poor white trash," a term used to denote attitude as well as poverty. The third social group to enter the mills were the true "poor whites." Some of them owned a few acres and a hovel, others were completely destitute. They had been pushed into the least productive areas of the South by the ever-advancing plantation well before the war and Reconstruction. Ignorant, poverty-stricken, and beset with malaria, hookworm, and other diseases, they had succumbed mentally to their environment, accepting their condition as inevitable. This acceptance separated the poor white from the tenant, whose lot might not have been any better materially. The division between the two was thin and often crossed, almost always by tenants sinking into the poor white class. The epithet "poor white" was despised by the Piedmont Southerner; indeed, it was a fighting term south of the Potomac and, thus, rarely used, for most of the poverty-stricken whites maintained their pride and their individual dignity. Though poor, they were in no sense a servile class ready to surrender all for a more affluent life.[6]

Whether constructed in an open field or in the South's largest urban areas, the mills initially recruited laborers from the farms of the immediate vicinity.[7] The dependence of Southern mills upon native white labor is strikingly illustrated by the records of the O'Dell Manufacturing Company of Chatham County, North Carolina. In June 1899, the mill's payroll contained the names of 155 workers representing forty-seven families. The Ellis family had eleven representatives; the Williams family, eight; the Andrews family, ten; the Campbell family, seven; and the Ferrel family, seven. Every name on the payroll was of Anglo-Saxon origin.[8] So successful was this practice that, before 1895, mill management never had to worry about a labor supply.[9] As the mills expanded, they simply enlarged the circumference of the area from which they recruited, which, like the growth rings of a tree, become a bit larger each year.

By 1895, however, a series of events had begun to put a slight strain on the available manpower in the immediate area of the Piedmont. Construction of gigantic, electrically powered mills prompted a meteoric rise in the number of the South's spindles and taxed even the Piedmont's ability to supply enough unskilled labor.[10] As the South began to increase its production of better quality cotton goods, including fine yarns and prints, more skilled operatives were needed. This was especially true of weavers, who were demanded in large numbers as the South continued to weave more and more of the yarn it produced. Such operatives often proved to be difficult to find.[11] Also, since many of the operatives had never accepted their break with the land, high cotton prices in a few good years such as 1904 drew some of them back to the farm.[12] This was less true of the urban operative, who was more completely immersed in the factory system than his rural counterpart. Some firms, particularly in the cities, were experiencing appreciable labor shortages by the turn of the century. At a Charlotte, North Carolina, meeting of Southern mill men in 1904, every man attending declared that he could employ from five to thirty more families in his mills.[13] Such declarations must be taken at somewhat less than face value, however, since management customarily overhired to insure a full force on any given work day. As this shortage, though never crucial, coincided with and was a causal factor in the rise of the National Union of Textile Workers (NUTW) throughout the Piedmont, mill men became alarmed. Several leading manufacturers toyed with the idea of attracting Europeans to the mills.[14] In 1906, South Carolina owners experimented unsuccessfully with Belgian immigrant laborers, some 500 in number, who were brought over on the *Wittekind*.[15]

However, the industry then found a whole new labor pool

nearer home in the Appalachian Mountains that lay just west of the Piedmont, populated by Anglo-Saxon Protestants.[16] Thus, the industry was able to retain a native white Southern work force. In 1900, therefore, 97.7 percent of the Southern textile laborers were native born of native parents, .6 percent were native born of foreign or mixed parents, and only .3 percent were foreign born. Negroes comprised the remaining 1.4 percent of the work force. In 1910, the percentage of native born of foreign or mixed parents had dropped to .4 percent; foreign born operatives continued to comprise .3 percent of the South's operatives.[17]

With the exception of poverty, the most common characteristic of the operatives was an abysmal lack of formal education. The antebellum South had regarded education as the responsibility of the individual, not the state. And although Reconstruction had led to a change in philosophy, at least in the rewritten constitutions of most Southern states, Bourbon penny-pinching had largely defeated attempts to establish effective public education systems. The result was a large, fundamentally unlettered population. New England manufacturers questioned, almost wishfully, the ability of the uneducated Southern farm laborer to engage successfully in cotton textile manufacturing.[18] One observer estimated that, by Massachusetts' standards, nearly two-thirds of Georgia's operatives were illiterate.[19] Mill owners were sensitive to such observations. Whereas, as late as 1905, North Carolina employers admitted that 50 percent of their adult work force could not read or write, most claimed that the majority of their own work force was literate.[20] Although employers probably exaggerated their operatives' literacy standards, improvements in school facilities in the quarter century from 1880 to 1905 certainly improved literacy statistics. Yet, large numbers of operatives in the South's mills, both adults and children, remained illiterate.[21] Furthermore, the operative did not possess any technical skills to offset his lack of formal education. Few of the workers who poured into the Southern mills had ever before seen a factory, inside or out. The inability to read or write proved to be of little hindrance in the operating of a "side" of spindles, and the machine had made technical skills unnecessary. Thus, a basically ignorant people became part of a modern industrial work force.

The Southern operative was, however, "sturdy in spirit, and reliable in disposition," and, most important, eager for work.[22] Since the cotton mills needed little skilled labor, rural workers were quickly transformed into competent operatives. This was particularly true of the spinning process, which required little more of the operatives than watchful eyes and deft hands. The training process for weavers, though more time-consuming, was not unreasonably difficult.[23] This rapidly trained labor force soon earned the praise of its employers. Few, however, surpassed Congressman Stanyarne Wilson of South Carolina, who commended the "splendid character, intelligence, and efficiency of the operatives. There are none like them in the world—native and to the manor born, moral, law-abiding, intelligent, homeloving, patriotic, and good citizens."[24] Such overblown oratory notwithstanding, the fact remains that, largely because of the industry's technological advances, thousands from the farms of the Southern Piedmont were transformed in a remarkably short time from tillers of the soil into surprisingly efficient laborers, who, by the turn of the century, were producing fine goods capable of competing with goods of the same type from New England.[25]

Just as the plantation and the farm had utilized the labor of the entire family, so did the mill. Throughout the quarter of a century under consideration in this study, the number of women and children in the mills exceeded the number of men. In 1880, the number of adult males in the South's mills was pathetically small. In Georgia, males over sixteen years of age comprised 31.3 percent of the work force; in South Carolina, 33.9 percent; and in North Carolina, only 26.2 percent.[26] Mill owners freely admitted that two-thirds or more of their operatives were women and children.[27] Since many children were too young to appear on the payroll (children as young as five years of age were carried on payrolls) but were permitted to "help" their mothers or sisters, the number was probably higher in many cases. As late as 1895, for example, a North Carolina factory with fifty-four operatives employed only six adult males; another firm had only thirty adult males in a work force of 125 hands. Furthermore, under North Carolina law, all persons above twelve years of age were considered adults.[28] By 1905, the percentage of adult males in Southern mills had risen considerably, largely because of the rapid increase in looms, which were usually operated by men. Nevertheless, women and children still constituted a majority of the labor force. In 1905, 49 percent of the South Carolina operatives, 43.8 percent of the North Carolina operatives, and 45 percent of the Georgia operatives were males above the age of sixteen.[29]

Several factors contributed to the dominant position of women and children in Southern mills. Not the least of these was that women and children could be hired for lower wages. For example, in 1890 North Carolina reported that average daily wages paid skilled men ranged from $1.00 to $2.50, that wages for skilled women ranged from 40 cents to $1.00, and that those for children ranged from 20 cents to 50 cents. In the same state in 1905, the range for men ran from 50 cents to $6.00 (extremely rare), while the range for women ran from 30 cents to $1.00. Children received from 25 cents to $1.00, the average being about 35 cents.[30] Cotton manufacturing technology also favored the small, quick hands of women and children, which were much more adept at mending broken threads than were the work-worn hands of fathers and husbands.[31] Some mill owners also considered women and children to be easier to train.[32] To insure an adequate number of women and children in the labor force, management often demanded that families occupying company housing provide so many workers per room.[33]

Although some have asserted that Southern management preferred women and children because they were "more tractable and less likely to strike," this is questionable.[34] Neither publicly nor privately did Southern owners express such opinions. Furthermore, the record does not bear out such an assumption. Although women did not respond to organization quite as readily as did men, women played a significant role in the South's textile labor unions and participated in all their major strikes. The Knights of Labor early enrolled female members, some of whom supported the organization with zealousness. Women comprised a major faction of the NUTW local in Columbia, South Carolina. The 1900 Alamance, North Carolina, strike was begun by a female member of the NUTW. Women also worked with their husbands in an effort to organize the industry.[35] If women had failed to respond to the organizational efforts of the Knights and the NUTW, hardly a single Southern textile local could have been organized, certainly none capable of engaging in a major strike.

The concept of the "family wage" also reinforced the industry's preference for women and child laborers. Mill management argued that the total annual income of a mill family was far greater than that of a farm family. Thus, the "family wage" was used as a cover for the low wages paid individuals. Spokesmen for management were correct in saying that a family working as a unit could make more in the mills in a month than many farm families could make in a year. Of course, the mill family had to purchase from its wages much of the goods that a farm family could produce for itself. There were other major differences between the "family wage" on the farm and in the mill. On the farm, the father was the major provider, the center of the household. The mill system destroyed the father's role as the major economic force in the family. Rather, it placed the family's economic responsibilities primarily on the wife and children and created a superfluous male population in the mill villages. Many fathers became loafers, openly living off the wages of their families. Others attempted to maintain their pride by becoming the family's errand boy and handy man.[36] Day in and day out, the children in the mills worked a more stringent schedule than did the farm child, and they did so in much less healthy surroundings. Cotton lint clogged the air within the mills, and humidifiers kept it continually moist to prevent threads from breaking in the spinning process.

The industry's emphasis on women and children, especially the latter, was not without its disadvantages for management. It was an important factor in bringing textile unions to the South. More work at better wages and shorter hours for the male operative was a major goal of the textile unions. For this reason, the unions made child labor one of their major targets for reform and used the male operatives' sentiment against this evil as a recruiting device.[37] Public opinion also failed to back management in this practice, especially toward the turn of the century. Reformers from various walks of life would eventually join organized labor in its attacks on the employment of children in the mills.

Life in the Mill and the Mill Village

"Average" working and living conditions in and around Southern mills simply cannot be described accurately. Conditions in the mills varied nearly as much as did the treatment of slaves on antebellum plantations. Hours, wages, housing, terms of payment, treatment by overseers—everything differed from mill to mill, even among mills within the same city. The size of the mills also varied tremendously, from the small, rural spinning mill with its meager work force to the modern "show mill" of the turn of the century which employed thousands. Yet, from the mass of available material, it is possible to obtain a fairly clear picture of the conditions in which the Southern

Table 3

Average Weekly Hours by State for Certain Textile Occupations[a]

State	Year	Male Loom Fixers	Female Spinners	Male Weavers	Female Weavers	Male Carders
S.C.	1903	66	66	66	66	66
	1896	66	66	66	66	66
	1891	69	68.25	68.62	67.90	68.82
N.C.	1903	66	66	66	66	66
	1896	66	66	66	66	66
	1891	66	66	66	66	66
Ga.	1903	66	66	66	66	66
	1896	66	66	66	66	66
	1891	66	66	66	66	66
Mass.	1903	58	58	58	58	58
	1896	60	58	58	58	58
	1891	60	60	60	60	60

[a] Figures do not take into account the age of the operatives.
Source: U.S. Bureau of Labor, Nineteenth Annual Report of the Commissioner of Labor, 1904, Wages and Hours of Labor (Washington, D.C.: Government Printing Office, 1905), 476–77 (hereafter cited as U.S. Commissioner of Labor, 1904 Report).

operatives worked and lived, provided one keeps in mind the wide discrepancies within the industry.

There was perhaps less variation in the number of hours that the operatives worked than in any other aspect of their working conditions. Long hours were standard throughout the South. During the 1880s and 1890s, the operatives worked the same hours as did the farmers—sunup to sundown.[38] Furthermore, the eleven to twelve hours of labor in the mills were but part of the working day for the mother and older children in the mill family. In the morning the children had to be awakened, clothed, and fed. In the evening, they had to be fed, bathed (if there was time), and put to bed. Before 1903, in North Carolina hours of work ran from sixty-three to seventy-five hours per week.[39] During this period, hours were about the same in Georgia and South Carolina.[40] Soon after the turn of the century, the three major Southern textile states all had laws limiting the working day to eleven hours, but the legislation was loosely enforced, if enforced at all, and many Southern workers labored a good deal more than this. Even if management rigidly adhered to the law, the average Southern operative continued to work eight more hours per week than his New England counterpart (see Table 3).

The Southern farmer who moved to the mill was familiar with long hours, but not with the rather rigid schedule forced upon him by factory life. As one Southern author expressed it,

We [the farmers] ourselves got up before daylight, but there was something alarming in being ordered to rise by a factory whistle. It was the command that frightened, the imperative in the note. . . . I thought it was terrible to spend six days of every week in a mill. I had never spent all of a day in any house in my life.[41]

Dissatisfaction over this long, rigid work schedule played a key role in Southern unionization activities, especially those of the NUTW.[42]

Table 4

Average Wages per Hour by State for Certain Textile Occupations[a]

State	Occupation	1890	1895	1900	1903
S.C.	Male Loom Fixers	13.28	12.26	13.19	13.23
	Female Spinners	3.03	2.81	3.58	5.25
	Male Weavers	6.85	5.44	6.98	8.32
	Female Weavers	6.15	5.01	6.04	7.13
N.C.	Male Loom Fixers	11.36	11.53	11.36	11.64
	Female Spinners	4.46	4.02	4.33	4.56
	Male Weavers	8.92	6.20	8.46	8.62
	Female Weavers	8.03	7.53	7.66	8.29
Ga.	Male Loom Fixers	13.38	13.22	13.33	13.26
	Female Spinners	5.23	4.96	4.86	5.87
	Male Weavers	6.99	8.31	8.45	9.79
	Female Weavers	6.96	7.84	7.98	8.67
Mass.	Male Loom Fixers	18.39	17.24	20.28	21.18
	Female Spinners	9.11	9.12	10.41	10.45
	Male Weavers	13.53	12.66	14.87	16.03
	Female Weavers	11.87	11.87	13.64	14.10

[a] All data are in cents per hour.
Source: U.S. Commissioner of Labor, 1904 Report, 480.

Wages were unquestionably the least stable element in the economic life of the operatives. They varied not only from year to year, but from state to state, region to region, and mill to mill, even within the same city. They seemed to have only two constant characteristics: they were always low and always extremely vulnerable whenever the industry experienced the slightest financial difficulty. The industry's piece wage system was in large part responsible for the variations in wages. Spinners were paid by the number of spindles, or "sides" they attended, but evidently there were no standard rates. Spinning hands could make anywhere from 30 cents to 60 cents per day. Weavers were paid by the "cut" of cloth. The cuts ranged in length from 47 to 53 yards, the length of the cut evidently having nothing to do with the piece wages paid. Some weavers received less for producing longer cuts than did fellow workers in other mills. North Carolina weavers in 1887, for example, received from 24 cents to 40 cents per cut.[43] At this rate, the average weaver could earn from 75 cents to $1.25 per day. And, as in New England, periodic inactivity of the mills, which occasionally, but infrequently, lasted as much as half a year, reduced the wages of Southern operatives.[44] In short, at all times the wages of the Southern operatives were substantially below those of the New England mill hands, sometimes nearly 50 percent lower, as is shown in Table 4. These data, compiled from not more than five mills per state, merely give an idea of the wage discrepancies between the two areas, for many factories paid wages considerably below those given in the table.

Southern manufacturers continually attempted to minimize this wide discrepancy, but few denied it. Apologists for the Southern mills argued that the cost of living in the South was much cheaper, as indeed it was.[45] But the differences in the cost of food, fuel, and shelter failed to cover the differences in wages, certainly not when it is realized that the Southern operative was receiving less per week for longer hours.[46] Southern management also maintained that the lower wages paid their operatives were necessary because they manufactured coarse goods, with little value added to the raw cotton, whereas the more skilled New England operatives produced fine cotton goods. The advent of fine cotton goods production in the South destroyed this argument. But even before this, Northern operatives producing the same type of cotton goods as their fellow workers in the South received much higher wages.[47]

Official federal and state reports on wages, revealing as they are, actually revise upward the wages received by Southern textile operatives. Because of the industry's penchant for liberal dividends and reinvesting profits in expansion programs, many firms faced serious shortages of operating funds. Management circumvented this hindrance by a number of practices that often reduced real wages. The use of scrip and the company store provided management with a combination that allowed them to operate with less cash, but drastically reduced the cash value of Southern wages. Scrip issued to operatives was usually redeemable only in company stores. Debts owed the store were deducted directly from the operatives' wages. Large-scale use of scrip, however, was primarily a phenomenon of the early mills; by the turn of the century, new sources of capital had made it an unnecessary practice for larger firms. Whereas, in 1887, nearly every North Carolina mill used the system, only one mill reported the use of scrip by 1895. However, the system was more widespread than the 1895 report indicated, since it survived in some areas until well into the twentieth century.[48] The scrip system was also used most heavily by rural mills, where the company store was the only store within any reasonable distance. Though used in the early urban mills, it was soon dropped. With the decline of the scrip wage, many urban mills also ceased to operate the company stores at which the scrip was redeemed.[49] Although resented by operatives and, in the more isolated mills, used as a weapon against unionization, scrip wages and the company store were not so corrupt as many of their critics claim.[50] A less subtle method used by mills to conserve cash was the practice of "docking," or reducing wages of individual operatives when flaws were found in the yarn or cloth they produced whether or not the flaws were the fault of the operative.[51] Some firms also increased their operating funds by delaying payment of wages. Factories paying cash wages often paid only once a month, some even less frequently. As late as 1905, there were Southern factories that paid their operatives only on demand. Like scrip wages, however, delayed payments were dropped by most mills as capital became more available.[52] The low wages paid by Southern mills were the major cause of the development of union sentiment among textile operatives. A dispute over wages lay behind almost every strike, whether of the Knights of Labor, the NUTW, or the UTWA.

The low wages paid by Southern mills have been justified by some on the grounds that the mills could afford to pay no more. Broadus Mitchell stated that "wages were really a question of what the factories could pay, rather than of what the people might ask."[53] In view of the rather high profits and the rapid expansion within the Southern cotton textile industry, this statement appears a bit questionable, to say the least. Profits of 15 percent and 20 percent on invested capital were not unusual during the 1870s.[54] Nearly everyone in the industry made money, and hundreds of investors rushed to partake in the spoils. As more and more mills appeared and competition increased, the returns of smaller and ill-managed factories grew less and less. Some factories were forced to close in periods of economic depression during the 1880s, especially during the period from 1884 to 1886.[55] However, in general, the South's mills seemed immune to the fluctuations of the national economy, and investments in the industry enabled it to continue to expand throughout the 1880s.

During the 1890s, when the mills of New England were constantly in trouble, Southern manufacturers experienced "exceeding prosperity," no curtailments in production, and continuous day and night operation. None were forced to auction their goods, as were some New England mills.[56] Writing in 1899, Daniel A. Tompkins stated that any well-managed mill should make a profit of from 10 percent to 30 percent.[57] Graniteville dividends averaged nearly 5 percent semiannually from 1880 until 1905, in addition to capital improvements on investments.[58] The earnings of Spartan Mills were equally high. Only once from 1893 to 1900 did the firm fail to pay dividends higher than the market rate of interest, and that failure occurred in July 1894 because of a shutdown for boiler repairs, not because of a depressed market. In 1895 the company recorded profits of nearly 20 percent of its total capital investments.[59] Holland Thompson described a North Carolina mill capitalized at $100,000 that, within less than eighteen months of operation, paid a 4 percent dividend, a practice which continued throughout the period under consideration. Within ten years after its establishment, this firm had also constructed a large addition to the original factory with funds taken from its earnings.[60]

Perhaps the most striking example of the high profits in the Southern industry is provided by the Dan River Mills of Danville, Virginia. Between 1882 and 1901, the company expanded from one factory of 6,000 spindles and 260 looms to seven factories with 67,650 spindles and 2,772 looms. The firm also purchased all but one possible water power site in the immediate Danville area on both sides of the river. Had an investor purchased 100 shares in the company in 1882, by 1901 his original investment would have grown to 278 shares of preferred and 55 shares of common stock in the firm. If these shares had been liquidated at par in 1901, the investor would have earned the equivalent of 36.7 percent per year on his original investment.[61] Obviously, the overall industry could have paid better wages simply by slowing its rate of expansion, reducing its dividends, or a combination of both measures.

Low wages and long hours were by no means the only grievances of the Southern operatives, although they certainly were

the most volatile. Several relatively minor factors contributed
to the hostility between management and labor. Perhaps the
chief among these lesser grievances was the native operatives'
resentment of overseers and superintendents, many of whom
were from New England and, as Yankees, naturally suspect.
Feuds between salaried mill officials and operatives antedated
the South's first experience with major union activity and continued to contribute to the friction between management and
both the Knights of Labor and the NUTW.[62] Another grievance in certain areas concerned the pass system, which required the operative to obtain the approval of his past employer
before a prospective employer would hire him. Management
most often used the pass system within cities, such as Augusta,
to prevent the operatives from constantly changing positions.[63]
Operatives also resented the misuse of recruiting agents and
advertisements. Many firms would actively recruit operatives
from the mills of the surrounding area during periods of peak
production to insure a surplus labor pool. Some even advanced
money to finance the operative's moving expenses and then
deducted it from his wages. At times, operatives were enticed
to mills when no jobs were available; in such cases the operatives were completely dependent on the mercies of charity.[64]
These three grievances were minor, but constant factors in
deteriorating labor-management relations. With the exception
of the first, however, they never caused strikes, but were often
topics discussed during strikes or strike threats.[65]

The living conditions the Southern operatives faced, like
their working conditions, differed greatly from mill to mill. But
the ubiquitous mill village provided a setting which encompassed
the variations and lent a sense of sameness to the lives of Southern Piedmont mill hands. The mill village was not, as some
have suggested, primarily a rural phenomenon. Located just
outside the city limits, most urban villages, like their rural counterparts, were unincorporated and privately owned. Thus, the
company not only escaped the city's higher tax rates, it acquired

greater control over the village and its inhabitants as well.[66] Proximity to urban areas did lessen management's control of village life somewhat by increasing the operatives' contacts with nonoperatives, whereas in the rural village nothing and no one was allowed within the village that did not meet with management's approval. The more varied life style of the city—more churches, merchants, entertainment, and available housing— presented a challenge to the village system. Throughout the South, however, the village and its paternalism dominated the life of the cotton textile operative.

Initially, management did not build the village as a means to control the operatives, although management was not unaware of this aspect of village life. Rather, the village's development was determined almost solely by economic considerations. Among them was the desire to escape city taxation and the opportunity of the company store to "get back in mercantile profit much of the money paid for wages."[67] The major cause of the village's rise, however, was simply that the thousands who poured into the mills had to be housed and only management had the capital to construct the required housing. This was especially true of rural mills, whose locations, usually determined by available water power sites, were frequently miles from the nearest town.

The pattern of variety also applied to mill village housing, with dwellings ranging from mere weather-boarded shacks to well-constructed, neat cottages. The former were most often found at small, rural mills, the latter at the urban "show mills" or an occasional large, progressively managed rural mill such as the Pelzer Mills in South Carolina.[68] Since economic considerations outweighed aesthetics, housing within a single village was usually built on a single plan, giving even the better villages a dull, drab appearance. Few villages were as bad as those described by such reformers as Clare de Graffenried and the Van Vorsts, who described the villages they visited as "sickly," "horrible," and "built on malarial soil."[69] However, more ob-

jective observers and persons familiar with Southern housing
were also less than impressed with the appearance of mill housing. Jerome Jones, business manager of an Atlanta labor paper,
testified before the United States Industrial Commission in
1900 that some of the mill housing around Atlanta was unfit
for family living. "The houses that I saw," he told the Commission, "I hardly think could be anything worse there [in the
village] or anywhere else." H. F. Garrett, President of the
Georgia State Federation of Labor, but not a mill hand, testified to the Commission that some mill housing was "simply
boarded up and down, with big cracks in them, and they are
in bad condition."[70] An English observer described "typical"
turn-of-the-century mill village housing as four-, five-, or six-
room wood tenements with outside wells and no water pipes
or sewerage systems. Their interiors had neither paint nor plas-
ter and were, in general, extremely untidy. Understandably, the
observer concluded that the tenements "did not impress one
very favorably."[71]

Naturally, mill officials always described company housing
as well-constructed, comfortable units, often preferable to the
average worker's home, urban or rural. Available evidence,
despite the denials of management, tends to support Harriet
Herring's description of village housing in the 1880–1900 era
as two-storied, often built on pillars because of the steepness
of the land, and usually without water and sewerage. Such
dwellings possessed "every element of deadly monotony . . .
with no curtain walls between the brick pillars . . . ranged in
two exact rows."[72]

Village housing rentals usually varied from 25 cents to 50
cents per room per week, although some operatives charged
that management demanded as high as 75 cents weekly. A few
firms furnished homes free of charge, especially rural firms,
and a very few of the large urban mills had no company housing. Some mills refused to hire operatives who would not rent
company housing; other mills in urban areas, even though

they maintained housing, did not require their operatives to live there. Rentals were deducted from the check of the family member most able to pay in any given pay period, a practice greatly resented by the operatives. Management claimed that the rents charged were comparable to or better than prevailing rates for private housing. Operatives frequently denied that this was the case.[73]

Sanitation was extremely poor within both the mill village and the homes of individual operatives. As has been observed, in most villages an outdoor well or hydrant served as the water supply for one or more houses, and sewerage systems were nonexistent. Only the larger urban mills constructed around the turn of the century built homes with indoor plumbing. Within single dwellings, overcrowding was common, particularly in the older urban villages where one and two families sometimes occupied a single room.[74] Such crowded conditions coupled with the operatives' almost complete lack of knowledge concerning personal hygiene created an unwholesome household. The operatives' appearance blended well with this unkept atmosphere. Often dirty and roughly dressed, the operatives' practice of dipping snuff and, because of their long working hours, sleeping in their clothes, did little to improve their appearance.[75] The Van Vorsts' description of the village home as a place of "confusion incarnate . . . and filthy disorder, tumbled beds, on the floor bits of food, vegetables, rags, dirty utensils and other domestic items," all enveloped by a "sickening odour" must, however, be balanced by descriptions of neat, tidy, clean homes such as those portrayed by Leonora Ellis.[76] And it must be remembered that farm homes, even Southern plantation homes, were never noted for their neatness. Although the farm homes from which the operatives came were seldom superior to those of the mill village, sanitation was probably better on the farm simply because of the farm dwelling's location in open country.

Whatever the aesthetic merits of mill village housing or its economic advantages or disadvantages for the operatives, its potential as a means of curbing labor organization was unmistakable. Control of the operatives' housing was management's most efficient weapon against the unions. This was especially true in rural mill villages where no other housing existed. In all the major strikes within the Southern textile industry, beginning with the 1886 Knights of Labor strike in Augusta, Georgia, management used eviction proceedings to defeat the strikers. Usually begun at the slightest sign of weakness within labor's ranks, eviction proceedings were invariably successful in destroying the operatives' will to offer further resistance. And once victory was achieved, workers who continued to exhibit sympathy for organized labor were subject to eviction. Thus, eviction was used as a means of suppressing potential organizational efforts.[77]

Even after scrip wages were abandoned by most Southern mills, the company store continued to be a major factor in the lives of most operatives. Only in some of the larger, newer mills in urban areas was the company store also abolished. Of eleven North Carolina counties reporting to the state Bureau of Labor in 1887, ten replied that every one of their mills owned a company store.[78] At the rural mills, operatives had no choice but to trade with the store, even though management did not require that they do so. Operatives at mills in more populous areas were often urged or forced to trade at the company store, although management at other mills allowed the operatives complete freedom of choice in the matter. Hominy, salt pork, flour, and molasses, the basic items of the slave's diet, were the staples carried by the company store. Rural operatives often supplemented this meager diet with such vegetables as collards, turnips, and potatoes grown in garden plots provided by management. In a few villages, operatives were allowed to keep a pig or a few chickens. Livestock, however, presented such sanitation problems that management was less than enthusiastic about this practice. Operatives worked these gardens in their limited spare time, and, since they had no time to devote to the canning of vegetables, their diet was enriched primarily in the late summer and fall. The operatives usually remained in debt to the company store for provisions.[79] Since outstanding accounts were deducted from wages earned, they were deprived of financial independence and made almost completely dependent upon management for daily essentials. Naturally, some of the operatives resented this dependence.[80] The store was also used as a weapon against labor, especially by rural mills. Faced with a threat from union activity, management would close the company store. The isolated operatives, far from the nearest town and with little or no cash, were thus forced to desert the union or starve.[81]

In addition to the housing units and the company store, every village had its church or churches. The social life of the mill hands centered around the church, and religion played a vital role in determining their thought and actions.[82] Invariably, the church was one of the three major evangelical Protestant denominations, most often Baptist or Methodist, occasionally Presbyterian. Many villages had several churches, some only one. The operatives readily attended churches of any of the three denominations, as all preached the same hellfire-and-damnation doctrine. Funds for the construction and upkeep of the church and the minister's salary often came, partly or wholly, from management. The operatives' spiritual needs, like his material needs, were, in a sense, partially provided for by management through a system with definite similarities to plantation practices. As a result, the pulpit seldom sided with labor against management.[83] In 1901, for example, the Reverend E. N. Joyner urged the operatives of Columbia, South Carolina, not to strike because the mill owners were their best friends and stated that time would prove whether any company policies "were not of God."[84] Thus, labor challenging management was pictured as both irrational and immoral.

The more astute and prosperous owners of the South's larger

mills initiated programs to provide social services and recreation for their operatives in an effort to obtain a more loyal, contented, and, thus, more productive work force.[85] Many, though by no means all, of the South's mill villages could boast schools. Like the churches, the schools were partially or wholly supported by management, which also usually hired the teachers.[86] Other facilities and diversions provided by management included libraries, hospitals, lyceums, athletic clubs, rifle clubs, literary clubs, and other services. Such social and athletic clubs and literary societies were often officered by management personnel, and, thus, they, along with the pulpit and the classroom, became a means of influencing the operatives' social, as well as economic, life. These services were also extremely effective in obtaining the allegiance of the Southern operatives for the company. In other words, the workers could not protest hours, wages, or child labor without endangering the availability of these services and diversions.[87] Of course, management did not hesitate to point to these services as examples of their concern for the worker. Fraternal organizations were also extremely popular with the operatives; the Red Men, Odd Fellows, Masons, and Knights of Pythias being the most popular. Management encouraged such organizations; mill officials often held offices within them.[88]

In short, the mill village was an almost completely paternalistic system. Management controlled outright when, where, for how long, and for what wages the operatives worked. It exerted a substantial influence over where the operatives lived, shopped, studied, played, and worshipped. In addition, management thoroughly policed the village, making sure that threats to the operatives' morality—liquor, prostitutes, and labor organizers —were kept at a safe distance.[89] Within some villages, management even went so far as to suppress local politics so that "no mayoralty elections, aldermanic squabbles," or ward politics "kept the people in ferment." State and national politics, which could not be prevented, were carefully watched. Management in such villages placed inspectors at the ballot box to see that each operative voted the right way. If an operative failed to vote for management's convictions, "he would bring down a lot of trouble upon himself."[90] In such a tightly organized and controlled environment, any unionization attempts were necessarily predisposed to failure.

Unquestionably, life in the early Southern mills was harsh. Long hours, low wages, and poor living conditions awaited all who entered the mills. Yet, they came, often in such large numbers that some were turned away. They came because the mills offered them the hope of a better life instead of the despair of farm life created by year after year of back-breaking labor that produced only mortgages and misery. The operatives were most attracted by the wages. Many farm families never saw as much as $100 in cash during an entire year. To such families who moved to the factory, their combined wages must have seemed phenomenal, making undreamed-of luxuries possible. The housing in the mill village was almost always as good as, and often better than that on the farm, and their wages allowed the operatives to improve both their diet and clothing.[91] Management's claim that cotton textile operatives were among the best fed and best clothed unskilled laborers in the South, though at best a modest claim, was borne out by the thousands who came to the mills and stayed.[92] This was the bedrock of management's defense of the status quo.

It was more than money, however, that drew the farmer to the factory. The nineteenth-century Southern farm was a lonely, isolated place. Sunday visits, an occasional trip to town, and revival meetings were the only events to break the monotony of farm life. The mill village, with its churches, schools, clubs, and neighbors, provided an exciting change. Many were drawn to the mills by their "inarticulate social instinct."[93] Others came to the mills to give their children a better life, including an improved opportunity to obtain an education. As one scholar observed, "It is probable that before 1900 larger percentages

of children living in mill villages had some sort of schooling
and had it closer at hand than most children . . . except those
living in towns of say, a thousand population or more."[94] The
Southern operatives were not unaware of this situation.[95]

The farmer who decided to desert the field for the factory
did not make his decision without due consideration. Ben Robertson touchingly recounts the reasons a tenant gave his uncle
for leaving the land. His motivations were the same as those of
thousands of others.

> What chance have I got to get ahead? What chance have I got
> ever to own any land of my own. . . . I could have money at
> the mill. . . . I ought to be able to save enough in no time to
> buy a few acres. . . . I don't know the folks who own the mill.
> They don't know me. I don't like to work for folks I don't know.
> . . . I want to improve my condition. I want to educate my chil-
> dren. I want them to have things better than I have had them.
> . . . I'm ambitious and I'm strong. I'm going to do it.[96]

Understandably, it was the same basic, very human desire to
create an even better life for themselves and their families
which led the more aggressive operatives to turn to organized
labor in an effort to challenge the status quo of the industrial
plantation.

3

The Mind of
Owner and Operative

Using the cotton mill as their agent, the disciples of Progress in the New South intentionally produced an industrial revolution in the Southern Piedmont. Almost overnight the mills created thriving commercial and industrial centers in such cities as Charlotte, Columbia, Danville, and Augusta. They pumped commercial life into numerous sleepy towns and converted open fields into manufacturing sites. They drew thousands from the farm who had never seen a factory and transformed them into an efficient labor force for what was to become the world's greatest cotton textile industry. But, in the words of Wilbur J. Cash,

There was no revolution in basic ideology and no intention of relinquishing the central Southern positions and surrendering bodily to Yankee civilization involved in the genesis of dream and program [of Progress], or in their acceptance by the South. . . . So far from representing a deliberate break with the past, the turn to Progress clearly flowed straight out of that past and constituted in a real sense an emanation from the will to maintain the South in its essential integrity.

In none of this [turn to Progress] was there any realization that the abandonment of the purely agricultural way and the fetching in of the machine would call for the remolding of the old purely agrarian mind . . .[1]

The ideology of the Old South unquestionably exerted a significant influence upon the concepts of both owner and operative concerning the place of the mill in the South, their role as individuals within the mills, and their position in Southern society in general. Many of the concepts held by the two groups were complementary or similar, but not quite identical. There was also a major difference in the application of these concepts to daily life. To a large degree, the operative was trapped by his past and a victim of it; he was ideologically adrift in the machine age. Management, on the other hand, adapted the ideology of the Old South to its own purposes while rapidly adopting the basic tenets of industrialism. The heritage of the past was consciously used by management as a tool with which to build the future. Yet, there was little if any hypocrisy in this practice, for management sincerely held its concepts of the South, the mills, and the role of the entrepreneur, whether they were rooted in the agrarian past, dreams of the industrial future, or a combination of the two. In brief, the entrepreneur believed wholeheartedly that what he thought best for the development of cotton manufacturing was best for the South, including the operatives. Believing as he did, he forcefully acted upon his assumptions while the operative struggled for a livelihood in a bewildering new socioeconomic system.

That Southern mill owners and officials quickly embraced the ideal of an industrial New South is not as surprising as the enthusiasm with which they did so. Since Southern mill owners seldom came from the old planter class, their acceptance of industrialism did not represent a sharp break with the past.

Rather, they most often represented low country commercial families, Piedmont merchants, or the larger yeoman farmers. Many, as has been observed, had direct connections with antebellum cotton manufacturing enterprises. Nearly all had been successful in some commercial endeavor before entering into the textile industry.[2] Freed from the restrictions of an almost completely agrarian society, these so-called Southern Yankees were determined to develop the cotton manufacturing potential of the old Confederacy to the fullest. Continued expansion obsessed them, becoming an end in itself, which justified virtually any means. Daniel A. Tompkins, who perhaps best represents the class to which he belonged, was mesmerized by the South's industrial progress. He once berated reporters on the staff of his *Charlotte Observer* for covering, in detail, the accidental death of a tramp killed by a north-bound train composed of thirty cars. The tramp's death, said Tompkins, was of little importance. "The real news was what the thirty cars were loaded with and why they were going North."[3]

Like his Northern counterpart, the Southern entrepreneur turned to the textile industry primarily because of the profits it offered, all statements to the contrary notwithstanding.[4] One of the largest investors in Dexter Converse's Glendale factory declared that "I would put my last dollar in cotton manufacturing. . . . The Northern mills are losing money . . . we are of course making handsome profits." H. H. Hickman, President of the Graniteville Manufacturing Company, frankly admitted that, if the conditions of the 1880s continued, "we will make a heap of money."[5] Daniel Tompkins was well aware that profits were the major concern of the entrepreneur in the cotton industry. "It has been abundantly proven by experience in the Carolinas," he wrote, "that cotton mills, on every class of goods manufactured there, can make a profit of 10 to 30 percent."[6] Even Francis W. Dawson, the editor of the *Charleston News and Courier* whom Broadus Mitchell credits with beginning the folk movement to save the South through the cotton mill, emphasized the profits to be made in the industry. The central theme of the February 10 issue of the *Charleston News and Courier* that began the cotton mill campaign of 1880 was the profits the industry had produced in the 1870s.[7] The profit motive, however, was not the only reason persons invested in the mills.

The vigor with which entrepreneurs rushed into the cotton textile industry was also prompted by the mentality of the "Lost Cause" which pervaded nearly every aspect of postwar Southern life. Mill owners and officers saw themselves as the Rebel vanguard in a second Civil War, a war that was being fought against the Northern foe in the industrial arena. "An industrial war is on between the North and the South," proclaimed the *Atlanta Constitution,* "and this time the South will win."[8] In this war, the ever-multiplying spindles of the South became, according to the *Columbus Enquirer,* "the weapons the peace gave us, and right trusty ones they are." The soldiers were native operatives and owners, who, in the words of Henry Grady, "began, in ragged and torn battalions, that march of restoration and development." The object of this second war, according to the *Raleigh News and Observer,* was to "force from the North that recognition of our worth and dignity of character to which people will always be blind unless they can see it through the medium of material strength."[9] The New South would be a creation "so rich and powerful that it might rest serene in its ancient positions, forever impregnable."[10]

Furthermore, the Southern cotton mill owners' rather strange blend of Social Darwinism and *noblesse oblige* cannot be discounted as a motivating factor. Originally men of family or position, all had some formal education, many had a college education, and most were community leaders.[11] Management never doubted their own superiority or questioned their position of leadership in the drive to create the New South. Like industrialists throughout the nation, they succumbed to the illusion that they, through the process of natural selection, had risen from the masses because of their ability and perseverance alone.[12] They were aware of the social responsibility of economic leadership, but did not, in the traditional meaning of *noblesse oblige,* try to better society because of it. Rather, they were convinced that in their struggle to expand profits and plants they were creating a better South for all. To Social Darwinism and the self-made-man theory, they added a new twist: a Southern view of Reconstruction. Reconstruction, they believed, had reduced all Southerners to "absolutely the same level of poverty."[13] Within this bleak economic setting, because of their ability, Southern manufacturers had risen to the top in an industry of their creation, and vastly improved the well-being of an entire region by doing so.

As a natural leader, it behooved the Southern manufacturer to become both protector and philanthropist, to protect the morals and provide for the social welfare of his people. By completely controlling the village, he zealously guarded the moral condition of his charges. In Graniteville, the company banned the sale of alcoholic beverages and frowned upon cigarette smoking.[14] Tompkins felt that management should eliminate "the drunken and lazy element" and the "notoriety seekers" from the midst of the "honest work people and their honest friends."[15] At times, management tried to prevent ideas hostile to their own from reaching the workers, to the point of eliminating village politics.[16] Even the owner's role of philanthropist had moral overtones. The various social services that the more progressive mill men of the region provided for their work force were designed to do more than meet specific needs within the village. Owners in North Carolina, who in 1900 pledged to provide schools, churches, libraries, and better sanitation systems for their workers, were attempting to "do all in our power to erect a high standard of morals and elevate and dignify labor."[17]

Mill officials did not engage in "welfare work" simply to prevent criticism or to retain the loyalty of their operatives, nor did they police village morals only to insure tranquility. They were well aware of these possibilities, just as they realized the value of welfare work as a public relations device. They immediately responded to criticism by citing their endeavors to aid the operatives.[18] As an apologist for paternalism put it as late as 1924, "It is paternalism in the South, but it is an intelligent and worthy paternalism, and so long as it continues *it would seem certain of success.*"[19] But, they also acted from a sense of obligation, because "it was an essential part of the Southern paternalistic tradition to look after the moral welfare of these people and get them safely into heaven . . . because it was so bound up with the Southern notions of the *good man,* of leadership, and of aristocracy."[20]

Significantly, at no time did Southern mill owners show a generous nature on the subject of wages and hours, nor did they brook any attempts by the operatives to influence policies in either area. It was not accidental that the North Carolina owners who pledged themselves to a program of social services neglected to mention either wages or hours of labor. This fact seems to contradict the image of the paternal owner, and if men were motivated solely by economic factors, the assumption of such a contradiction would be justified. Certainly mill owners believed that higher wages and shorter hours would reduce profits, and this belief just as certainly helped determine their attitude toward these issues. Yet, most owners were truly convinced they knew what was best for the operatives, and that, as natural leaders, their advice should be taken. Columbia owners were dumbfounded by a 1901 strike partially because they had just voted to help build a church, school, public hall, and library for their labor force.[21] Most mill owners also genuinely cared for their workers. "The fact is sometimes lost sight of, however, that the cotton mill operatives are not a class unto themselves. They are as human as any other humanity, and are entitled to individual consideration on individual merit, as other humanity is."[22] These are the views of Daniel Tompkins, who had no qualms about admitting that "welfare work" was also in the owner's self-interest.

A major reason for the entrepreneur's hatred for unions was this stubborn conviction that he knew what was best for his operatives. Union labor directly challenged this conviction, especially in the field in which management was most unwilling to have it challenged—the determination of policies regarding hours and wages. The union's challenge frankly startled management, which sincerely expected "sympathy, not criticism, confidence, not suspicion, not enmity, but friendship" from the operatives.[23]

Closely related to the owner's belief that he was a product of natural selection was the concept of the operative and himself as members of a common, native Anglo-Saxon stock. Although it excluded the Negro, this belief was strikingly similar to and obviously descended from the planters' argument that slaves were merely part of a congenial, larger family. Owners continually stressed the close blood ties between themselves and the workers, and largely attributed the South's lack of labor troubles to this factor.[24] Because they realized that it was correct in the ethnological, but not in the sociological, sense, the "one big family" concept was among the most useful held by mill officials. It allowed them to identify with the worker, to assert that their interests were the same as his. Management deliberately dwelt upon the South's ethnically homogeneous white population in an effort to discourage the seemingly obvious class differences stemming from the socioeconomic stratification within the region. The family concept also allowed the owner to believe that a familiar kind of democracy existed within the paternalistic system. One spokesman for the mills put it this way:

> While the system in the Southern mill is paternal, there is a democracy greater than to be found perhaps in any other industry. Feeling that he or she is of as good stock as the employer, the mill worker has no hesitancy about going into the boss' office,

sitting down alongside his desk and asking advice on some matter
or voicing a protest. They're all of one family. They're all of one
community. They are all of the mill.[25]

Perhaps most important, the family concept could be applied
to the racial problem. The South's large Negro population constantly posed a potential economic and social threat to whites
of lower socioeconomic status, tending to curb their willingness
to challenge their financial betters. At the same time, this racial
economic conflict made it easy for management to champion the
cause of the white worker against the blacks. Above all else, the
owner shared with the operative membership in the "superior"
Anglo-Saxon race. All social and economic barriers between
mill hand and mill owner faded in the belief that they faced the
same enemy.

Although the owner publicly emphasized his kinship to the
operative, privately he often expressed the opinion that the
operative was of a lower "class," much beneath himself. The
idea that the operatives were a separate class in the minds of
the owners is unmistakable, despite Tompkins' denial. Kohn
continually used the phrase "these people" when he referred
to the mill operatives.[26] Time and again the word "class" oc-
curs in the owners' descriptions of laborers that Broadus Mitchell
recorded.[27] Indeed, some owners believed the operatives to
"have an inborn inclination" to be loyal to their employers.
When the operative attempted to rise above his socioeconomic
status, the owner belittled him for trying to emulate his betters.[28]

Xenophobia complemented the owner's consistent use of the
homogeneous South theme. Directed largely at the North, his
fear of things foreign reached ludicrous proportions. In the
eyes of the Southern mill owner, the United States north of
the Potomac was populated mainly by non-Anglo-Saxon Europeans. Ranged against the homogeneous, native, enterprising,
individualistic Southern worker, he saw the heterogeneous,
foreign, socialistic, union laborer of the North. The owner

often and vehemently expressed his fear that the "foreign" doctrine of unionism which was growing in the North would contaminate his "pure" Southern work force. One employer suggested an "anti-immigration bureau" to prevent "the whole world from dumping its scum on our shores. . . . Unless something is done to stop foreigners . . . our country will be ruled by anarchists and such cattle."[29]

Another spokesman for the mills said the South must be saved from the invasion of "the scum of Europe," and that the Southern manufacturers "must not yoke themselves to those of other sections." Indeed, the South, already blessed with "the most favorable conditions of the whole world of labor, with the sweetest, brightest homes, and loveliest wives, and sweethearts and children in the country" could easily "work out our own salvation, prosperity, and happiness in our own way and to our own satisfaction."[30] Northern, foreign-inspired unions with their demands of higher wages, shorter hours, and the abolishment of child labor could only disturb the excellent management-labor relations of the South and, thus, do great harm to the Southern mill hand.[31] Besides, how could such foreigners and Yankees possibly know the needs of the Southern operative as well as his employer and fellow Southerner? In addition, Southern owners were convinced that textile union activity in their region was largely the result of an attempt by New England manufacturers to reduce competition.[32] Thus, unionism was viewed as a plot directed, at least in part, by forces with which the Southern owner believed himself at commercial war.

Like most American entrepreneurs of the era, the Southern mill owner stoutly believed in and defended his version of laissez-faire economics. Believing that he had risen to the top in a free enterprise system solely because of his natural ability and hard work, the Southern owner resisted any attempt to change, however slightly, the economic system that he thought had produced him. With the exception of a few farsighted men, the owners opposed any attempts by government to regulate their business.[33] Any hint of regulation of the industry's low wages and long hours alarmed mill officials, for since the 1870s they had believed these to be their major advantage in the industrial war with the North. They continued to hold this belief throughout the period under consideration.[34] They furiously opposed any effort by government, unions, or any other force to change either wages or hours. Mill men also feared that government intervention would strengthen the hand of organized labor, or at the very least, encourage its growth. As management saw it, regulatory legislation could lay the "mud sills upon which will germinate unions and all the attendant evils connected with the same."[35]

In their unabashed belief that the mill was their private property to run as they saw fit, mill officials resembled both the plantation owners of the past and the contemporary industrialists of the North. And, as in the case of the planter and Northern industrialist, their views reflected economic reality. Quite frequently the mills were, for all practical purposes, their own property. Although hundreds, perhaps thousands, invested small sums in the industry, the larger firms were controlled by a handful of "captains of industry." These men pioneered and created the industry they controlled. John Montgomery, Dexter E. Converse, Edwin M. Holt, W. B. Smith Whaley, James and Eugene Verdery, and others had large investments in numerous textile firms. The industry was also a family industry, just as the plantation had been. A small number of families, sometimes even a single family, dominated the industry within a given locality, and they were, in turn, connected with other such families either through marriage or business arrangements. The daughter of Ellison A. Smyth, for example, became the wife, mother, aunt, and sister-in-law of cotton mill executives. This characteristic of the industry became more noticeable toward the turn of the century and, despite a series of financial reverses and recoveries in the twentieth century, remains evident to the present.[36]

Like his Northern counterpart, the Southern industrialist was somewhat inconsistent in his application of the laissez-faire philosophy. Most refused to bargain with the operatives except as individuals, holding to the theory that the operatives could seek work elsewhere if they did not like the terms they were offered.[37] Others were willing to acquiesce in unionization so long as the unions were "controlled by good motives and good men" and did not become too "theoretical" or seek to dictate hours or wages.[38] Yet, management itself constantly sought to organize to reduce competition and to present a united front to labor, well before organized labor appeared in the mills.[39] Furthermore, management was not adverse to legislation that might enhance its control over the worker or lessen the possibilities of effective union organization. Some even suggested laws forbidding operatives to organize.[40] Naturally, the industry never objected to governmental activity in its behalf. Mill officials lobbied effectively for tax privileges, which they obtained from both state and local governments. Most owners were also protectionists and ardent advocates of an expansionist foreign policy in areas where large textile markets were expected, such as Asia.[41]

The several facets of the mind of the Southern mill official were welded into one interlocking complex by his conceptions of Reconstruction, the South's unifying myth. The owner saw Reconstruction as a devastating, traumatic experience, economic and social, which the South, with tremendous fortitude, had conquered with his leadership, only after years of bitter struggle. Daniel Tompkins felt the Civil War had reduced the region's population en masse to the depths of poverty and loosed a barbarian, the Negro, within its midst. Reconstruction, according to Tompkins, was a quarter-century struggle requiring all the moral and physical courage that the white man could muster "to save civilization."[42] T. C. Guthrie echoed Tompkins' views in a speech to the 1902 Southern Cotton Spinners Association convention. The war, maintained Guthrie, "destroyed the capital and property of the South, left grinding poverty in its wake, the fight for mere subsistence employed all the energies of the people." Then came the struggle against carpetbag government. Fortunately, this "school of adversity" developed strong individuals, most of whom saw the grand opening of cotton manufacturing, took it, and succeeded. In this manner, the Southern manufacturer acquired a right to his vital interest in good government, the moral and educational advancement of all classes, and the South's continued industrial development.[43] Like all enduring myths, this one proved the more useful because it was not totally lacking a factual basis.

This view of Reconstruction flattered the owner and ill prepared him for criticism. In this view, he was the savior of the South, the leader who came forward in a time of social and economic crisis to open a road to material wealth and social security for his poverty-stricken people. Since his methods had succeeded in establishing the industry, they must be correct for all time and for other areas. It buttressed his xenophobia. Only a Southerner, especially a Southern industrial leader, could understand what the South had gone through and what problems it faced. Therefore, no outsider could intelligently criticize the industry he had created. This was especially true of Northerners, who had brought the South to ruin and were jealous of its recovery and industrial progress. As the South's savior, the mill owner expected obedience from the saved. Believing that hard work and natural ability had lifted him to the top, he saw any attempt at unionization as socialistic, basically dishonest, and "un-Southern." Without this interpretation of Reconstruction, the Southern owner would have found it difficult to justify his almost absolute paternalism. With it, he not only justified paternalism and expected it to go unchallenged, but he felt it should be appreciated.

Opinions of the mill hands are much more difficult to determine than those of management. Largely uneducated, they left few written expressions of their thoughts and aspirations. But, on occasion, letters from literate workers appear in mill records or in the reports of the North Carolina Bureau of Labor. The early Southern labor press was usually more attuned to the concerns of the artisan laborer than to those of the mill worker, and few of these papers have been preserved. Not a single issue remains of the only textile labor paper of the era, the *Southern Unionist,* published in Columbus, Georgia. Only bits and pieces of information can be gleaned from those papers that were preserved.

Government investigatory bodies ignored the rank-and-file textile laborer and his leaders as well. For example, of the Southern labor leaders who testified before the United States Industrial Commission in 1899 and 1900, not one represented a textile local, although the NUTW was at its peak in these years and was controlled by Southerners. The skilled laborers who did appear, however, represented local or state labor federations which contained textile locals, and were personally acquainted with operatives. Occasionally, someone who was reared in a Piedmont mill town and was personally familiar with its inhabitants' customs and mores wrote a book of recollections about the past. Northern journalists of the era constantly toured the villages and often published excerpts from interviews with individual operatives. Material garnered from these varied sources fortunately can be used to construct a fairly accurate description of the Southern operatives' basic outlook on their economic and social positions in society.

Coming directly from the land, the cotton mill operatives brought the prejudices, customs, and traditions of the Old South into the mills. This clinging to the agrarian ideal, this inability to escape the thought patterns of the rural South, was at least as significant in determining the operatives' response to management and organized labor as were the economic conditions they faced within the industry. Unlike management, which recognized the permanency of the factory in their lives, mill hands often viewed the mill as a means of temporary relief. Many hoped that after earning some cash in the mill they could return to the land, and a few did so in the years that raw cotton prices made considerable advances.[44] Since cotton prices throughout the period under study were usually depressingly low, the mill hands had no meaningful economic alternative to the factory. No other industry bid against the cotton mill for their labor, which would have made their services more valuable and would have given them some bargaining power. Rather, thousands stood eager to desert the farms for the mills. In such an economic situation, only through rigid organization could the laborer even hope to force management to raise wages, shorten hours, or improve working conditions. However, almost everything in the mill workers' past militated against their acceptance of organized labor.

As has been observed in the previous chapter, a serious lack of formal education was a common characteristic of the laborers, and was, perhaps, the most damaging legacy they inherited from the Old South. The operatives' lack of formal education was complemented by an almost total ignorance of the workings of an industrial society. The lack of a formal education had not proven a serious burden on the Southern farm, which was rarely a model of scientific agriculture, nor did it prove a major hindrance to the performing of individual jobs within the mills. But in the industrial world, it proved to be the key to the operatives' lack of political, social, and economic astuteness, and a major difficulty in their attempts to adjust to their new positions.

On the farm, the operative had always worked as an individual; solidarity with his fellow workers was an idea completely beyond his frame of reference when he first entered the mill.[45] As late as 1910, a government survey revealed that the majority of women in the South's cotton mills held no opinion about organized labor because of ignorance of the subject. In Georgia, 122 of 159 reporting women pleaded ignorance; in North Carolina, 210 of 295; and in South Carolina, 159 of

199.[46] Organizers often complained of the operatives' appalling ignorance of the principles of unionism. Printed matter could not be relied upon; organizers had to be kept constantly in the fields explaining the ideals of the union to gatherings of mill hands. Some, becoming discouraged, felt that organizational efforts were useless until the laborers were better educated.[47] Keeping organizers in the field as teachers as well as organizers was an expensive proposition, especially in view of the fact that the funds required to do so came from outside the South.

Unaccustomed to a cash economy, the mill worker responded to it much like a child with a few pennies in a candy store. He squandered his wages on consumer goods and luxuries that he had longed for on the farm, and thus remained constantly in debt.[48] He rarely saved any of his wages. In 1887, North Carolina owners reported that as few as 5 percent of their operatives saved; most estimated that from 10 percent to 20 percent saved a portion of their earnings.[49] The poverty and futility of farm life had taught the worker to enjoy the fruits of his labor immediately. Since they felt no need for personal savings, the mill workers saw no reason to build a strong union treasury. In addition, they were unaware of the possible continuance of their economic difficulties. Rather, they often saw the union as a refuge in time of trouble instead of as a means for continually strengthening their ability to obtain concessions from management. As a result, the financial condition of Southern textile locals was always vulnerable.

The Southern operative suffered from an acute "great man" complex, accepting the role of the benevolent protector that the entrepreneur had created. Although partially caused by lack of education, much of this acceptance stemmed from the almost feudal social system of the Old South. Like the old planters, the mill owners and officials were considered people of "quality." In daily life, they stood apart from, yet somehow remained a part of, general village society.[50] Clare de Graffenried sensed this strange relationship between owner and oper-

ative in 1891 when she wrote that the operatives lacked aggressiveness because of their ignorance and an unshakable trust
in the rectitude of the employer.[51] Among many of the operatives, this unshakable trust was almost pathetic. One poor
operative seeking employment wrote his prospective employer,
"as to pay, you know what the job is worth, and what you can
pay for it. It [sic] is your work and I have no rite [sic] to fix
it."[52] Another operative told a touring Northerner that his employer "treats us right."[53] The operatives' reliance on the owner,
which was constantly reinforced by preachers, editors, and
politicians of the South, even affected the operatives' personal
lives. Disputes within families were often brought to the mill
president, and his advice was taken in all matters from religion to lynchings.[54]

An extremely powerful social phenomenon buttressing this
acceptance of the entrepreneur as provider and protector was
what has been called the "negative class consciousness" of the
mill hands. Negative class consciousness was a result of the
suspicion and scorn with which the rest of Southern society
viewed the mill hands. Even the farmers, the class from which
the mill workers came, looked down upon them. Despite the
poverty and isolation of farm life, those who lived it were
strongly imbued with the concept of Jeffersonian agrarian democracy. Many felt that those who deserted farm for factory
betrayed the basic Southern concept that the agrarian life
was the free life, much to be preferred over the confinement of
the factory. Ben Robertson, who was raised in the Southern
agrarian tradition, described how mill workers "made me feel
they had been captured, that they were imprisoned, that they
had given up being free."[55] Ben Tillman, the leader of the
agrarian reform movement in South Carolina during the 1890s,
gave voice to the farmers' disrespect for the mill hand when
he referred to them as "that damned factory class."[56] The emotional impact of leaving the farm was almost traumatic and
was the major reason operatives continued to dream of return-

ing to the farm. A laborer who ignored the advice of his friends and family and left the land described his departure as being "like a funeral."[57]

Furthermore, the mill hands in urban mills were not accepted by the townspeople, who applied to them such epithets as "lint-head," "cotton-tails," "factory rats," and "cotton mill trash." Such an attitude on the part of the middle and upper classes was not uniquely Southern, but it was probably strengthened by the Southern agrarian tradition and a belief, which developed with slavery, that to work with one's hands at the command of another was degrading. This attitude was also reinforced by the physical separation of the mill village from the remainder of the community.[58] Deserted by the farmer of the rural South and the white collar worker of the urban South, the mill hands developed a strong social class consciousness, viewing the mill owner and officials as their champions. In an "us versus them" situation, management was accepted as a part of the "us." Although the alienation of the operatives was slight compared to that of the slave, their plight was not without a degree of similarity.

Religion, another important factor in shaping the mind of the mill worker, was also a foe of organization. This was true largely because the operatives, like most Southerners, attended the more evangelical churches, especially the Baptist and Methodist. By and large, ministers of these denominations preached sin and salvation of souls, not the social gospel. To them, life's goal was Heaven, rather than the affluent life. In the words of one of the era's divines who ministered to mill workers, "It was better to hunger like Jesus than to have fulness and forgetfulness."[59] The emphasis the pulpit placed on nontemporal values contributed to the laborers' acceptance of their circumstances in this world and their hope of better fortunes in the next. For most operatives, "that old time religion" was beyond question. In their minds, "Heaven and hell were localities as real and material in their make-up as Georgia and Florida."[60]

Religion involved the process of getting an individual's soul into the one place rather than the other, and did not concern labor-management disputes.

It also must be remembered that most mill village churches were subsidized by management, so that no criticism of the mill hands' state of affairs could be expected from the church. Nor did management's influence within the religious establishment end at the mill village pulpit; the church's entire organizational structure was controlled by the class from which management sprang. Such manufacturers as H. H. Hickman, who served a term as president of the Southern Baptist Association, were extremely active in the hierarchy of the South's major Protestant churches.[61] Surprisingly, at least two ministers were among the more prominent labor leaders in the industry.[62] They realized, as did only a few others, that the church would not plead the mill hands' case in any major labor-management dispute.[63] In the eyes of management and the press, these ministers ceased to be men of the cloth and became renegades. Although ardent union advocates proposed the teaching of labor union principles in the village churches and one went so far as to declare that "a man who does not believe in a union does not believe in the Bible, and should be called an infidel," they could not alter the entrenched otherworldly religious concepts of most operatives.[64]

Caught in a paternalistic social system that they neither created nor controlled, the Southern operatives were partially prevented by their individualism from grasping the potential of organization as a means of obtaining some voice in the operation of the industry. As cotton farmers moved to the mill, they were inclined to deal with the overseer and other mill officials as they had dealt with the landlord or county merchant, on a personal level. They failed to realize that the superintendent or overseer were but agents of the company, that they were no longer working for an individual as an individual. They also feared unions, which represented organization, partly because they did not understand them, partly because, as farmers, they had always worked as individuals, and partly because they believed unions to be a threat to their freedom to act as individuals.[65]

The entrepreneur cleverly used the operatives' fear that union organization would require him to surrender his liberty. In 1901, for example, when the AFL and NUTW were exerting a tremendous effort to obtain approval of a child labor bill in South Carolina, management was able to convince hundreds of operatives to sign petitions against the measure. Their petitions requested the "right" to be permitted, "as others are, to make our own contracts, control our own families."[66] Although they were isolated from the rest of Southern society, the operatives' individualism kept them from developing the economic class consciousness necessary to force from management a greater share of the wealth they created.

Management, however, did not escape detrimental effects from the operatives' individualism, for the operatives often refused to work on a given day if they felt other things, such as going fishing, were more important at the moment.[67] Although hampered in urban areas by the pass system, operatives often changed jobs with less than a moment's notice, usually moving to another mill within the same general area.[68] One male operative boasted he had worked at fifty-six different mills.[69] A small percentage of the operatives, known as "floaters," constantly moved from mill to mill. Naturally, such workers were seldom hired as permanent employees by the larger mills or urban mills where adequate work forces existed. But, they were frequently hired by even major firms as a means of insuring a surplus work force. Such migratory habits on the part of the industry's laborers also contributed to the failure of Southern unions to obtain a firm foothold, especially in rural areas.

No understanding of the mind of the Southern operative can be achieved without a thorough examination of his almost pathological fear of the Negro as a social and economic competitor. Like the tip of a gigantic iceberg, the relatively few racial incidents in the mills belied the depth and power of the operatives' racial prejudice and fear constantly lurking beneath the surface of his consciousness. In his unswerving determination to keep Negroes out of the mills, the Southern white showed a class awareness that, had it been based on purely economic principles, would have warmed the heart of any Marxist. To insure that he would never have to compete with the Negro in the mills, the white worker either had to accept offered terms of employment willingly or achieve some other method of preventing the employment of thousands of blacks who were in even more destitute economic circumstances than he. Even if the latter had been possible, to most whites it was unthinkable. So, the operative looked to management for protection from the blacks at the same time he was seeking improved hours of labor and wages.

The threat Negro labor posed to the white cotton mill worker was, for the most part, a potential, rather than immediate threat. As long as the white labor supply remained adequate and made no demands, management relied upon it almost exclusively. Although slaves were used in some antebellum factories, the pioneers of the industry such as William Gregg and Edwin M. Holt had used white labor. After the war, the industry continued in the pattern they had established, partly because plenty of white labor was available and partly because entrepreneurs did feel a sense of responsibility for their fellow whites. Negroes were, with rare exceptions, employed only in the most menial positions. They performed heavy tasks requiring no skills in the machine shops and in boiler rooms of steam-powered factories. They worked as scrub men and teamsters, as grounds keepers, and, occasionally, as strippers (those who tore the burlap or jute bagging from the bales of raw cotton). All of these jobs had two things in common: they were carried out in peripheral areas, not actually within the mills, and they were performed exclusively by males. Positions within the mill areas, such as weavers, spinners, loom fixers, and others, were never filled by Negroes, and under no circumstances did Negroes work in the presence of white women except in a janitorial capacity.[70]

Yet, for the operative, the threat of a black work force was ever present, and time and again Southern management, even while championing the cause of the white laborer, displayed an interest in the possibility of utilizing Negro labor. Although some mill officials maintained the Negro lacked the intelligence and discipline to become an effective industrial worker, most thought otherwise. As early as 1880, manufacturers expressed the belief that Negro laborers could be used profitably in the mills, provided they were adequately supervised by whites. Some felt Negro labor would prove to be less expensive than white.[71] Few actually experimented with Negro labor because they realized that to do so would seriously disrupt their white labor force, and, as long as an unlimited supply of whites seemed to exist, experiments with Negro labor were not worth the effort. When it began to be apparent in the late 1890s that the supply of whites in the immediate Piedmont area was not inexhaustible, management began to test its theories about the Negro.

In 1896, manufacturers at Rome, Georgia, attempted to use Negroes inside the mills, and in 1898, an Atlanta firm employed a large number of Negro women in positions previously reserved for whites. In 1899, officials of a Griffin, Georgia, mill moved Negroes into positions normally occupied by whites.[72] Three separate attempts were made in Charleston to use Negro labor between 1896 and 1899. The most prominent of these was the Vesta Cotton Mill experiment of 1899, which was financed by one of South Carolina's leading textile manufacturers, John H. Montgomery. White capital also financed a mill proposed in 1897 by black entrepreneurs in Columbia, South

Carolina, and a mill established by blacks in Concord, North Carolina, in the same year. The Concord mill was manned exclusively by Negroes except for major managerial personnel.[73]

Technically, these experiments were failures, for the mills run by Negro labor proved unprofitable. However, in no case did their failure seem to be caused primarily by any deficiency of the Negro as an industrial laborer, as some contemporaries claimed. The Charleston mills had failed twice with white labor, the Concord mill lacked capital and operated under the additional burdens of secondhand machinery and inexperienced management, and the Columbia mill never began operations. Most Southern labor historians agree there was no reason that the Negro could not be trained to become an efficient operative.[74] While the failure of the Negro mills caused some industrialists to argue that the Negro was incapable of industrial labor, many continued to state openly their belief that Negroes could be profitably employed. Even John Montgomery attributed the failure of the Vesta experiment to factors other than the supposed inability of the Negro labor force.[75]

Southern management's interest in Negro labor was prompted by two closely related factors, the first being the desire to maintain a surplus labor supply. More than a decade before the first signs that white labor in the immediate Piedmont area was becoming scarce, manufacturers had eyed the Negro populace as a hedge against such an eventuality. As one author so aptly expressed it, "If a greater extension of manufacturing operations should make larger demands for labor than the native white population of the state could supply . . . there is the negro population."[76] In the 1890s, the employer's fear of a dwindling white labor source and his interest in the Negro reached a peak. In 1895, Daniel Tompkins proposed that 100 manufacturers each contribute $1,500 to finance an experiment with Negro labor, since the industry's continued expansion would soon exhaust the supply of white labor.[77] With few exceptions, Southern owners testifying before the United States

Industrial Commission in 1899 and 1900 revealed the same concerns. Almost invariably, mill officials professed that they would continue to employ whites exclusively so long as they could supply their demands for workers.[78] Some attempted to remove any hint of possible racial economic competition by asserting that whites could be used in the more skilled positions associated with the increasing Southern production of fine goods while the unskilled Negroes would be used only to manufacture coarse goods.[79]

Despite their public allegiance to the white operative, the mill owners' interest in the Negro was also prompted by the recognition that the Negro could be used as a threat to keep the whites from seeking increased wages and benefits. It is far from coincidental that management's experiments with Negro labor came at the peak of the NUTW's activity in the South. Such experiments constantly reminded white operatives that management was well aware that "the colored man is now knocking at the door of cotton mills asking for work at lower wages than white men could think of." Mill officials stood ready to use the Negro the instant white workers spurned their terms of employment.[80]

In their private correspondence and in their testimony before the Industrial Commission, mill officials revealed such a calculated approach to Negro labor as a buffer against organization that it is hard to believe they genuinely preferred to employ white labor. Indeed, employers had expressed the belief that Negro labor would be easily controlled and not prone to strike as early as 1880.[81] Dexter E. Converse warned New England manufacturers supporting child labor laws that the Southern owners could use Negro labor to assure low wages, if need be.[82] Daniel Tompkins believed that if the Negro could be used in the mills, the South's labor problems would be solved for at least a quarter of a century. Otherwise, "we will without doubt have the same laws, the same experiences, and the same accessories of new labor from various sources that New England has had."[83] John H. Montgomery graphically expressed the owners' willingness to hire the Negro if whites gave trouble. Success at Vesta, he wrote a friend, would "make the South and all New England wild—that the Negro mill problem has been settled—no more trouble about labor—no more strikes, labor unions, etc. among the whites for fear that the Negro will step in and take their places."[84]

No other managerial representative who spoke on the question quite equalled the bluntness found in the testimony that John P. Coffin, Vice-President of the Southern Industrial Convention, gave to the Industrial Commission in 1900. The Negro, Coffin explained, was "a reserve force in case of strikes and labor troubles and combinations against capital in the South." A buffer against "injustice," the Negro

> is absolutely loyal to his employer, he is not given to strikes; he does his work faithfully, and can be depended on. . . . is a thing that will keep out much of the agitation of labor in the South, because the Southern people and manufacturers of the South will, before they submit to unjust domination by unions, negroize their industries. . . . If labor is reasonable, if labor will work for anything within reason, white labor will dominate the South forever; but they [management] will not submit to such outrages as have been frequently committed by organized labor.

When asked if he was holding up the Negro as a threat, not to prevent unjust demands by the whites, but to force whites to accept any terms offered, Coffin's reply was brief and to the point. "The employer must have something to hold over union organizations, or just turn his business over to the union and let them run it." In closing, he stated his opposition to the employment of Negroes in the mills. "I believe in white labor as far as possible, but I also believe in justice."[85]

The white mill workers' reactions to the use of Negro labor varied from vocal protest to violence, and it always materialized rapidly. In Charleston, where cotton manufacturing was not a major economic factor, whites protested the use of Negroes at the Vesta mill, but took no direct action. Company officials noted the opposition of Charlestonian working classes, but were more worried about reaction in upstate mills, where the factory was the only alternative to the farm. Here, one official believed, white opposition would have made such an experiment impossible.[86] Whites in Rome, Georgia, succeeded in persuading company officials to discharge recently hired Negroes by threatening to strike and hiring a lawyer. Led by the women in 1898, white employees at an Atlanta firm struck in a successful effort to obtain the dismissal of forty Negro women hired in the folding department.[87]

The next year white operatives at Griffin, Georgia, organized the Labor Regulatory Society to resist management's efforts to employ Negroes at Kincaid Mills. Member workers flogged the Negro employees, beat a number of Negroes who were not employed by the firm, warned the mill superintendent to leave town, and asked local merchants to fire their Negro employees and replace them with whites. The state militia had to be called out to stop the rampaging white mill hands.[88] Will H. Winn, an organizer for the AFL who worked vigorously to organize the mills, expressed the operatives' sentiments when he advocated that the South's Negroes be colonized in Cuba. This plan, he believed, had the backing of all the whites except mill owners and their managerial personnel, and 98 percent of the blacks. Only his latter figure was incorrect.[89]

Because of the white laborers' inability to overcome their racial prejudices, management was able to play the role of their protector against the blacks while, at the same time, using the blacks as a threat to keep wages depressed and hours of labor unchanged. Mill officials skillfully encouraged the mill hands' hatred of the Negro and manipulated that hatred to their own ends. During the South's successful campaign to disenfranchise the Negro through the "Grandfather Clause," which allowed illiterate white voters to escape state requirements that voters be literate by proving they were the direct lineal descendants of voters registered prior to the ratification of the Fourteenth Amendment, proponents of the clause sought the operatives' support, encouraging them to form white supremacy clubs.

The following description of ceremonies in such a club in a North Carolina mill village speaks volumes about the operatives' irrational fear of the Negro. After a Negro had allegedly assaulted a young white girl in the village, the operatives gave a shirt to the local sheriff as a token of their appreciation for his efforts to find the attacker. The shirt was presented

> by three beautiful little ten-year-old factory girls, handsomely arrayed in white dresses trimmed with red. These bore the red shirt, and after commanding the sheriff to kneel, each one of the trio, in faultless style, repeated beautiful, heroic, pathetic poetry, selected for and adapted to the scene. Then they advanced and placed the shirt on the sheriff. On its front, on one side, were inscribed these magic words, "White Supremacy," on the other "Our Sheriff."

The sheriff, a "kind-hearted, whole-souled, Christian gentleman, and a faithful minister of the gospel," then wept, recovered, and delivered a blistering denouncement of the Negro race. The shirt he was presented had been made by the girls of the weave room, "all or nearly all of the young ladies weaving a few threads and sewing a few stitches until the beautiful garment was complete in every particular."[90]

While the operatives fumed over supposed threats to white supremacy, management was gutting child labor legislation and branding union organizers as advocates of racial equality.[91] Organizers had little hope of coping with such powerful social forces. Economic realism had little chance in such a supercharged emotional atmosphere.[92] The Southern operative, one writer noted, "is considered in this order, a Democrat, a Carolinian, an American, and last, spiritually, a laboring man."[93] Had the writer added "white man" before "Democrat," his summation would have been even more accurate. Another early observer remarked that the Southern laborer did "not feel that the spinner in Fall River or the weaver in Lowell are closer to him than the people of his own section even though they pursue different occupations."[94]

Extreme individualism, lack of education, and deep racial prejudices, all heritages of the Old South, seriously hampered the development of a traditional economic class consciousness among Southern mill workers. For those who overcame these handicaps and realized the need for organization if they were to improve their condition, management's overwhelming power and the lack of any real economic alternatives loomed as formidable barriers. That thousands rejected their agrarian legacy of individualism and the entrepreneur's myth of Reconstruction to challenge the paternalism of the mill village demonstrates the operatives' determination to obtain a better life for themselves and their children. Their struggles to obtain a larger share of the New South's wealth, which was the creation of their labors, drew the condemnation of the region's most powerful social, economic, and political forces, and were defeated. Yet, they were the first to question seriously the heirs of the planter class, Southern cotton mill management. Their action in face of such opposition was hardly the mark of a docile, submissive labor force.

4

The Knights of Labor: Trailblazers

During the decade of the 1880s, the Noble Order of the Knights of Labor penetrated into the South's cotton textile mills, inaugurating the concept of modern labor organization in the industry.[1] The Knights presented management with its first serious challenge from union labor about basic issues of labor-management relations. The operatives' hours of labor, the industry's low wages, the practice of child labor, and the entire system of mill village paternalism were explicitly questioned by the Knights.

Perhaps as significantly, the Knights implicitly challenged both the owner's image of himself as a benevolent employer and his view of the operatives as his grateful, docile charges. Throughout the Piedmont, textile workers willingly explored the possibilities for the improvement of their circumstances that the Knights seemed to offer. Management's original response varied from adamant resistance to almost total indifference. However, as the power of the Knights grew, management, unwilling to have its policies questioned and appalled at the willingness of the operatives to explore the possibilities of organization, reacted swiftly to the threat posed by the Knights. By closing ranks and adopting the policies of those mill officials most violently opposed to unionization, management succeeded in completely exterminating the union in the South's textile mills by the close of the year 1888.

Labor-management disputes, including strikes, had occurred within the South before the appearance of the Knights. But, they were usually strictly local affairs, a spontaneous response by the workers to some grievance. Confined to one company and of short duration, they were easily squelched. A dispute at Graniteville in 1875, which lasted a month, was an exception to the generalization concerning the length of such strikes.

In the summer of that year, the Graniteville Manufacturing Company decided to reduce wages when one of its major selling agents in Charleston declared bankruptcy. Refusing to accept the reduction, the operatives struck the Graniteville firm under the leadership of James Friday, one of their number. The strike was a spontaneous expression of the operatives' resentment over the declared wage cut and was conducted without the support or encouragement of any outside labor organization. Violence erupted when mill superintendent S. W. Howland was struck in the neck by a shotgun blast. Fortunately, he was not seriously injured. After the operatives were out for an entire month, the strike was finally broken. The wage reduction was retained and the mill's directors instructed the President, H. H. Hickman, to close the mill completely if further violence occurred.[2] Despite its failure, the strike portended the success the Knights would have organizing operatives in Graniteville, South Carolina, as well as in Augusta, Georgia, an area with an established textile tradition.

As the major national labor union during the 1870s and 1880s, the Knights of Labor were among the most naive, most incongruous labor organizations in American history. Deeply rooted in the antebellum reform movements rather than in labor

unionism, the Knights excluded from membership only law-
yers, bankers, gamblers, stockbrokers, and liquor dealers.[3] As
a result, its members included Socialists, trade unionists, ex-
Greenbackers, farmers, social reformers, and would-be politicians. On paper, the Knights' organizational structure was
highly centralized, with the executive directors elected by the
organization's annual General Assembly in control of the entire
edifice. Beneath the General Assembly were state, district, and
local assemblies. In areas where few locals existed, the locals
often directly affiliated with the General Assembly.[4] Although
Terence V. Powderly, the Knights' Grand Master Workman
from 1879 until 1893, led the directors, neither he nor the directors ever exercised full control over district and local assemblies, which often did as they pleased without fear of expulsion.[5]

Theoretically, the Knights were basically an industrial union.
Union members affiliated directly with the order, not through
affiliation with some member union. A large faction of the
Knights, however, favored craft organization to trade unionism,
despite the objections of Powderly and other leaders. This
problem was only partially resolved by allowing trade unions
to affiliate with the Knights under the title of "trade districts,"
which were, of course, composed of trade locals. This compromise failed to settle the question, and the continuing dispute
over the place of the trade union within the order would
weaken the Knights and eventually play a major role in their
national decline.

Actually, the Knights were more of a fraternal order of laborers than an industrial union or federation of industrial unions. In their desire to reach the nation's entire laboring populace, the order's leadership promoted the mixed local assembly,
which accepted anyone eligible for membership regardless of
his trade. Mixed locals often not only contained members of
various crafts within a single industry, but members of various
industries as well. By 1886, the majority of the Knights' locals
were mixed assemblies.[6] Such a loose organizational structure

encouraged the order's growth in nonindustrial areas because it allowed the few laborers in various occupations to coalesce under one banner. In the South, mixed assemblies were by far the most numerous, with true industrial assemblies second in number and the craft locals, a poor third.[7]

Despite its emphasis on industrial unionism, the Knights of Labor refused to accept the role of the worker in a modern industrial society. Rather, the Knights rejected outright American industrialism's reduction of the laborer to an economic entity and sought to destroy the wage system. The Knights hoped to return to the productive system of the past in which the producer was his own employer, capable of feeling an identity with, and a sense of pride in, the product he produced.[8]

Powderly dominated the determination of the Knights' ideology, and, as a result, the order offered an extremely naive program to the laborer. Powderly's program was centered around the principles of education and cooperation, and he sought to avoid direct confrontation with management, if at all possible. His ideology well represented the American reformer's faith that education, not violence and radicalism, was the answer to nearly any problem. In other words, the worker, largely ignorant of social, economic, and political "truths," must be educated before he could demand his rightful place in society.[9] It was the task of the Knights to educate the worker to these "truths." Such educational work would be time-consuming, but to attempt to destroy the wage system without it would be folly.[10]

The principal truth Powderly believed the laborer must learn was that of cooperation. Through cooperatives, the laborer could be restored to his proprietary role. Indeed, cooperation was "the only means whereby the poor can obtain a just share of the profits and honors of advancing civilization."[11] Throughout the 1880s, the Knights attempted to establish producer and consumer cooperatives, with little success. Lacking in operating capital, discriminated against by competitors, and suffering from inexperienced management, most of the cooperatives the Knights established soon failed. Yet, cooperation continued to be one of Powderly's dreams, because, without it, the Knights had no alternative to the wage system with which they were at odds.[12]

Partly because of his vain egotism and partly because of his basically middle-class attitudes, Powderly was vitally interested in politics. A successful candidate himself, he served as mayor of Scranton, Pennsylvania, from 1878 until 1884. Nevertheless, he attempted to keep the Knights from becoming a political organization until the advent of Populism, by which time the Knights were well on the road to oblivion.[13] Prior to 1892, the order had theoretically adopted a policy of rewarding its friends and punishing its enemies without participating in politics as a union.[14] The national leadership of the Knights forbade locals even to discuss politics as an item of official business.[15] Completely ignoring such admonishments, locals throughout the nation actively participated in politics, especially after 1886.[16] Southern Knights were no exception.

A veteran of the disastrous industrial warfare of the 1870s, Powderly was convinced that "strikes are a failure. Ask any old veteran in the labor movement and he will say the same. I shudder at the thought of a strike, and I have good reason."[17] Such views were also totally in keeping with his educational, cooperative, nonviolent methodology. Powderly vigorously opposed strikes and lockouts as "harassing details" which drained a "great deal of valuable time" from the main tasks of education and cooperative enterprises. At best, he believed, strikes gave the worker only temporary relief.[18] Accordingly, immediately upon his election as Grand Master Workman in 1879, Powderly used his influence to cripple the union's defense fund. He diverted 70 percent of it into educational and cooperative efforts. Although an Assistance Fund was established in 1882, Powderly's opposition to the strike continued. The fund was to be financed by a compulsory monthly assessment of five cents per member levied against local assemblies. The order's national administration made little effort to see that the assessments were collected. During the financial year of 1885-1886, local assemblies paid in only $600 to the fund. At the end of June, 1886, the Assistance Fund had a balance on hand of only fourteen dollars and thirty cents. As a result of failing to build an adequate strike fund, in the tumultuous year of 1886 the order was forced to issue special appeals and assessments in a desperate attempt to save locals which rushed into strikes only to find that they faced total defeat without help from the national organization.[19]

The Knights also adopted a strike policy that made it almost impossible for locals to obtain the national union's official approval for a strike. Only the executive board, in consultation with the Grand Master Workman, could officially authorize a strike. Authorization was not even considered until both the local and the district assembly involved had attempted to settle the dispute by arbitration.[20] After 1886, a two-thirds vote of a local was required to initiate a strike and, at any time during the strike, the general, state, district, or local assembly could demand another vote. Unless a majority of the members decided to continue, the strike had to be settled immediately on the best terms obtainable.[21] Powderly and other leaders of the order incessantly preached arbitration. Here their naïveté reached, perhaps, its greatest height, for arbitration was impossible as long as the employer refused to recognize the locals. In the face of the opposition that the Knights often met, arbitration became a joke.[22] This was certainly true of the order's attempts to obtain arbitrated settlements from Southern mill officials.

As basically idealistic advocates of social justice, Powderly and the Knights took a liberal approach to the problem of the Negro laborer, a stance that hindered the union's growth in the South. Although the Negro was organized into separate assemblies in the South, on the national level he was afforded equal treatment. At general assemblies, delegations from Southern Negro assemblies were received just as were white delegations; no efforts were made to segregate them. Even the 1886 General Assembly held in Richmond, Virginia, was completely integrated. Powderly's racial attitudes were based on both moral and economic considerations, for he perceptively realized that

> Southern labor, regardless of its color, must learn to read and write . . . while this race [the Negro] continues to increase in ignorance and numbers, prosperity will not even knock at the door of the Southern laborer.[23]

Southern critics of the Knights were quick to charge them with favoring the Negro and promoting racial equality. The Richmond General Assembly triggered vicious editorial attacks on the order by much of the Southern press. Whites seemed most upset because a Northern delegation had insisted upon equal treatment for its Negro members at theaters, hotels, and restaurants.[24] The issue was agitated so much that, in 1887, an Oxford, North Carolina, member reported that in his area, "Nigger and Knight have become synonymous terms."[25] Their progressive racial policies seriously handicapped the Knights in the South, for even their white Southern membership found it difficult, and at times impossible, to accept such liberal views. Editors of official Knights of Labor papers in the South agreed with the national order on the need to improve the Negro economically, but refused to endorse social equality and, at times, portrayed blacks in a most unflattering manner. Some Southern Knights continued to discriminate against the Negro economically. In Richmond, for example, white Knights in the building trades succeeded in denying employment to black laborers on municipal construction projects.[26] In any case, the racial problem was undoubtedly a major barrier to the Knights' efforts to enroll Southern laborers in their cause.

The Knights' interest in the South began immediately upon the formation of the General Assembly in 1878. In 1878 and

1879, the Knights commissioned fifteen organizers for the South: seven were placed in Alabama, five in Kentucky, and one each in Florida, Georgia, and North Carolina.[27] South Carolina was completely ignored. The order's original strongholds in the South were Mobile and Birmingham, Alabama, but, by 1883, interest in the Knights expressed by artisan laborers of the Southern seaboard states demanded further attention. In July of that year, Georgia had five locals; both North Carolina and South Carolina had one.[28] Within a year, new assemblies were formed at Atlanta and Charlotte.[29] At the 1884 General Assembly, General Secretary Frederick Turner reported receiving numerous requests for information concerning methods of forming locals from laborers throughout Alabama, Florida, and North Carolina. Turner recommended placing a "good, live organizer" in the South. John Ray, a delegate from Raleigh, North Carolina, expanded Turner's recommendation by asking the Assembly to put paid organizers in each Southern state. The Assembly failed to act upon either request.[30]

Two events of the mid-1880s proved to be significant factors in the Knights' successful efforts to gain footholds in the South. First, in the year 1884–1885, the South began to feel the effects of the general depression of 1883. Laborers saw the Knights as a means to prevent reductions in wages or the loss of positions. The second was the order's successful strike in the spring of 1885 against Jay Gould's midwestern railway system, which forced the railways to rescind announced wage reductions. Against a backdrop of two depression years, this short-lived victory caused workers throughout the nation, including the South, to view the Knights as their most likely means of economic salvation. Thousands rallied to the order's banner, hoping that somehow Terence Powderly could lead them out of their personal economic wilderness.

As Southern interest in the Knights increased, the order's national leadership began to pay more attention to the region. Before 1885, organizational work in the South had been done by natives; some were paid organizers, but most were volunteers.[31] In January 1885, however, Powderly and Richard F. Trevelick, veteran labor agitator and national organizer for the Knights, toured parts of the South, stopping at Raleigh, Atlanta, Columbus, and Augusta, but not visiting South Carolina.[32] In the spring of 1886, Trevelick visited South Carolina, Georgia, North Carolina, and other Southern states. Ralph Beaumont, former Greenbacker and member of the Knights' National Legislative Committee, made the Southern tour in the spring of 1887.[33] At that year's General Assembly, the Southern seaboard states east of the Mississippi were represented by delegates from five states and ten district assemblies.[34] The order's increased interest and success in Dixie were amply demonstrated by the holding of the 1886 General Assembly in Richmond and the General Assembly of 1889 in Atlanta.

Although the Knights had made a special effort to organize the Northern textile worker as early as 1883, they paid little attention to the organizational needs of the Southern operative until 1885.[35] By the end of the latter year, individual Southern cotton mill hands were probably members of mixed locals in such textile manufacturing areas as Raleigh, Durham, and Charlotte, North Carolina; Danville, Virginia; and Roswell and Atlanta, Georgia.[36] Such locals, however, largely comprised masons, painters, carpenters, and other skilled urban laborers.[37]

After a four-year boom period, by late 1884 and early 1885, the Southern cotton manufacturing industry was beginning to feel the effects of the depression of 1883. Only rarely were mills forced to close, but declining orders caused many firms to reduce wages and production in an effort to conserve operating capital, a commodity that Southern mills were often short of, even in the best of times.[38]

Like laborers across the nation, Southern mill hands turned to the Knights for protection. The national organization continued to devote more attention to locals dominated by artisans, but did encourage members of such locals to recruit textile workers or aid them in forming their own assemblies. As a result, by 1886, in the Piedmont crescent stretching from Danville, Virginia, to Columbus, Georgia, the Knights had established numerous mixed locals containing large numbers of operatives and over twenty textile trade assemblies.[39] The order would eventually establish textile assemblies in Alabama and Mississippi.[40] Even so, the order was most active within the industry in the three major Southern textile states of Georgia, North Carolina, and South Carolina.

The Knights of Labor appear to have been as strong in North Carolina as they were anywhere in the South, with the possible exception of Virginia. The union established a local in Charlotte in June 1883, but the state organization grew from locals formed in the Raleigh-Durham area in 1884.[41] This area, which was the heart of the state's Fourth Congressional District, was so well organized in 1886 that it elected the State Master Workman, John Nichols of Raleigh, to Congress as an Independent.[42] Locals existed in all regions of the state, and several newspapers voiced the doctrines and aspirations of the order. The Knights made their presence felt in the politics of several municipalities. They were also able to exert enough political pressure to obtain the passage of a bill creating a state bureau of labor. Yet, the union's strength rested largely in the hands of artisan and agrarian groups. The Knights lagged in their organization of the textile worker, and those operatives that did join proved less militant than their counterparts further south.[43] These facts reflect the state's large agrarian population and its small number of urban mills with large labor forces. Textile operatives managed, nevertheless, to become involved in much of the order's activity within the state.

Textile operatives who responded to the Knights after the Southwest strikes because the order seemed to offer some hope for improved conditions quickly found such hopes to be slim ones, yet they continued to hold on to them. Mill workers probably first joined the Knights as individual members of mixed assemblies such as the Raleigh locals, since no trade assemblies existed in the state until well into 1886. By July of that year, the Knights had established locals in Alamance County, the state's textile heartland, at Graham, and at Burlington (then called Company Shops).[44] These locals were also mixed assemblies, but were largely composed of operatives.

They ran into immediate opposition from mill officials. W. A. Fogleman, Master Workman of Local 8293, Company Shops, informed Powderly early in October that superintendents were discriminating against union members. When the local protested to the owner, "he would not give us no satisfaction and says he will not do nothing so we ask your advice." Fogleman told Powderly that the Knights were strong enough to close the mills, and that "we have got to come down to 11 hours per day." Powderly answered the plea in mid-November. With the order inundated by strikes, he warned the operatives to avoid a strike at all costs. As a new local, they should expect difficulty. He told them not to strike, or ask for the discharge of the superintendent, for the national organization could not support a strike or lockout. Instead, they should continue to organize as secretly as possible "and give no cause for such action [the firing of members] and it will come right in time."[45] The Alamance operatives evidently accepted this advice, for organizing continued both there and elsewhere in North Carolina, including the towns of Charlotte and Hickory, both of which were in the midst of the textile manufacturing belt.[46]

Before the end of the year, mixed locals definitely containing textile operatives existed at Fayetteville and Mount Holly. Mill hands were probably members of mixed assemblies in the mill towns of Concord, Salisbury, and Henderson. Textile trade assemblies existed at Lowell and Mountain Island.[47] By 1887, the Knights had established mixed assemblies in Greensboro, Swepsonville, and Winston, with large numbers of operatives in the locals of the two latter towns. Swepsonville was in Alamance County, Greensboro in the neighboring county of Guilford. Another assembly composed largely of operatives was established at the Columbia factory, thirty miles south of Greensboro, early in 1888.[48] Yet, the number of operatives in these locals, even the trade assemblies, must have been small. Despite W. A. Fogleman's boast that the Knights could close the mills of Company Shops, they avoided direct conflict with management. Powderly's advice might have had some influence, but, had the Knights existed in many mills in large numbers, management's policy of harassing and discharging Knights inevitably would have led to serious conflicts.

The Knights, with one possible exception, never led a textile strike in North Carolina, despite this widespread organization.[49] This possible exception occurred, significantly, in Alamance County, home of the Holt mills and, in the 1880s, the state's leading and best organized textile center. In April 1887, the Knights in Burlington unsuccessfully backed a slate of candidates for municipal offices. There is no evidence to establish a connection, but the political defeat probably sparked a strike just after the election against the Falls of the Neuse Manufacturing Company in Swepsonville, another Alamance County town, located outside Burlington.

The operatives hoped to force the company to reduce its hours, as it required a seventy-five-hour week, but the company maintained such hours were justified because it charged no rent for company housing. The mill hands asked for a sixty-six-hour week and the privilege of paying rent. Management refused and the operatives struck. Although no positive evidence shows that the Knights were involved in the strike, it is unlikely that an assembly of Knights composed largely of operatives located in the town remained passive. If the Knights were involved, they were doubly defeated, for the strike ended in failure.[50] Despite the defeat of their only strike, however, one author notes that the North Carolina Bureau of Labor in its 1893 report credited the Knights with securing voluntary reductions of hours at other mills.[51]

While the North Carolina Knights failed to engage in any major strike activity, they were able to bring pressure to bear on the mills through the state's labor press. The order had a number of papers scattered throughout the state, including the *Fayetteville Messenger,* their official paper, the *Charlotte Craftsman,* the *Durham Workman,* the *Raleigh Workman,* the *Greensboro Craftsman,* and the *Wilmington Index.*[52] Though most of these newspapers had brief lives, they occasionally aroused the ire of the cotton manufacturer. In May 1887, C. F. King, editor of the *Charlotte Craftsman,* copied an article describing conditions in a Durham cotton mill from the *Richmond Labor Herald.* According to the article, mill hands were overworked and mistreated; even small children received brutal whippings. The officers of the mill sued King for criminal libel, and on June 18, King appeared in Durham to stand trial with witnesses to attest to the truth of the article. The owners promptly had the case postponed and urged King to simply apologize. Backed by Congressman John Nichols, State Master Workman, King refused. The charges were discreetly dropped.[53]

The order's press attempted to counter attacks on the Knights made by anti-labor papers. This was especially true of attacks based on the racial issue, which, for reasons already discussed, could seriously damage the order's reputation among operatives. The *Messenger* fought a continual verbal war with the state's leading Democratic paper, the *Raleigh News and Observer.* It consistently denied the *Observer*'s charge that the Knights advocated social equality for Negroes, that the Knights were led by a Negro, and that they hoped to see Negroes in control of the state's government. "The subsidized press," charged the *Messenger,* had caused many to feel that a Knight was "a horribly depraved specimen of humanity to be shunned and dreaded." But, because of the courage of a few, asserted the *Messenger* hopefully, people were beginning to "understand and endorse the principals [*sic*] of the Knights."[54]

To a larger degree than the Knights of any other Southern

state, the Knights of North Carolina participated in a national revolt of laborers against the political establishment. By 1886 national labor troubles, including the Knights' second major strike against Gould's southwestern railway system and the Haymarket Riot, had resulted in a groundswell of anti-union public opinion. Reacting to this negative sentiment, state legislatures passed bills to hinder labor's organizational efforts and courts convicted ever larger numbers of union members of conspiracy and rioting. As a means of self-protection, labor turned to political action, especially in major urban areas. In what has been called the "Great Upheaval," workers in New York, Chicago, and several New England towns entered labor candidates in the municipal elections of 1886. The most significant of these candidates was Henry George, who ran for the office of mayor of New York on the ticket of a labor coalition party, the Progressive Democracy. This tendency of the Knights to rush into partisan politics in support of independent labor candidates ran directly counter to Powderly's policy of cautious nonpartisanship.[55] In North Carolina, State Master Workman John Nichols was elected to Congress from the Fourth District primarily by combining the votes of the Knights and disgruntled agrarian elements. Indeed, Nichols went so far in wooing the rural vote as to liken the Knights to the Agricultural Wheel of Arkansas, a farmers' organization that later merged with the Southern Farmers' Alliance. His election clearly presaged the coming fusion of the Populists and the Republicans in the mid-1890s.[56] Yet, despite his emphasis on the agrarian vote, he received substantial support from the industrial laborer. The vote in Alamance County, home of the state's oldest textile mills and a major cotton manufacturing center, indicated that the operative voted for Nichols rather than his Democratic opponent, John Graham. Alamance was one of the four counties Graham carried, but he did so by only thirty-one votes. The narrowness of his victory is extremely significant since he had the backing of the Alamance mills. In

addition, Thomas Holt, a member of the area's leading textile
family, ran successfully on the same ticket for a seat in the
county's delegation to the state house of representatives. Holt
himself narrowly escaped defeat, even though he was backed
by his firm's tremendous financial resources. The *News and
Observer,* the major spokesman for the Democrats in the East,
committed itself during this campaign to a rabidly anti-Knights
position and had backed both Graham and Holt vigorously.[57]

After their victory in the Nichols campaign, the Knights'
state assembly met in January 1887 in Raleigh and decided to
lobby for a state ten-hour-day law, a child labor law, and the
creation of a bureau of labor. They were able to introduce the
ten-hour and child labor bills, but both were lost. (To have
requested an eight-hour day, as did organized labor throughout the northern states, would have been laughable in the
South.) The Knights' efforts were not, however, completely in
vain. Largely because of their lobbying, the legislature passed
a bill establishing a state bureau of labor.[58] Created as a part
of the Department of Agriculture, Immigration, and Statistics,
the Bureau of Labor Statistics was the only bureau of its kind
in the South until the turn of the century.[59] A Commissioner
of Labor was appointed for two years by the governor at a
salary of $1,500 per year. After an initial appropriation of
$5,000, the Bureau received $2,000 per year. The Commissioner was to "collect information on the subject of labor, its
relation to capital, the hours of labor, the earnings of laboring
men and women, their educational, moral, and financial condition; and the best means of promoting their mental, material,
social, and moral prosperity."[60] The Bureau's lack of regulatory powers made its establishment a hollow victory for the
Knights. Yet, it served notice on the manufacturers that their
actions were no longer above question, and the information it
provided was later instrumental in the adoption of child labor
laws.

In 1888, vastly overestimating their political power, the

Knights followed the lead of labor groups across the country
and plunged headlong into politics with heady optimism. Actually, their optimism was not entirely unfounded. Nichols' election in 1886 had shown support from both agrarian and labor
groups, and agrarian unrest was rising. The Knights had beaten
the Durham mills in a libel suit, obtained the passage of the
labor bureau bill, and were continuing to establish locals
throughout the state. In addition, the state had a large Republican element whose votes might be enticed. Thus, their unsuccessful attempt to elect members of the Burlington municipal government in 1887, discussed earlier in this chapter,
rather than discouraging the Knights merely served as a prel-
ude to their large-scale involvement in the state's political
wars the following year.

Recovering from the Burlington defeat, the Alamance Knights
renewed their political activity and "forced the issues of the
[1888] campaign to be fought on the Knights of Labor plat-
form."[61] At Mount Holly, where the local assembly had over
eighty members, mostly operatives, the Knights nominated
their own candidates for local and state offices.[62] The *Messenger* audaciously backed the National Union Labor party's
national ticket of A. J. Streeter, President of the Northern
Farmers' Alliance, and Charles Cunningham. Fayetteville
Knights formed a local Union Labor party and ran their own
slate for county and state positions, including a cotton mill
hand named Warren Carver for the state house of representatives.[63] Nichols, still the State Master Workman, stood for reelection to Congress from the Fourth District.

For the Knights, the campaign of 1888 centered around the
congressional contest between John Nichols and Democratic
candidate Captain Benjamin H. Bunn, a contest in which
the textile industry was deeply involved. The *Raleigh News and
Observer* and the *Messenger* championed the cause of their
respective candidates while castigating the opposition. The
Raleigh paper used the racial issue unsparingly against candi-

dates the Knights supported, especially Nichols. Should their candidates win, charged the *Observer,* the entire state would be delivered to Negro rule. Playing on the Southerner's hatred of Reconstruction, the paper also attempted to link labor candidates and the Knights in general with the Republican party.[64] This charge was not without foundation, for the Knights were seeking Republican backing for their friends. But the order also refused to support any party per se, insisting that members should vote for laboring men, regardless of party affiliation. Although the *Messenger* favored a state Union Labor party ticket, it supported Nichols who ran as an Independent.[65]

The *Messenger* vehemently denied the *Observer*'s allegations, while striking hard at Benjamin Bunn, President of the Rocky Mount Cotton Mills, as a foe of labor. Bunn, claimed the *Messenger,* had enforced such arbitrary regulations at his factory that many hands had left his employ rather than "submit to his tyranny." He had informed his employees that if they joined the Knights they would be immediately discharged. Bunn was "merely the tool of the plaid trust [the Holt interests]" who opposed child labor legislation because he employed children in his own mill.[66] The charge that Bunn was the tool of the Holts was lent credibility by the fact that Thomas Holt was running for the lieutenant governorship as a Democrat. Officials in the Holt mills were accused of threatening to fire operatives who did not vote the Democratic ticket.[67] The *Messenger* was obviously trying to hold the vote of the district's mill hands for Nichols hoping that, combined with the vote of discontented farmers, it would provide him the margin of victory.

The labors of the *Messenger* and the Knights proved inadequate; their candidates were defeated throughout the state. Nichols failed in a second effort to tap the building agrarian discontent that in less than a decade would sweep the state into the Populist camp, and carried only Wake County in his bid for reelection.[68] Yet, the *Messenger*'s efforts were not without effect. Nichols' opponent received his smallest majority in Alamance County, even with Holt on the ticket, a strong indication that large numbers of operatives continued to support Nichols. In Fayetteville, the entire Union Labor ticket was handily defeated. Although the *Messenger* blamed the defeat on "intimidation, illegal voting, bribery, and miscounting," it failed to substantiate the charge except for noting that a Union Labor candidate had been told to leave town. The *Messenger* ruefully admitted that organized labor had suffered a severe setback in North Carolina. Other local labor efforts must have fared poorly also, for the *Messenger* failed to report the election results in Burlington and Mount Holly. Had the Knights scored victories at either town, they would have been publicized. The paper tried to encourage the rank and file without success. Disillusioned laborers left the order, and the *Messenger* soon folded for lack of subscribers.[69] The Knights had staked too much of their future on the hope of winning in the political arena in 1888. The defeat they received there proved to be the *coup de grace* for the order in North Carolina's textile mills, although assemblies of farm laborers and artisans lasted well into the 1890s.

Stirrings of organizational activity among South Carolina's cotton mill workers prompted by the Knights evoked an immediate and vigorously hostile response from management. The Knights first appeared in the state among the artisans of the towns of Florence and Columbia.[70] From there they spread westward into the Piedmont where they soon began to obtain members among the operatives, especially those in larger mills who had seen their wages reduced. Organizers also crossed the border from Augusta, Georgia, to recruit mill hands from the tier of the state's southwestern counties.[71]

Sometime early in 1886 the Knights ran afoul of the Graniteville Manufacturing Company, the state's oldest textile firm. The Knights attempted to organize operatives at the company mill in Vaucluse, a little town, like Graniteville, just a few miles north of the border from Augusta, Georgia, in a region called Horse Creek Valley. In April, the Vaucluse laborers unsuccessfully petitioned for wage increases, indicating the Knights had met with at least partial organizational success.[72]

At the same time, Ellison A. Smyth informed mill owner Henry Hammett of signs of labor organizations at his factory in Pelzer, a mill village just south of Greenville and approximately a hundred miles northwest of Graniteville. His operatives' favorable response to the Knights thoroughly alarmed Smyth, whose first reaction was to suggest the formation of a manufacturer's organization to confront the union. He requested Hammett to support a meeting of mill men to consider this and other methods of combating the Knights' increasing organizational activities. Hammett dismissed as premature such a meeting until some "demonstration" occurred or the operatives were "demoralized" by events outside the state. Yet, Hammett was more concerned about the Knights than his reply to Smyth indicated. As early as March, Hammett had written to Dexter E. Converse, asking, "Do you apprehend trouble in the end from labor organizations or will they break down of their own weight—without a revolution?" In addition, he had already ordered his superintendents at the Piedmont and Caperdown mills, both located a few miles from Greenville, to "nip in the bud" any "Yankee-inspired" organizational activity by discharging operatives engaged in it.[73]

Hammett, easily the most militant anti-union mill owner in the state, possessed an almost psychotic contempt for organized labor that led him into a personal crusade against the Knights. Events on the national labor scene only increased his apprehension. The Haymarket Riot fed his fears of revolution and his conviction that the Knights were a serious menace to the property rights of businessmen.[74] In addition, his growing concern over the Knights in South Carolina was nourished by their success just across the border in the mills of Augusta, Georgia, where trouble between the union and management had been in the offing since April 1886. By June, the Augusta dispute had erupted into what became the Knights' major Southern cotton textile strike. Hammett immediately offered the Augusta mill presidents his support, and throughout the strike acted as their self-appointed advisor. "Crush the Knights beyond resurrection," he argued; they presented a greater threat to the mills than "the depression of the last two or three years, or any threat in the last twenty years." To support the Augusta manufacturers, he sent them a copy of a proposed area wage scale and promised to attempt to obtain approval of it by mill owners throughout South Carolina.[75]

Although Hammett's fears of revolution were the product of an overactive imagination, his concern that a strong Augusta union might spread to South Carolina was well founded. Four Charleston locals established early in 1886, at least one of which contained textile operatives, had lent the Augusta strikers their moral and financial support.[76] Of much greater concern to Hammett, however, were the recruiting activities of the Reverend J. Simmions Meynardie, leader of the Augusta strike. Not only was Meynardie holding the Augusta Knights together in the face of determined resistance, he had also crossed into South Carolina and succeeded in organizing a number of operatives at both Vaucluse and Graniteville.[77]

No stranger to the area, Meynardie, the son of a prominent Charleston Methodist divine, and himself a Baptist minister, had previously preached in the South Carolina Piedmont and had evidently attempted to organize the area's operatives in addition to ministering to their spiritual needs. Hammett, ever the alarmist, characterized Meynardie's previous efforts as "black and disgraceful." The *Carolina Spartan* embellished the portrait: Meynardie was a man "of anarchist tendencies, who never did a fair day's work—giving trouble wherever he goes."[78]

The *Spartan* was correct about Meynardie's connection with trouble. It erupted among the Knights at the Graniteville company's Vaucluse plant, a local Meynardie had organized, when its leader, Robert Butler, was discharged for interference in the weaving department. When the company brought James Rearden from Graniteville to replace Butler, the Vaucluse Knights, about half of the labor force, displayed their resentment. Surrounding Rearden as he came to work, they directed a barrage of taunts at him. One female Knight called Rearden a "damned red-headed son-of-a-bitch," threatened his life, and gave him twenty-four hours to leave town. Rearden bought a pistol and stayed. The woman's threats expressed feelings more intense than those of her fellow Knights, for no further incidents occurred.[79] Evidently, the Knights believed that further resistance was futile, and, rather than conduct an unsuccessful strike, they accepted Rearden. Although partially defeated, the local at least continued to exist.

Undaunted by their setback at Vaucluse, the Knights continued their efforts to organize the South Carolina mills, beginning in October during the height of the Augusta strike. Although no evidence exists to link directly the Augusta Knights with this second effort to recruit Carolina operatives, such a connection is probable. The Knights began this effort by attempting to penetrate Hammett's carefully guarded Piedmont mills with little success. Hammett, fearful that unionization would endanger the price of the mill's capital stock, ordered his superintendent to discharge and refuse to rehire all those connected with the Knights. He also instructed him to close the mill at any further signs of organizational activity.[80]

Meanwhile, the Knights had been successful in organizing textile trade assemblies at Smyth's Pelzer Mills and Converse's Clifton Mills, two of the firms clustered within the general Greenville-Spartanburg textile complex. In addition, they had organized a mixed assembly within the city of Greenville, which included textile operatives among its members. Learning of the forty-five-member Pelzer assembly and the Clifton local, Hammett encouraged both Smyth and Converse to resist the Knights. When he destroyed the Clifton assembly by discharging union members, Converse received Hammett's hearty congratulations and an expression of hope that Smyth would follow his example.[81] Hammett's hopes were not misplaced. Although the Pelzer operatives attempted to organize secretly, Smyth was able to obtain the names of members, all of whom were immediately discharged. Members of the order were mystified as to how Smyth obtained their names and appealed to Powderly for help. Their appeal was never answered. Smyth evidently also used physical intimidation to disrupt the local, for the organizer at Pelzer "got frightened and ran away."[82]

Despite management's staunch resistance, the Knights stubbornly persisted in their efforts to organize the state's mills. Knights were still active in a Charleston mill as late as June 1887.[83] In July of the same year the *Carolina Spartan* reported that "walking delegates" (commissioned organizers) from various Southern assemblies were in Greenville, Pickens, Laurens, and other textile counties of the Piedmont sowing a "crop of organized labor, distrust, race antagonisms, menace." The paper directed its heaviest criticism at the order's willingness to work with the Negro. By appealing for cooperation among the two races, said the *Spartan,* the Knights were "playing with fire."[84] The *Spartan*'s criticisms may have had some effect, but the organizers succeeded in reviving or establishing white locals at Rock Hill, Graniteville, and Vaucluse. Although these locals were mixed rather than trade assemblies, their membership probably included individual textile operatives.[85] Late in the year, however, the order suffered defeats at Fishing Creek and, again, at Clifton, that proved fatal to its efforts to organize the industry in South Carolina.

Sometime in 1887, the Knights succeeded in a second effort to organize the operatives of Clifton. The revived assembly again drew a hostile reception from mill officials, who began to discharge its members immediately upon learning their identity. Since the local had made no demands concerning hours, wages, or working conditions, management's discharge policy prompted the Knights, who only sought recognition of their right to organize, to strike the Clifton plant in September. Proclaiming that they had done the operatives no injustice and that, therefore, the operatives had no need for a union, management steadfastly refused to alter its position. Then, what was to become management's dual ultimate weapons throughout the South were employed as the Clifton management moved to eradicate every remnant of organization. All Knights, real and suspected, were locked out of the mills and eviction proceedings were begun to remove the families of twenty-six Knights from company housing. To replace the locked-out Knights, new hands were successfully recruited from the surrounding area.[86] Without money, jobs, or housing, the more than 100 Clifton strikers appealed in desperation to the Knights' national executive board for aid. Seeking help closer to home, they also asked other Southern locals for financial support. The *Messenger,* the Knights' official paper in North Carolina, carried appeals for the Clifton members in both November and December.[87] These pleas were never answered, the local was defeated, and its members dispersed. After December 1887, no reference to the Clifton strike is to be found in the *Messenger,* the *Carolina Spartan,* or the *Journal of United Labor,* the Knights' national paper.

Already seriously weakened by their reverses of 1886, the Knights' defeat at Clifton further hastened the decline of the order in South Carolina's mills. In December 1887, some thirty Spartanburg Knights formed an emigration colony and left the Piedmont to seek an area more hospitable to organized labor. Most likely, some of the Knights from Clifton, which is just outside Spartanburg, joined the colony, since their positions had been filled and several had expressed the desire to seek employment elsewhere.[88]

A second major setback for the order followed on the heels of the Clifton episode. In the fall of 1887, the management of a cotton mill at Fishing Creek discharged and refused to reinstate members of a recently organized textile local. Intervening on behalf of the locked-out operatives, Local 8053 of Mount Holly, North Carolina, requested the order's national executive board to try to obtain a settlement. The board sent one of its members, T. B. Barry, to investigate the lockout. Barry, who arrived in November, reported that management had organized scab laborers into a vigilante group called the "Jayhawks" and encouraged them to fight the union. The Jayhawks marched on the homes of two active members of the local, intending to hang them. The two escaped the mob only by fleeing to the woods where they remained in hiding for two weeks. Faced with such violent opposition, the other members either disavowed the order and returned to work or left for positions elsewhere. The 1888 General Assembly voted to boycott the firm's products, but, by then, the order had been completely driven from the mills.[89] An inconsequential disturbance in that year at Greenville proved to be the last gasp of the Knights in their efforts to organize the South Carolina cotton textile industry.[90]

The Knights established their first assembly in Georgia among the artisans of Atlanta in 1883.[91] During the next three years, the order grew until it had assemblies in all of Georgia's major cities, in most of her towns, and in many rural areas. As in North Carolina, the union was somewhat a forerunner of the Southern Farmers' Alliance and of Populism, recruiting discontented tenant farmers, black and white, in addition to its artisan members of urban areas. Unlike either North Carolina or South Carolina, Georgia had several urban areas containing both artisan laborers and large concentrations of textile operatives. In the urban industrial areas of Columbus, Atlanta, and Augusta, the Knights obtained a firm foothold, establishing district assemblies in each by 1887.[92] Here, the urban operatives, especially those of Augusta, were more integrated into the industrial economy than any other mill workers in the South and responded to the concept of organization. They proved to

be the most militant Southern Knights and presented Southern
cotton manufacturers their most serious challenge until the
turn of the century.

By the fall of 1886, the Georgia Knights had made considerable inroads into the textile industry. At least one of the Atlanta district assembly's twenty-eight locals was a textile trade
assembly.[93] W. M. Harbin, an Atlanta Knight and Methodist
minister, organized several Columbus locals which later formed
a district assembly. At least three of these locals were textile
trade assemblies.[94] Augusta had a textile assembly as early as
1884 and, in 1886, its major textile assembly, Local 5030,
claimed well over 2,000 members. There were also three mixed
assemblies in Augusta that may have contained operatives,
and a textile trade assembly existed at Macon.[95] Mixed locals
at Barton and Roswell definitely contained operatives, and
mixed locals at Rome and Stone Mountain probably included
individual textile mill hands.[96]

The Augusta Knights deserve special attention. By far the
largest Southern textile assembly, Augusta Local 5030 was also
the South's most militant local. Indeed, as this local became
the very symbol of textile unionism in the entire Southern Piedmont, its fate determined the fate of the entire Southern movement. It was with this local that Southern management fought
and won its major battle with the Knights.

With the possible exception of Columbus, Augusta, with
nine cotton mills, was the only Southern urban area with such
a large concentration of mills in the 1880s. It had been a textile center since before the Civil War. Thus, like the rural
Graniteville or Alamance County, it possessed a work force
with at least something of an industrial tradition. This tradition had reduced the Augusta operatives' agrarian individualism
and implanted within them the seeds of class consciousness.
Living in an urban area, Augusta workers were further removed
from the land, more aware of the likelihood that they would
never return to the farm, and more dependent on the mill for a

livelihood than was the average Southern cotton mill hand. They were better prepared mentally to respond to unionization efforts than their counterparts in rural areas and small towns. It was also much more difficult for management to prevent "walking delegates" from proselytizing among the Augusta workers as could be done in the rigidly policed, rural, company-owned villages. In short, circumstances in Augusta were by far the most favorable to a successful unionization attempt in the Southern mill region.

A short-lived Augusta textile local formed early in 1884 set the pattern for management-union relationships. The assembly was badly needed, because that year the manufacturers of the town, faced with a declining market, cut wages and reduced production. They also attempted to organize a Southern and Western Manufacturing Association to insure the operatives' acceptance of these changes. The attempt failed only because a major Columbus firm, the Eagle and Phoenix Manufacturing Company, refused to cooperate with Augusta mill owners, believing that wage and production reductions "would hurt needy operatives and engender strikes."[97] The Columbus firm proved to be a good prophet, for in November 1884 the Augusta Knights of Labor led a strike at the Augusta factory to protest wage cuts. The entire work force went out, completely halting production. President Charles H. Phinizy immediately stated that he would receive "followers" back, but that the strike's "ringleaders" would never be rehired. This forceful policy of divide and conquer broke the strike in one day and evidently crushed the union, since no records of textile locals in Augusta can be found again until 1886.[98]

By 1886, however, the textile market was rapidly improving and the need to curtail production ceased, although the mills had not yet resumed dividend payments.[99] As the market continued to improve, rank-and-file laborers began to voice hopes of restoring wages to their 1884 levels. Management was determined to hold the line to make up for the past three lean years.[100] Management's determination was increased when, in late March and early April, high water on the Savannah River damaged seven of the nine Augusta mills. (Two of them, Riverside and Algernon, were flooded by more than ten feet of water.)[101] The Augusta manufacturers' unbending wage policy was dealt a severe blow, however, when the large Eagle and Phoenix Manufacturing Company of Columbus decided to increase wages by 10 percent for its more than 2,000 employees on May 1, 1886.[102] The Columbus workers made no known demands, but it must be remembered that the Knights had at least three textile trade assemblies there and the owners and management of the Eagle and Phoenix Manufacturing Company had been desirous of avoiding strikes even in the depression of 1884. Very likely, the Knights at least encouraged the drive for a wage increase, if they did not provoke it outright.

The situation in Augusta in the spring of 1886 was made more volatile by the presence of the large Knights of Labor textile Local 5030, three other mixed assemblies, and a local press that, however mildly, supported the right of labor to organize.[103] These locals had all been organized since January 1886 by the Reverend J. Simmions Meynardie. A Baptist minister, Meynardie had been hounded out of his native South Carolina by a hostile press and individual mill owners for his attempts to organize the operatives of that state.[104] In Augusta, however, Meynardie's almost fanatical organizational efforts bore fruit, and he became the Master Workman of Local 5030.

As the newly formed Local 5030 grew during the spring of 1886, tension between it and management continually mounted, nearly reaching a breaking point late in April.[105] Early in that month, Meynardie and the executive board of Local 5030 had drawn up petitions to present to the presidents of the city's mills. They requested the mills to discontinue the pass system, abolish the two weeks notice requirement, replace superintendents who discriminated against members of the union, and fill all future vacancies with union men. The Knights also suggested that, since the market for cotton goods had improved, the mills should increase wages. They asked that their petition be answered by May 1 and planned a picnic and celebration for that day. On April 13, Meynardie wrote Powderly, informing him of the local's plans and asking his advice. He said that management was organized and unrelenting in its efforts to weaken the local. The mill officials wrongly believed the order to be weak because it was "conservative." Meynardie admitted the operatives were too poor to stay out on a protracted strike and recognized that assistance from the national union would not be available until the local was six months old. He also noted that if the operatives did not receive "outside help" they would not benefit from the order. He exhibited great concern over the coming struggle, explaining that he hoped to approach the problem "legally, judiciously, and expediently." He believed that if he made a mistake and lost the fight to have the petitions adopted it might be fatal for the local. In addition, he maintained that thousands in South Carolina were watching and waiting for the results of the local's requests. "If we fail to carry our point we are done."[106] Powderly failed to answer.

The mill presidents replied to the Knights' petitions on April 20 in a circular distributed to all mill hands. After an appeal for "calm and consideration," the circular got right to what management considered the major issues involved. The presidents refused "most positively to recognize any outside interference between our employees and ourselves . . . the right to employ or not to employ another is absolute and incontestable. We will not allow any outside parties to manage our affairs." They warned the operatives that heavy past losses made any wage increases impossible. However, since they believed that wages were "a fair subject of discussion between employer and employee," they agreed to confer with the hands individually and "as employees only" about wages or other matters. The Knights responded the same day by voting to "absolutely and positively decline to confer with the Presidents, or any other persons, except through our Executive Board."

The local press joined the issue by admonishing the Knights to concentrate on the issue of wages and the reduction of hours rather than "fritter their energies away on false issues and imaginations." But, it also cautioned the Knights not to push too hard for immediate wage increases, for the mills' shareholders would hardly approve such increases until they began receiving dividends once more.[107]

Faced with a united opposition, realizing that the national could not help them if they struck, and having received no reply from Powderly, the union evidently temporarily decided to accept this advice. With the April crisis played out, the hardening of the stances of both management and the Knights was its only result.

The next month, Meynardie attended a special session of the General Assembly in Cleveland, called primarily to deal with the problems caused by the order's recent phenomenal growth, one of the most pressing being a rash of strikes by locals across the country. Meynardie claimed to represent some 5,000 Augusta operatives, a claim which must be taken in its broadest sense, for the local had hardly half that many members. Meynardie, however, was convinced that he spoke for all the operatives in the Augusta area. Indeed, his major weakness as a leader seems to have been more than just a touch of a messianic complex. He was primarily interested in talking with the order's national officials about the situation in Augusta, and it can be safely assumed that he did so. It can also be reasonably assumed that he was encouraged to take the most conservative approach possible, for the leadership was desperately trying to avoid major strikes.

In his zeal to find support for his efforts to improve the lot of the Augusta workers, Meynardie took his case to the Cleveland press. He criticized the long hours and low wages of the mill hands and vigorously denounced the practice of child labor. He revealed that he had personally buried on the average of two children a day for the past month because of a severe measles epidemic. The health of working children in general, he asserted, was extremely poor. Further, he implied that the Knights' desire for a 15 percent pay raise was more than justified, saying that wages had been reduced as much as 25 percent in 1884. He also warned the mill owners not to drive the operatives too far.[108]

The national press quickly picked up and carried Meynardie's bitter denouncement of the Augusta mill presidents, and detailed reports of the speech were soon carried in the *Augusta Chronicle*. Management's reaction was a predictable chorus of angry denials. One president went so far as to charge Meynardie with saying that Augusta's operatives were armed and ready for trouble, an absolutely groundless accusation. Others explained that the 1884 reductions had been only 10 percent and that their operatives' working conditions compared favorably with those of the Northern textile worker. Management took special pains to counter Meynardie's indictments of child labor. The presidents denied that children under seven years of age were on their payrolls, as had been charged.[109] None, however, mentioned the Southern practice of allowing children under seven to "help" their mothers or sisters, although the names of such "helpers" were not included on the payrolls.

The tension created by Meynardie's speech and the resulting national publicity it received did not subside. Instead, it only reinforced management's decision to refuse to recognize the union and served to increase the militancy of the workers, whose determination management seriously underestimated. On June 11, the weavers at the Algernon Mill struck when the mill refused to honor their request to discharge overseer D. E. Mc-Gaw, whom they accused of being an abusive tyrant. The weavers denied that their strike was connected with the Knights. In fact, they maintained that the Knights' leadership had advised caution, as indeed they had. Closing ranks, the mill presidents met immediately after the strike began and decided to shut all the mills unless the striking Algernon weavers returned to work by June 14. This decision was heartily condemned by the *Augusta Chronicle* because it meant that nonunion operatives would be forced off the job. The impasse was resolved, however, when McGaw volunteered his resignation, which was accepted.[110] But, this settlement failed to alter the basic issues—the Knights' desire for wage increases and management's refusal to recognize the union. The tension between the operatives and the mill presidents continued.

Management's refusal to recognize the union prompted the next round in the slowly escalating struggle. On June 18, the spinning room operatives at the Riverside Mill struck because the overseer had discharged two Knights. The strike failed to close the mill completely, but enough of the work force left to reduce by one-half the amount of machinery the mill could operate, and that was far from being adequately manned. This time the strike was openly led by rank-and-file Knights, who correctly believed that other operatives, including nonunion men, could not be induced to fill their vacant positions. The Knights' local leadership, however, opposed the strike, advising the operatives to proceed with extreme caution. Their advice, determined by the order's emphasis on arbitration and the local's lack of resources to support a major strike, proved sound. Once more the strike was evidently settled, for it is not mentioned in the *Augusta Chronicle* again. In a major concession which implied partial recognition of the Knights, management agreed to allow representatives from both the Knights and the mill presidents to investigate the McGaw dispute. The committee was formed and carried out its task, finding McGaw to be honest and stating that the entire June 11 "misunderstanding" could have been prevented had the presidents joined the Knights' executive board in a prompt investigation of the matter. Again, management demonstrated a desire to placate the operatives, acquiescing in a report that placed the responsibility for the McGaw dispute primarily on the shoulders of management.[111]

In the next episode, management revealed that it had no intention of recognizing the union, but was trying to buy time. The laborers responded by increasing their demands. On July 6, the weavers at the King Mill walked out because an overseer discharged some union men. The workers also demanded a 20 percent pay raise, thus for the first time publicly acknowledging that wages were a fundamental issue in Augusta's labor-management feuds. When the mill gave a conditional 10 percent raise on the following day, the weavers returned. The mill agreed to retain the raise if its first six months' profits for 1886, which would be known by the end of the month, indicated that the retention of the increased wages was feasible. In still another major concession, the mill rehired the discharged Knights. At this point, Knights in the other mills, seeing the partial success of their fellows at the Riverside, Algernon, and, now, King mills, also began to demand a 10 percent wage increase.[112]

The tension between management and labor finally passed the breaking point when, on July 9, Charles H. Phinizy, President of the Augusta factory, posted a notice indicating that wage increases would not be forthcoming. The mill hands in the picker room reacted by striking immediately, and, since the mill's other departments were dependent on them, the entire work force of 650 hands had to leave the mill. In keeping with the Knights' anti-strike policy, Meynardie attempted to prevent the strike. But he was rapidly losing his ability to temper the militancy of the rank and file. He immediately made it clear that the local executive board had advised against the strike and offered to confer with Phinizy. Phinizy's response was less than encouraging. He gave no assurance that he would recognize the order. But hoping to avoid a strike, he promised to increase wages as soon as the mill's business warranted it, while

giving no indication when that might be. Only fourteen men in
the picker room had actually struck, but they refused to return on such nebulous terms. Once again the rank-and-file
operatives, union and nonunion, showed an amazing solidarity.
The mill failed to persuade anyone to fill the fourteen vacant
positions. Unable to get the men to return, yet desiring a negotiated settlement, Meynardie called for aid from the national
organization. His request was quickly answered. William H.
Mullen, editor of the *Richmond Labor Herald* and a member
of the Knights' executive board, arrived in Augusta on July
13.[113]

Phinizy agreed to meet Mullen and local representatives of
the Knights, but warned that the mill's directors would not
deal with or officially recognize the union. At the meeting,
which was attended by Mullen, Meynardie, M. M. Connor, and
a local physician for the Knights and Phinizy and Major Joseph
Cunningham for the Augusta Mill, Mullen asked for a 15 percent raise. In return, he would guarantee that another increase
would not be requested for at least a year. Phinizy refused the
request. Later, Mullen countered with a 10 percent compromise and again Phinizy refused to accept his offer.[114]

Meanwhile, a strike over requested wage increases in the
card room of another Augusta firm, the Enterprise Mill, had
closed that plant. Before departing for Richmond, Mullen authorized a strike against the Augusta Mill for a 10 percent increase, but ordered the Enterprise hands back to work. Under
Meynardie's leadership, they complied, showing an amazing
amount of discipline for Southerners largely uneducated in the
procedures of organized labor.[115] Obviously, both management
and labor wanted to make the Augusta Mill strike a test case,
and their attention centered there. By this time, the operatives
at the Augusta Mill were leaving the city in search of jobs elsewhere and the union had established a relief committee which
was aiding those who remained.

The Knights were not alone in bringing in outside advice,

however. Arriving in Augusta on the same day as Mullen was Henry P. Hammett, who came ostensibly to discuss the affairs of the Atlantic, Western and Greenville Railroad, of which he was president. His real motive, no doubt, was to bolster the Augusta management's will to resist the Knights. Hammett was furious over their willingness to talk to the operatives and grant them minor concessions. He had previously branded the Algernon settlement of June a complete victory for the Knights and declared that if the Augusta Mills could not manage their own affairs without being dictated to by their help, "the sooner they shut down permanently the better—for every one who has their money invested in the property."[116]

Hammett probably urged the Augusta owners to unite against the Knights, promising the support of South Carolina manufacturers should they do so. Soon after Mullen left Augusta, the presidents of Augusta and the Horse Creek Valley, South Carolina, area mills began holding secret meetings. These meetings resulted in the formation of the Southern Manufacturers Association, of which H. H. Hickman of Graniteville and Charles Goodrich of Augusta were elected president and secretary, respectively.[117] Faced with a determined opponent in the Knights, the Augusta management was beginning to accept Hammett's hard line.

With labor and management now firmly organized into two hostile camps, each determined not to surrender, the situation steadily deteriorated. Nine card strippers struck the Sibley Mill for increased wages on July 29. As no one would replace them, the entire mill was forced to close. Two of Augusta's nine mills, the Sibley and Augusta mills, were now completely idle. On July 31, the King Mill announced that it would retain the 10 percent conditional wage increase granted earlier in the month, but claimed that to do so would mean operating at a loss. This announcement indicated that differences of opinion still existed among the city's mill officials, and unanimity was necessary before Hammett's policies could be effectively applied. Still, tension remained high among the 1,300 or so mill hands now out of work, and the operatives remaining on the job were showing signs of restlessness. Meanwhile, the mayor, Patrick Walsh, also the editor of the *Chronicle,* was desperately trying to get the two strikes settled, for he realized a bitter, protracted strike might have unpleasant political consequences. And, merchants who had been issuing the strikers supplies on credit were demonstrating signs of uneasiness and pressuring for some type of settlement.[118]

Faced with two strikes and the possibility of the operatives of the town's other seven mills striking at any moment, the Southern Manufacturers Association decided "to make a square issue here and now." Evidently, the King Mill management was convinced that this was the best policy, for on Saturday, August 7, all the Augusta presidents announced the formation of the Association "in self-defense." The Association included both the Augusta and Horse Creek Valley area mills. They also announced that unless the striking operatives returned to work on August 10, all the Augusta mills would close the following day. Such a maneuver would obviously deprive the strikers of any financial aid from those operatives still at work.[119]

Stunned by the Association's announcement, the leadership of Local 5030 nevertheless began preparations for a major strike-lockout. Aware that financial assistance from the national was an absolute necessity, on the eve of the lockout Meynardie dispatched an impassioned plea for aid to Powderly, urging him to come to Augusta if at all possible. He explained that in addition to the Association's plan to close all of Augusta's mills unless the strikes were stopped, the presidents of nearby South Carolina mills had informed their operatives that "if they contributed one cent to support the Augusta lock-out, they [the Presidents] would close the mills against them." Further, continued Meynardie:

These tyrants declare they will down the "socialistic mob" in the

South before it goes any further! They intend to throttle it in its infancy. . . . If they force us to disband by starving out our members; and force them to terms by lockouts and Boycotts, then we are done. Then with bitter wail may we chant the requiem of our noble—our dearly beloved order, in the South.

The Southern Mill Association claims that you will never recognize any Southern institution. That we are only a tool to help support northern moves etc., this talk is heard and believed by many; and your presence will forever bury in eternal oblivion this infamous lie. . . . The condition of these Southern tyrants is such, that they cannot hold out long. They have little or no surplus: and they know we have none, therefore, they whisper it around that they can starve out and break us up in a month.

Do give us all the help you can. . . . Don't let us sink! It will not take a great deal to carry us: as we are used to hard times and scanty living. We have carried 650 strikers and families on three and four hundred dollars a week. The lock-out will turn about 3,000 operatives out of employment: All of these are Knights and children of Knights who are not old enough to join our order.[120]

Mullen agreed with Meynardie on the importance of the Augusta strike. Writing Powderly on August 14, he expressed his willingness to go to Augusta, but noted that "if it is possible for you to go to Augusta, I no doubt [sic] but what it would do a vast deal of good." He saw the lockout as a "direct blow at the existence of the Order in the South. . . . The result of this conflict means Knights of Labor or no Knights of Labor in the South. God bless and sustain these people."[121]

The prompt closing of all the mills was followed by a three-month war of attrition which the Knights, at the mercy of strikebreakers from the surrounding area, with woefully inadequate financial resources, and without experienced leadership, were bound to lose. Their defeat was hastened, however, by their humane but irrational policy of accepting all applicants for membership, who, faced with the lockout, now came in droves seeking provisions from the relief committee. Already in debt to local merchants, the committee had no hope of providing for the new members.

Merchants and other townspeople, fearful of the effect the lockout would have on the town's economy, increased their pressure on Mayor Walsh to obtain a settlement. Responding to the pressure, Walsh also requested Powderly to come to Augusta. Powderly failed to come, but sent Mullen and National Secretary Frederick Turner to the city in mid-August. For the second time, Mullen made an attempt to arbitrate the strike.[122] The mill presidents received Mullen, Turner, Meynardie, and other Knights at a meeting that was also attended by Mayor Walsh. Turner offered a plan to "adjust" the salaries of mill officials in order to obtain wage increases for the operatives without increasing the mills' payrolls. The presidents refused the offer. Turner continued his unsuccessful efforts to settle the strike through arbitration until August 19, when he and Mullen departed Augusta after turning control of the strike back to the local executive board.[123]

By this time, Augusta grocers were becoming reluctant to fill the relief committee's credit orders, as the committee had built a staggering debt of more than $20,000. More mill hands were leaving the area to seek new jobs; the Riverside and Augusta mills had been reopened to nonunion labor early in September. A few local workers, protected by the police, began to return to their jobs. The Knights did nothing to stop them, although they branded them as scabs.[124] If the owners had hoped that the opening of the Augusta Mill would cause labor's ranks to break, they were proved wrong. Most of the workers refused to admit defeat.

The Augusta presidents' decision to talk with the Knights elicited a barrage of adverse criticism from Hammett. Just before Mullen and Turner arrived in Augusta, he had written William E. McCoy, President of the Riverside Mill, a blistering letter blaming the entire situation on earlier yielding to the Knights. He warned McCoy that "to yield to them now is to yield the whole management of the mills, manufacturing, commercial and financial to them." Refuse to treat with the Knights, he advised,

> stamp out the Knights then and now, and make it amongst them [the operatives] discreditable for one to admit that they ever belonged to the organization. When they get good and starved out and miserable and utterly ruined, they will turn upon and murder Meynardie and other leaders of the organization.

Above all, he admonished, ignore the merchants of Augusta and the local press, who criticized the lockout, for they merely wanted the mills' payrolls started again and had no concern for the mills' true interest.[125] Writing McCoy on August 19, he repeated his warning against bending to the pressure of the townspeople to end the lockout. Stand firm, he urged, and victory will be yours in sixty days. The Augusta hands, he advised, would not leave the city in large numbers, despite the lockout.[126]

However, Hammett realized that the Augusta manufacturers would like more than verbal support. So, early in September he sent the presidents a list of wages, which he said other South Carolina firms had adopted, and advised the Augusta mills to adopt and post the same schedule. If the operatives refused to accept the posted wages, Hammett advised the adoption of an eviction policy. Above all, he cautioned, "Whip and crush the Knights, to yield is ruin."[127] In mid-September, Hammett repeated his advice to begin eviction proceedings and assured the Augusta presidents that the strikers had received no financial aid from the national organization, despite rumors to the contrary. Furthermore, he expressed the belief that the Knights' hope for such aid was completely unfounded.[128] His assessment of the situation proved amazingly accurate.

By the end of August, the strikers were in desperate circumstances. They had received no financial aid from the national organization. Turner and Mullen had failed to settle the strike-lockout through arbitration, and management showed not the slightest indication of altering its position. On August 30, Meynardie again wrote Powderly, imploring him to obtain financial aid for the workers. Both the letter's content and its author's script revealed that the pressures of leadership were beginning to affect Meynardie. Some of the hands, he wrote, had been unemployed for eight weeks. The Association was determined to break the Knights in the South, and was leaving no stones unturned in its effort to do so.

> We do most earnestly and ardently implore your intervention in our behalf—We sorely need financial assistance this *self same moment*—Do for God's sake render us such assistance as will hush the *bitter wails of hungry* children and *poor ill-treated widows* and thin *little orphan children*—General M. W. You may think this an overdrawn picture, but God knows "the half is not told." . . . The *Lock Out*—has been examined and endorsed by our General Executive Board and we do feel that we should receive some substantial assistance from the *Board*. Endorsement and sympathy *alone* we find a poor substitute for meat and bread in this time of dire need and distress.

Meynardie ended his appeal by requesting Powderly to issue a circular letter to the order to obtain funds for the strikers until the national executive board acted.[129]

Since the Assistance Fund was by this time nonexistent, the national administration was incapable of rendering the Augusta strikers immediate financial aid. But, prompted by the reports of Mullen, Turner, and Meynardie and a number of similar requests from striking locals across the nation, the General Executive Board early in September issued an appeal for financial aid to the entire order. By the end of the month over $8,000 had been collected, $2,000 of which was sent to Augusta on September 15. The arrival of the funds sparked the strikers' hopes of obtaining more aid and temporarily boosted their morale. But as the days passed and no further aid was received, the strikers' spirits began to decline. Sensing weakness in labor's camp and probably bolstered by Hammett's advice and support, the Association announced an eviction policy which became operational on September 20. More mills also opened their doors to nonunion labor, including strikers who would desert the union. The Knights recognized the legality of the maneuver and did what they could to find shelter for those operatives forced to leave company housing. No violence occurred.[130]

Early in October Meynardie left for Richmond to attend the General Assembly, leaving the strikers without a strong leader and disappointed in the failure of the national executive board to send more funds. And, prior to departing, he had introduced an internal political dispute among the Knights by openly supporting the regular Democratic ticket in a municipal election, thus opposing a faction of the Knights who hoped to end the strike by electing a slate of independent labor candidates.

In addition, the spectre of race raised at the Richmond General Assembly hurt the Augusta local. The *Augusta Chronicle* accused the New York delegation to the Assembly of implying that Negroes were barred from economic progress in the South. The *Chronicle* denied the alleged implication, noting that the greatest competition between blacks and whites was in the South. The editorial stated that the South placed few barriers to the Negroes' economic progress and that, if there was money to be made in a field, Negroes could be found there. Sparked by news reports of the Assembly and the *Chronicle's* editorial, rumors that Negroes were going to be hired swept the mill communities, causing even prominent Knights to return to work and renounce the union.[131]

The growing number of hands returning to the mills was bolstered by operatives recruited from South Carolina. Some mills imported token forces of strikebreakers from New Jersey.[132] However, the initial impact of eviction and the racial rumors only caused labor's ranks to waver; they did not break.

Despite the internal differences and external pressures, the strikers held together. Enough operatives remained out so that the production of the operating mills was only a fraction of their capacity, since they were unable to obtain workers in large numbers.

The total collapse of the strike was finally brought about by the collapse of its leader. Meynardie had left his obviously shaken forces to attend the Knights' General Assembly in Richmond in the midst of a family crisis. He must have realized that his absence might injure the local, but probably felt he must make an attempt to obtain immediately further funds from the national union for the strikers' depleted relief fund. If this was his hope, he was disappointed. He returned on October 12, before the General Assembly ended and after a major personal confrontation with Powderly, "almost crazy" from "mental exhaustion." Apparently, he was suffering from a nervous breakdown. His illness, believed by many to be alcoholism (and there is some indication that, under pressure, Meynardie might have overindulged), coupled with the fact that no money seemed to be forthcoming from the national, completely demoralized the Knights.[133]

Various rumors flew in all directions. Large numbers of workers now expressed their desire to return to work. At this point, the local executive board removed Meynardie from the office of Master Workman and replaced him with M. M. Connor. This maneuver only split the Knights between the Connor and Meynardie forces, a split which Meynardie attempted to heal by agreeing that Connor should replace him because of his illness. But Connor proved to be unable to control the strikers as well as Meynardie had. The number of Knights returning to work continued to increase. It was becoming painfully apparent that the strike was collapsing as a result of management's eviction policy, the rumors concerning Negro laborers, the union's financial problems, and, finally, the loss of Meynardie's leadership.[134]

Realizing that the strike was disintegrating, the local executive board evidently appealed again to the national for additional financial aid, as it had received only $2,000 from the national during the entire strike, and Southern locals had provided only slightly more. Since the funds requested by the national executive board's September appeal were still being collected (over $6,600 in October, in addition to the more than $8,000 collected in September), it is difficult to understand why the national board failed to forward more funds to Augusta. There are, however, several factors which possibly explain why the board chose this course. First, Powderly and the board basically opposed strikes. In addition, Powderly and other national officers were convinced that most of the strikes of 1886 had been the result of ill-considered actions by new unions composed of laborers seeking immediate relief, not reform. Such strikes, national leaders believed, were devouring resources that could be put to better use. And finally, whatever occurred between Powderly and Meynardie at Richmond had caused Powderly to have grave misgivings about the strike's leadership.[135] Had funds been sent to Augusta, morale would have climbed and the strike might have continued for several more months. This development, perhaps, is what Powderly and the board wished to avoid, especially if, after seeing Meynardie in Richmond, they had come to believe the strikers incapable of winning.

Whatever the rationale of Powderly and the board, by the end of October they had evidently determined to end the strike on the best terms available. At the behest of the board, on October 27 National Committeeman James A. Wright arrived in Augusta. First, he examined the local relief committee's $30,000 debt and promised to pay all these bills he adjudged legitimate, much to the relief of the local merchants. To obtain the needed funds, the General Executive Board levied a twenty-five cents per capita special assessment on member locals, an action which possibly would have produced much more bene-

ficial results had it come in July, or even in September. Upon
examining the records of the local executive board, Wright
found "gross mismanagement" of relief funds, outright embez-
zlement, outrageously high officers' salaries, too liberal initiation
policies, and the elevation of nonlaborers to positions of leadership. In short, Wright found the local assembly's executive
board, with the exception of Meynardie, who was still ill, totally
incapable of directing the strike.[136]

Faced with such facts, Wright had little choice but to negotiate with the mill presidents and hope to salvage something
from the strike. The mill presidents were willing to talk, and
the negotiations were begun. They led to a six-point settlement
that spelled almost complete defeat for the Knights on the wage
issue, but granted them minor concessions and, at best, tacit
recognition. The settlement, announced on November 4, called
for the following: (1) abolishment by the mills of the pass
system and petty tyrannies, (2) no discrimination against the
Knights when the mills opened, (3) the mills to remit rent due
on company housing from August 11 to November 6, (4)
future disputes to be settled by a four-man committee composed of two laborers, who did not have to be Knights, and
two mill presidents, (5) positions of operatives fired "for cause"
not to be boycotted by other operatives, and (6) the mills to
open November 8, 1886.[137] In a strike-lockout that cost over
$50,000, the Knights of Augusta had been effectively curbed,
as Hammett advised.[138] The rest of the South could breathe
easier.

As damaging as the Augusta defeat itself was the acrimony
and dissension it engendered, reaching from the ranks of Local 5030 to the order's national councils. In December, Meynardie wrote Powderly that the local had thrice requested him
to resume his position as Master Workman. He had finally done
so, but certain Knights, with aid from national officials, were
trying to "down" him. He apologized for his conduct at Richmond, which he said he could not remember, and asked for

support. Powderly sent a curt reply. "I prefer not having anything to do with the matter you bring to my attention."[139] In a series of letters, M. M. Connor denied charges of fraud filed against him by Wright and requested reinstatement as a commissioned organizer. Powderly sided with Wright.[140]

Furthermore, Mullen was piqued at Powderly's failure to send him to Augusta for the third time and was highly critical of Wright's settlement. He criticized the national executive board's performance and charged that the order had given a "cold shoulder" to the South. Many Southerners felt the order could have won in Augusta had it invested more. Powderly defended Wright and the board, which he claimed forwarded $41,000 to Augusta. He noted that another $22,000 was sent the strikers from "various parts of the Order." He said that the board had never refused to comply with Southern requests, and, indeed, had sent most of the funds raised by the last general assessment to Augusta. Mullen also criticized Meynardie for urging the workers to strike by promising them millions from the national. This flatly contradicted Meynardie's earlier letters to Powderly and is made even more suspect since the charge was made only after the strike's defeat.[141]

The money the Knights spent in Augusta did not completely eradicate the strikers' bills. In a final chapter to the strike and its bitter legacy, some Augusta operatives attempted to sue the Knights in an effort to force the order to pay the remaining debts. The reaction of Charles H. Litchman, General Secretary, to this maneuver speaks volumes about the national leadership's attitude toward Augusta. "Of all the cheek and conglomeration of human depravity certainly this in Augusta takes the whole bakery. After swindling the Order out of $50,000 or $60,000 they now undertake to blackmail for enough more to settle their rum bills. May the devil take them and all their tribe!"[142] Powderly instructed General Treasurer Frederick Turner to pay the operatives nothing. "I will not allow the order to be blackmailed without a trial, this is an attempt to swindle the order out of money which they could not beat us out of."[143] The suit fell through, evidently, for the bills were never paid. In March 1887, a former officer of Local 5030 wrote Powderly, explaining that Wright had endorsed the relief committee's actions and every order of the committee had carried an approved signature. He wrote that persons signing, such as himself, were being held personally responsible for remaining debts. He wanted to know if Powderly could come to their aid. Significantly, Powderly stamped the letter "NO ANSWER REQUIRED."[144]

Pathetic attempts at unionization in Georgia's textile industry continued after the Augusta defeat. The Augusta locals tried to rebuild, but the bitterness of the strike made it almost impossible to do so. In 1888, one of their members wrote the *Journal of United Labor* that "the work of organizing is slowly but surely progressing. . . . They [the operatives] are beginning to understand that there is more important work to perform than rushing into strikes." He admitted, however, that the movement was faced "with bitter opposition and oppression."[145] In late 1889, there was a strike led by the Knights as a result of the discharge of one of their members at a mill in Roswell, Georgia.[146] It was probably crushed, for the state press failed to record it. This was the last textile strike in Georgia led by the Knights. The locals in Atlanta, Macon, Columbus, and other towns faded into oblivion. Although some agrarian and artisan assemblies remained, the Knights of Labor had been driven from Georgia's textile industry.

The Knights appeared briefly in the mills of Mississippi and Alabama, but their efforts there were minor and quickly smothered. The Wesson Cotton Mills of Wesson, Mississippi, were organized in mid-1886. Members of the Knights immediately encountered a discharge policy, although they looked upon the order as more of a fraternal organization than a labor union. The assembly's Master Workman attempted to explain to management that members had made no demands, but had taken the position that "the Knights of Labor were an honorable society . . . that they would much rather build the Mississippi Mills up than do anything against their interests." Such sentiments failed to impress management. The owner replied that "he would break up the order in Wesson if he had to discharge every Knight of Labor in the mills and if it was necessary he would close the mills for 12 months."[147]

The local appealed to Powderly for advice. Powderly replied that if members were being discharged, "you had better send back your charter and give up the order at once for it will come to that in the end."[148] He was right. Management simply evicted all employees suspected of having connections with the Knights and persuaded other businessmen in town to refuse to employ them. No strike occurred, probably because of Powderly's advice. But the Knights of Alabama, primarily artisans, miners, and iron workers, boycotted the firm's goods, to no avail.[149]

Operatives of the Cottondale, Alabama, mills organized in 1887 and were evidently tolerated as long as they made no demands. Though tolerated, they enjoyed little respect. An inebriated foreman early in 1888 rode a horse into the local's meeting hall and cursed the members, both male and female. The local took the man to court. During the court proceedings the Cottondale firms reduced wages. When the Knights protested, they were locked out until they agreed to sign yellow dog contracts. (Pledges to quit and refrain from returning to the union during a specific term of employment. Yellow dog contracts took their name from the term used by union men to describe workers who signed them.) The Knights' state assembly called a boycott of goods manufactured at Cottondale, but it had no effect. The local was destroyed.[150] The order could hardly have succeeded in Alabama and Mississippi after having failed in the South's major cotton textile manufacturing centers.

After their defeat in Augusta, the Knights' efforts to organize Southern mills had no hope of success. This was forcefully demonstrated by the fate of the order in South Carolina in 1887. The national leadership had been seriously compromised in the eyes of the Southern worker by the Augusta strike and its aftermath. Yet, Powderly continued to evidence a hope that the Knights might regain the support of the operatives. In August 1888, he appointed John O'Keefe, a Rhode Island textile worker, as "lecturer" in West Virginia, Virginia, North Carolina, South Carolina, and Georgia. That a Northerner should be sent as an organizer of Southern operatives shows the absolutely futile nature of this gesture.[151] The spark of hope the order had once ignited within the cotton textile industry's operatives had been temporarily snuffed out.

A number of varied, complex, and interrelated factors resulted in the ultimate failure of the Knights of Labor in the South's cotton textile industry. Mill village paternalism and the determined resistance of Southern management to the very concept of organization were the most significant. Both were enhanced by the operatives' position as a small, economically and politically weak industrial working class, engulfed in a mass of discontented agrarian laborers. The racial question proved to be a stumbling block to the Southern Knights in general, and the textile industry was no exception. Inept leadership and unnecessary involvement in politics also hurt the Knights. Both of these failings were directly related to the reform ideology of the order, an ideology that failed to aid the operatives to obtain immediate goals. And, finally, the operatives' almost total ignorance of organized labor, even of an industrial society, proved to be a serious handicap.

Southern management's determination to resist unionization was perhaps best exemplified by the actions of Hammett and other South Carolina mill presidents. This resistance was the major immediate cause of the Knights' defeat. When the Augusta presidents, aided and abetted by their South Carolina counterparts, decided on a policy of confrontation, organized to implement their decision, and finally accepted Hammett's unyielding policies, the Knights were dealt a mortal blow. Even had the Knights been better led and financed, at this early stage of Southern labor organization it is unlikely that they could have defeated the Southern Manufacturers Association.

Mill village paternalism buttressed management's determination to resist because it presented officials with a ready-made strategy of resistance. Although management constructed the village system with the vague understanding that it could prove of value in warding off organization, they used the system against the Knights primarily because it was there and could be used. Mill village paternalism prevented the order from ever obtaining a foothold in rural and small town mills such as those controlled by Hammett or those in Alabama and Mississippi. Under such conditions, suspected organizers were quickly thrown off the premises.

Secret organization, advised by Powderly, was impossible in such a closed community. Hammett boasted that organizers could not work in secret because "we have too many traps set for them." If organizers attempted to hold meetings in areas adjacent to the village, operatives attending were invariably identified and discharged.[152]

Control of the operatives' housing proved extremely effective in combating strikes, even in urban Augusta, as is evidenced by the success of management's eviction policy there as well as in small towns such as Clifton, South Carolina, and Wesson, Mississippi.

Furthermore, the national order's stand on the racial issue hindered its acceptance in the South. Foes of organization, especially the press, pictured the union as a supporter of social equality for the Negro and likened it to the Republican party of Reconstruction. The Knights were never able to overcome the white Southerner's basic fear of the Negro. The failure of Nichols' bid for reelection in North Carolina in a campaign based on the premise of uniting the votes of operatives, artisans, and farmers was partially a result of the success of his opponent's use of the racial issue. Also, the threat of the Negro strikebreaker was always in the background. Once activated, it could be devastating, as was demonstrated by the rumors and near panic that swept the Augusta strikers in 1886 as a result of racial incidents during the Richmond General Assembly.

Clearly, however, much of the blame for the Knights' defeat lies at their own door. Failure to build adequate strike funds before participating in strikes hurt them seriously at Clifton and Augusta. Numerous other locals which were never involved in strikes or lockouts also continually experienced financial difficulty. By accepting the droves of operatives who sought admission to the union after the 1886 lockout began, the Augusta local's leadership only compounded its financial problems. Inept leadership and outright dishonesty were serious shortcomings that plagued many locals.[153] The national leadership handled the Augusta strike poorly. By refusing to send funds until the last of October they practically insured the strikers' defeat. In short, the national paid the operatives' bills only after admitting defeat. Had the same amount of money been distributed during the strike, the Knights would probably have failed to obtain the desired wage increases, but would have certainly been in a better bargaining position on other issues. They might even have been able to obtain a settlement that could have been interpreted as a moral victory. Certainly, the bitterness that the strike engendered would have been avoided.

The Knights' proclivity for political involvement also had its detriments. In North Carolina, more time was spent on politics than on organization. Member operatives were deeply involved in these political activities, which is one reason the Knights, with one possible exception, never were involved in textile strike activity in the state. The overwhelming defeat of their candidates in the 1888 election, including operatives who were running for office, sealed the fate of the order in North Carolina. More specifically, Meynardie's public endorsement of

Democratic candidates in opposition to many of the rank and file who favored a labor ticket introduced a split in the Augusta local at a time when unity was badly needed.

In the final analysis, the reform character of the Knights, coupled with the basic naïveté of the Southern operatives, led to the Knights' decline. Southern mill hands were looking for a savior in the mid-1880s, and they wanted immediate salvation. The Knights seemed to offer hope. The order had the ideals, the vision, and originally even the fervor of a militant religious sect. "The ideas of the Knights of Labor," proclaimed a Southern Knight, "will be to the working world what Christianity has been to the world."[154] This zeal enabled persons such as Meynardie to drive themselves to mental and physical exhaustion in an effort to achieve a more just economic order. But the rank-and-file operatives joined because of the victorious strike against Jay Gould's midwestern railway system in 1885. They wanted shorter hours, increased wages, better working conditions, and an end to child labor. Because of the Knights' original success against the Gould railways, they hoped that the order would provide a means to obtain them. Education, cooperation, and arbitration proved to be inadequate means to accomplish these ends. Defeated at Swepsonville, Clifton, and Augusta and faced with management's unrelenting opposition, Southern operatives were forced to realize that believing the order would "be crowned with success in the triumph of right and justice" did not make it so.[155] Disillusioned at Powderly's and the union's inability to produce immediate, tangible benefits, they departed its ranks.[156] Had the Knights won wage increases in Augusta, or even other major concessions, the history of organized labor in the industry might have been altered. But they lost, thus becoming merely the first of several unions to fail to organize Southern operatives.

Had the Knights been less prone to rush unprepared into strikes, had they concentrated on organization until they created a stronger base, had they built stronger treasuries and tightened membership requirements, they might have accomplished more in their struggles with textile management. But, it must be remembered that Southern operatives were almost totally ignorant of the concepts of organized labor and just as inexperienced at wielding the power, however slight, that organization could bring. Nor did their wages allow them to finance a strong union program. In addition, the vast majority of the hands retained an agrarian mind set; they had developed no true economic class consciousness. Yet, had such a consciousness been fully developed, the Knights still would have been defeated.

In Augusta, a genuine class consciousness did develop, for, there, even nonunion workers refused to fill positions vacated by striking or discharged Knights. However, Augusta was the urban exception in an overwhelmingly rural and small town industry. Even in Augusta, operatives were at the mercy of farm hands and operatives in more rural areas just across the Savannah River who proved willing to act as strikebreakers against their fellow workers. The basic economics of the region dictated the union's failure. In the midst of a pool of surplus labor, in an industry that required minimum skills, the operative, if he made demands, was expendable.

Despite its failure, the legacy of the Knights is not without its positive aspects. It was the first labor organization to challenge the hitherto sacrosanct position of the South's new cotton mill aristocracy. It was the first labor organization to press for legislation to improve working conditions, shorten hours, halt child labor, and demand the installation of safety devices. Although most of their efforts failed, the Knights were directly responsible for the establishment of the North Carolina Bureau of Labor. And their demands for reforms set valuable precedents.

The Knights introduced the concept of unionism to Southern industry and instilled a degree of economic class consciousness, however minute, in the cotton mill hands at a time when it required real courage to join an assembly at Pelzer, Clifton, Swepsonville, or Augusta. They initiated the mill hands to the experience of industrial warfare. And most significantly, they put the first dent in the generally accepted thesis that the laborers of the industrial plantation were content with the status quo. Unfortunately, they also demonstrated to management that a thorough, determined policy of organization, lockouts, and evictions could crush organized labor if it dared protest. Management never forgot this lesson.

5

The National Union
of Textile Workers:
Establishing Footholds

For nearly a decade after the defeat of the Knights, the South's cotton textile industry was almost completely free of organizational activity. For numerous reasons, the future appeared bleak to those operatives who advocated organization. Many mill hands who had responded to the Knights' organizational efforts were disillusioned by their failure and saw little hope for future unionization attempts.

Generally, the early 1890s were good years for the industry. As a result, wages, though low, were steady. No wage cuts prodded the operatives to organize in self-defense. On the farm, however, the reverse was true. The depressed state of Southern agriculture reached a peak during these years, sending thousands of farmers into the mills. Their numbers more than adequately filled the growing cotton textile industry's demand for laborers. Also, before 1895, neither the American Federation of Labor (AFL) nor the National Union of Textile Workers (NUTW) evidenced the slightest interest in organizing the

Southern textile operatives, who, inexperienced in unionism, were incapable of successful organization without some assistance from these national unions. Yet beneath this placid exterior, some Southern operatives nourished resentments about the continuing long hours, low wages, and child labor practices of the mills. This discontent briefly surfaced in conjunction with the agrarian reform movements of the late 1880s and early 1890s in North Carolina, South Carolina, and Georgia, but social and economic factors held it in check. However, by the mid-1890s, changing economic conditions and the active support of the AFL and NUTW combined to create the most intensive unionization efforts in Southern textiles prior to the depression of the 1920s and the advent of the New Deal.

Although possessing great potential as a means of forcing concessions from the manufacturer, the Southern agrarian reform movement failed to benefit the operative, largely because it had little concern for or understanding of the position of labor. Despite their lip service to the goals of labor, the Southern Farmers' Alliance and the Southern Populist party resented the operative as the representative of an alien industrial society.[1] Benjamin R. Tillman, leader of the South Carolina agrarian reformers, referred to the operative as "that damned factory class."[2] Winthrop, South Carolina's college for women established under the Tillman aegis, was to train for higher stations the "vast army [of girls who] have had no other avenues open to them except as seamstresses or in cotton factories." Indeed, according to Tillman, a young woman should seek work in a cotton mill "only as the dernier resort."[3] Leonidas L. Polk, founder of the North Carolina Alliance, President of the Southern Farmers' Alliance, and Populist politician, showed little interest in the plight of the operative and "cared as little for the strikes of labor unions as he did for the 'domineering assumptions of greedy capital.' "[4]

Rank and file Southern farmers shared this anti-industrial attitude of leaders like Tillman and Polk.[5] As early as 1888, laborers sensed that the Alliance, representing the employing farmer, was "nothing more or less than oppression and death to the laborer."[6] Since the farmer often used child labor and worked his help well over ten hours a day, he was in no position to deny the mill owner to do the same. Indeed, the yeoman farmer saw the mill as a competitor, a lucrative corporation which lured away his labor while paying little for raw cotton. James L. Orr, successor to Hammett as president of Piedmont Mills, realized this when he wrote a friend: "There is a widespread feeling among farmers that the factories are making a great deal of money and are taking and will continue to take their best tenants, by giving larger wages than they can pay."[7]

Nevertheless, in their desire to appear anti-Bourbon, the agrarian politicians could use the mills as a stalking horse. Tillman and his lieutenants did so in their 1892 campaign when they verbally flayed management so severely that management feared their campaign oratory would trigger strikes.[8] Such oratory was designed to appeal to agrarian, rather than industrial, constituents, however, for Tillman and others were well aware of the farmers' distaste for the factory. For several reasons, they dared not seriously inconvenience the mills. Tillman borrowed funds from some of South Carolina's most prominent owners, as did many of his lieutenants like Stanyarne Wilson, Tillmanite member of the state legislature and, later, congressman. Wilson, who had specifically sought the vote of the operative, held stock in various mills.[9] Polk, a former middle-class entrepreneur and real estate promoter turned politician-reformer, was on friendly terms with leading North Carolina industrialists.[10] Eager to seize the reins of power from the Bourbon democracy, the agrarians were willing to accept the laborers' support, but unwilling to seek seriously to relieve their condition through legislation.

Power politics also entered the picture. The operatives simply lacked the political power to force the agrarians to consider their plight. They had no political organization, and no idea of how to exert their influence on those few members of the various state legislatures that their votes helped to elect. Management, on the other hand, was very adept at political maneuvering, and unsparingly used its influence to halt what it felt to be adverse labor legislation. When the North Carolina Populists fused with the Republicans to gain control of the state in 1895, they naturally had to make concessions to the Republicans. A mill owner who had voted Republican in 1894 candidly told a member of the 1895 fusion legislature that any radical labor bill or "foolish legislation" would "hurt Republican support among the mill owners." If they wished to retain their power, the Populist-Republicans were warned to consult with mill owners before passing any labor legislation.[11] In South Carolina, mill owners were also able to use political maneuvering to emasculate labor legislation proposed to legislatures that were controlled by agrarian reformers.[12]

In Georgia, the Alliance and Populists simply could not break the power of the Bourbon Democrats. The Alliance legislature of 1890 sent old Bourbon war horse, General John B. Gordon, back to the Senate. Yet, they sarcastically characterized him as "first, a railroad lawyer; second, a railroad promoter; third, a railroad president; and fourth, the farmer's best friend."[13] Bourbon politicians literally stole victory from Thomas Watson, the South's foremost Populist, in his 1892 congressional race. Out of a possible poll of 11,240 in Richmond County, which encompassed Augusta, Watson's opponent scored a majority of 13,780 votes.[14] Against such opposition, the Populists would have achieved little, even if they had ardently championed the cause of the industrial worker.

The sparsity of legislation passed by the agrarian reformers to aid the industrial worker clearly reflects both their lack of concern for labor and management's ability to protect its interests. Some of the Tillmanites attempted to deal with the South Carolina operatives' grievances. Stanyarne Wilson of Spartanburg County in 1890 openly solicited the operatives' vote in a successful bid for a seat in the state house of representatives. There, he introduced a bill limiting the factory work day for women to ten hours and forbidding the employment of children under the age of sixteen. Wilson, along with Tillmanite representatives John G. Evans of Aiken and Coleman Blease of Newberry, obtained petitions supporting the bill from operatives in their counties. Opposed vigorously by management, especially the state's "Big Four" (Ellison A. Smyth of Pelzer Mills, John Montgomery of Spartan Mills, Dexter E. Converse of the Clifton and Glendale mills, and Henry P. Hammett of Piedmont Mills), the bill passed the House only to be killed in the Senate.[15]

In the election of 1892, Tillman and Wilson, successful candidates, respectively, for the governorship and the state senate, both flayed management severely for opposing the 1890 bill.[16] Management, meanwhile, was rallying its forces to oppose any limitations on child labor. James L. Orr, who had replaced the late Henry P. Hammett as president of Piedmont Mills, wrote a colleague:

> I do not dread the labor law for hours as much as I do for ages. A law prohibiting the working of children under 16 years old, would increase the cost of production about 25%, and if the age were fixed at 14 the cost would be increased by at least 10% . . . from 12 to 16 they make the best spinners and doffers and I don't see how we could get along in the Spinning room without that class.[17]

The Tillmanites again introduced a ten-hour bill in 1892. Management, led by the "Big Four," with Orr in Hammett's position, began their opposition to the bill. More afraid of possible child labor legislation than a bill reducing hours, however, they agreed to a "compromise bill." They would offer only mild opposition to an eleven-hour bill in return for a promise by Wilson and others to halt child labor legislation attempts.

The Tillman forces immediately accepted the offer. No compromise in actuality, the terms of the bill were practically dictated by Orr and the other mill presidents.[18] Management also planned to use the bill to justify any future wage cuts. As passed, the bill failed to mention either women or children, provided no enforcement machinery, and called for an eleven-hour day, but allowed the mills to operate up to 110 hours per week to make up time lost to accidents, necessary repairs, cleaning the machinery, and other "unavoidables."[19]

Bills to limit the factory work day to ten hours were also supported by the agrarian reformers in North Carolina. In the 1891 legislature, which was controlled by the Farmers' Alliance, a ten-hour, anti-child-labor bill was introduced, but killed by an unfavorable report from the House judiciary committee. This same legislature, however, met the demands of the farmer by passing legislation to regulate railroads, to establish a normal school for girls, to increase school taxes, and to increase appropriations to the University of North Carolina and the state colleges. The Populists called for a ten-hour bill during their unsuccessful campaign for state offices in 1892. But when a fusion of Populists and Republicans won complete control of the 1895 legislature, another attempt to pass a ten-hour bill failed. Although the bill was supported by petitions from Charlotte operatives, the bill's passage would have angered Republican manufacturers.[20]

In Georgia, events even more closely paralleled those of South Carolina's reform movement. In 1889, the legislature passed an eleven-hour bill. Like the South Carolina law, it made no provisions for women and children, had no enforcement features, and allowed management liberal make-up time.[21] That was practically the extent of the Georgia movement's aid to the operative. The 1890 legislature, completely controlled by the Farmers' Alliance, failed to pass any legislation designed specifically to benefit the industrial worker. Instead, "the Alliancemen spent their fight against big business and monopoly in

railroad legislation: they hardly touched the throttle of industrial capitalism, of which they were the avowed enemies."[22]

In spite of this, the Georgia movement received some support
from the mill operatives. In an 1890 Democratic congressional
primary, Thomas Watson drew his heaviest support in Augusta
from the operatives' wards. But his opponent, George T. Barnes,
carried the city, the center of his political machine, partially
because management marched their operatives to the polls to
see that they voted for him.[23] Running for Congress in an unsuccessful bid for reelection as a Populist in 1892, Watson
again got his heaviest Augusta vote from textile workers in an
election replete with "ballot-box stuffing and burning, intimidation, bloodshed, and bribery." Again, management used the
"job lash" to keep operatives loyal to the Democratic party, and
some were discharged for continuing to support Watson.[24]

Clearly, those operatives who supported Watson and other
Populists showed marked determination, especially in view of
the returns they received for their efforts. A small minority of
the population with no political or economic organization, the
operatives were unable to counter the effects of the agrarians'
anti-industrial prejudice and management's political power.
Thus, a few campaign pledges, some occasional anti-manage-
ment rhetoric, and two ineffective laws regulating hours were all
the operative received from the Southern agrarian reform movement.

Neither the Populists nor the Knights of Labor, however,
represented the mainstream of the American labor movement.
Instead, it was the American Federation of Labor (AFL) that
forcefully stamped its imprint on the development of organized
labor. Unlike either the Knights, who were more interested in
reforming American industrial society than in improving the
worker's conditions in it, or the Populists, who were agrarian
reformers that looked with suspicion on American industrialism,
the AFL believed it necessary for labor to compete with management within the economic framework of the existing indus-

trial society. Under the pragmatic leadership of its president, Samuel Gompers, the AFL adhered rigidly to "business unionism." Its goals were simply to obtain more of America's wealth for the laborer: higher wages, shorter hours, and improved working conditions. An informal debate between Gompers and Morris Hillquit, noted Socialist leader, before the United States Commission on Industrial Relations in 1914 clearly and concisely revealed Gompers' labor program:

> *Mr. Hillquit:* Then, the object of the labor union is to obtain complete social justice for themselves and for their wives and children?
> *Mr. Gompers:* It is the effort to obtain a better life every day.
> *Mr. Hillquit:* Every day and always—
> *Mr. Gompers:* Every day. That does not limit it.
> *Mr. Hillquit:* Until such time—
> *Mr. Gompers:* Not until any time.
> *Mr. Hillquit:* In other words—
> *Mr. Gompers:* [Interrupting] In other words, we go further than you. [Laughter and applause in the audience.] You have an end; we do not.[25]

To achieve these goals, Gompers insisted upon adherence to policies determined by his experiences in the Cigar Makers Union. Active in the labor movements of the 1870s, Gompers was exposed to the policies of the Knights, the Socialists, and other reformers, but he rejected their ideals and turned to pragmatic action on the economic front. He learned through the painful experience of lost strikes that high dues, the maintenance of a full union treasury, and the avoidance of radical political schemes were essential. A skilled craftsman himself, Gompers believed that organization had to begin with the skilled, and championed the craft, or trade union. Such workers were harder to replace in strikes and earned more with which to support Gompers' rigid financial policies. Although opposed to violence, he defended the use of the strike and boycott. He regarded the strike as the ultimate weapon, to be used only when all other attempts to settle disputes had failed, and only when conditions indicated that the chances of a union winning a strike were very good. Convinced that labor, once organized, could fend for itself in the economic arena without governmental aid, Gompers demanded that the AFL and its affiliates refrain from engaging directly in politics. To do so, he believed, would bring impotency and decay to any labor organization.[26]

Organized in 1890 and controlled largely by Massachusetts locals, the National Union of Textile Workers (NUTW) was the major AFL textile affiliate. Basically a craft union, the NUTW was strongest among the skilled Northern operatives, such as the weavers, loom fixers, and carders. The NUTW's organizational structure was flexible, however, approaching a modified industrial unionism at times. Such a structure was ideally suited to attract the Southern operative, for it allowed the skilled operatives to spearhead organizational efforts while also providing for the organization of the unskilled. Yet, neither the NUTW nor the AFL had paid any attention to the plight of the Southern worker before 1895.[27] In that year, a chain of events presaged the coming involvement of both unions in the Southern cotton textile industry.

The AFL's interest in Southern mill hands was largely the result of Gompers' ideological warfare with the Socialists. At the Federation's annual convention late in 1894, against a background of events that included the Pullman strike, the march of Coxey's army on Washington, the Cripple Creek War, and continuing economic depression, the differences between the Socialists and the trade unionists within the Federation came to a head. In a move to gain control of the union, the Socialists sought to convince the AFL's membership that political action was needed if labor was to improve its condition. Led by Gompers, the trade unionists defeated the Socialists' proposal to commit the Federation to a political program. To avenge this defeat, the Socialists merged with the miners to elect their candidate, John McBride, to the presidency of the Federation, the first and only time that Gompers lost the office.[28] This power struggle continued at the Federation's 1895 national convention, where Gompers out-maneuvered his Socialist opposition in an open battle for control of the Federation and regained the presidency. His election caused the Socialists to bolt the Federation and, under the leadership of Daniel De Leon, to found the Socialist Trade and Labor Alliance (STLA) as a competitor of the AFL. Correctly believing that De Leon planned to bring the textile workers into the STLA and use them as "the entering wedge to split the Federation," Gompers began to encourage AFL organizational efforts among Southern operatives. He had toured the South during his 1895 "leave of absence," recognized the operatives' lack of organization, and realized that they might respond to the STLA.[29] At the urging of Robert Howard, a delegate of the Mule Spinners Union from Massachusetts, the Federation's 1895 convention voted to appropriate not more than $500 to put two part-time organizers in the Southern textile field.[30] Gompers appointed Howard and Will H. Winn, a printer from Columbus, Georgia, to these positions.[31] Thus, a power struggle between Socialists and trade unionists within the AFL, a struggle that would soon be repeated within the NUTW, prompted the Federation's first real interest in the Southern operative.

Although the fear of socialism, especially De Leon's STLA, spurred the Federation to action, a less immediate but equally menacing consideration prompted the Federation's concern for the Southern mill worker. By 1895, the South was seriously challenging New England for supremacy in the production of coarse cotton goods and was beginning to constitute a threat in the production of fine goods. Fully aware of the growing Southern threat, New England manufacturers hoped for and even encouraged unionization in the South to reduce that region's competitive advantages.[32] During the years from 1895 to 1900, the appeal from Northern management for Southern unionization rose to a crescendo. As the *Boston Commercial Bulletin* put it:

> If the national labor organizations really wish to aid [the New England cotton industry], as they say they do, let them force, as they can force, a working week of not over fifty hours in every other state. We cannot level Massachusetts down; let the labor unions raise the other states up.[33]

There was an awareness within the Federation, especially among a few of the leaders of the Northern textile locals, that unless Southern labor could be organized, its wages raised, its hours lowered, and the practice of child labor halted, New England manufacturers would cut wages in an attempt to reduce the South's advantages. This realization added extra incentive to the Federation's Southern organizational drive.[34]

In 1896–1897, the AFL worked to organize the South through the NUTW and to keep the NUTW from Socialist control. Will Winn evidently started his organizational work immediately after his appointment, for a local weaver's union, unaffiliated with the national, was established in Columbus by January 1896.[35] Whether by accident or design, Eugene Debs, already ideologically in the Socialist camp, appeared on February 29 in Columbus, which was becoming a center of unionization activity in the South. Debs told his audience that "Government is on strike against labor." Therefore, strikes by labor were unfortunate, but necessary.[36] The city's artisans and, especially, railroad workers, received him enthusiastically, for Debs was still president of the American Railway Union. The city's operatives, however, were less ardent in their reception.

Not Eugene Debs, but management gave Winn the greatest assistance in his organizational efforts. Columbus' major cotton mill, the Eagle and Phoenix Manufacturing Company, announced a 10 percent wage cut in late March for the production of certain types of goods. The decrease, which was to become effective April 6, affected the weavers most. Upon learning of the planned reductions, the weavers began to hold secret meetings, and on March 28, they sent a protest committee to the mill's management. The committee was brusquely dismissed. Undaunted, the weavers struck, and were followed out of the mill by the vast majority of the other operatives. Management continued to refuse to consider a settlement, claiming that even with the reduction in wages, Eagle and Phoenix operatives received 16 percent more pay than did the operatives of the Carolinas. If the weavers did not like the wages offered, they could find jobs elsewhere. On March 30, management closed the Eagle and Phoenix mill; some 1,700 people were put out of work.[37]

While refusing to acknowledge that the operatives would, without "outside agitation," challenge their pronouncements, management prepared to wait out the strike. The company's president, John Bigby, insisted that it was "the insidious work of that man [Debs] which is the prime cause of all this trouble," a statement which, if believed, revealed a woeful lack of comprehension of the workers' reasons for striking. The mayor of the town advised the operatives to exercise "prudent judgement," but the operatives continued to organize. By early April, recruiting agents from other Georgia and Alabama mill towns were successfully operating in Columbus.[38] On April 9, the strikers again sent a delegation to President John Bigby and requested a compromise wage scale. Again, Bigby refused to entertain the committee. The mill continued to stand idle while Bigby was trying, unsuccessfully, to import help from the outlying areas to reopen it. Meanwhile, the Columbus operatives had applied for affiliation with the NUTW, and NUTW secretary, T. P. Cahill, had forwarded them their charter.[39] Resistance to a local wage reduction had led to the formation of the NUTW's first Southern assembly.

By mid-May, however, Bigby's dogmatic resistance to compromise had begun to bear fruit. On May 11, the company was able to reopen a spinning mill successfully. The sight of the returning spinning hands took much of the confidence out of the weavers and other more determined strikers, and they capitulated on May 14. In return for their acceptance of the reduced wage scale, management promised only that the reduction would be rescinded "as soon as conditions improve and the business outlook is sufficient to warrant it."[40]

Even though it ended in defeat, the 1896 strike aroused the Columbus operatives to the possibilities of organization and encouraged the incipient unionization drive there. The workers had failed to obtain their immediate objective, but the union had weathered the strike without being destroyed. Management made no effort to crush the fledgling unions organized during the strike by refusing to rehire union members. On May 17, Debs again spoke in Columbus, receiving a somewhat warmer welcome from the mill hands than he had in February. This time, he emphasized the textile workers' need for organization. He warned against rushing into strikes without adequate preparation, noting that management could close the mills and live off accumulated capital while the laborer frequently could not afford to remain out of work for extended periods of time.[41] Winn of the AFL was also active in Columbus immediately following the strike. As a result of his efforts and the influence of the strike, five textile unions were organized by the summer of 1896: the loom fixers, the carders and spinners, the dressers and finishers, the dyers, and the weavers.[42] In his report to the Federation in August 1896, Winn stated that, elsewhere, his organizational activities had produced results but slowly. But, he urged the AFL to "keep an eye on Columbus."[43] Winn's organizational efforts were supplemented in the late fall and winter of 1896 by Robert Howard's tour of the Southern textile states.[44]

Continued organizational activity in Columbus following the spring strike of 1896 was probably aided by the Eagle and Phoenix scandal which broke in June when the company was forced into receivership. Sparked by charges of corruption lodged by large Columbus stockholders, subsequent investigation revealed that President John Bigby, who was from Atlanta, had placed enough of his relatives on the company's board of trustees to constitute a majority and had been siphoning off thousands of dollars of the company's earnings. Bigby had also greatly increased the salaries of management (his presidential salary had been raised from $10,000 to $20,000 per year early in 1896), initiated an impractically optimistic dividend schedule, and misappropriated $59,292.56 of the company's funds for his personal use. Such financial policies were necessarily partially responsible for the wage reductions which sparked the 1896 strike. They also placed the company so far in debt that, once Bigby was removed and the company reorganized, the new management was forced to adopt strict financial measures, including the retention of the reduced wage scale.[45]

In 1897, however, the pace of organizational activity definitely slowed as the Southern unions found themselves caught in the struggle between trade unionists and Socialists within the AFL. Immediately upon his reelection in 1895, Gompers had declared war on the Socialists in the Federation's ranks. The Socialists had responded by forming the STLA. As Gompers had feared, the STLA had tried to gain control of the NUTW, and had shown amazing success. By the end of 1895, the Socialists were so powerful in the NUTW that many of the craft union locals based in Massachusetts and other New England states, which supported Gompers' trade union policies, seceded from the national union.[46]

At the 1896 spring convention of the NUTW, the STLA made an open bid to control the union, trying to induce the NUTW to leave the AFL and affiliate with it. But Gompers learned in advance of the STLA's plans and was able to rush P. J. McGuire, a Federation vice-president, to the NUTW convention as a trouble-shooter. McGuire succeeded in preventing the convention from voting to leave the AFL, but the convention did vote to hold a referendum on the issue.[47] Still, the STLA continued to exert a powerful influence within the NUTW, becoming influential in the Southern unions formed by trade unionists Winn and Robert Howard.[48]

Early in 1897, the NUTW national secretary, a Socialist, founded the small Socialist Labor party in Columbus with the aid of some of the members of the Columbus locals.[49] The STLA, according to Gompers, "ruthlessly destroyed" the results of the AFL's "painfully slow efforts in Georgia." Stung by these successes and the success of the STLA among some Northern textile unions, Gompers, now firmly in control of the AFL, determined to drive the STLA from the ranks of the NUTW. When the NUTW convention met in May 1897, Gompers again had an AFL representative present. The NUTW was bluntly informed that unless it disavowed the STLA and began organizing operatives solely on a craft basis, the AFL would do so without the aid of the NUTW. This amounted to a threat by the AFL to create another textile national. Faced with the prospect of another national backed by the AFL, the NUTW repudiated its ties with the Socialists.[50]

In an organizational shuffle that occurred sometime after the May convention, NUTW President J. P. Gleeson of Philadelphia resigned and Vice-President Prince W. Greene, a weaver from Columbus, Georgia, and a supporter of Gompers, stepped into the union's chief executive position. With both the Socialists and the larger New England craft locals out of the union, Greene and the Southerners found themselves in charge of the AFL's national textile affiliate.[51] Greene, who served as president until 1900, kept the NUTW loyal to the AFL, kept the South in control of the NUTW, which still retained some Northern locals, and fought to keep the NUTW in control of textile unionism.[52] After the summer of 1897, the Federation, assured of the loyalty of the NUTW, promised to render the NUTW "all possible aid and sympathy," a promise that was not adequately honored. At the December 1897 AFL convention,

Gompers recommended "renewed organizational efforts" in the textile field. A resolution calling for two full-time Southern textile organizers was introduced, but failed to pass, despite Gompers' backing. Its defeat was prompted by the fact that the convention felt that the money to support the proposed organizers could not be spared.[53]

Meanwhile, continued Southern labor unrest was preparing the way for further organizational efforts, despite the Federation's hesitation to finance them. At the time of the 1897 AFL convention, an Atlanta strike occurred which bolstered textile organization there. Atlanta's textile industry centered around the huge Fulton Bag and Cotton Mills, which employed 1,400 operatives. On August 4, 1897, company president Jacob Elsas hired twenty Negro women to work in the folding department of one of the mills. Led by women workers, the entire white work force immediately struck. The strike quickly turned into a riot led by John O'Connor, one of the striking operatives. Police were rushed to the scene, where they attempted to arrest O'Connor. Cries of "don't let 'em have him" and a shower of rocks greeted their attempts. The rock throwers were quickly clubbed into submission and O'Connor was arrested. Crowds of angry strikers stayed at the mills until late into the night, however. The authorities evidently released O'Connor during the night, and he quickly joined Socialist S. M. White in organizing operatives into the Textile Workers' Protective Union. The newly formed union sent a committee to negotiate with Elsas, who refused to arbitrate the matter. He was running his own business, he said, and the whites had "no rights even to enquire about it." Realizing the strength of the operatives' racial prejudice, however, Elsas agreed to discharge the Negroes and rehire the strikers without discrimination. This offer he made to the workers on the condition that they agree to work overtime to meet increased orders, which was the reason Elsas had given for hiring the Negroes. The operatives agreed and the strike was settled by noon, August 5.[54]

After the strike, the newly organized textile local did not disband, nor did it retain its Socialist ties. Instead, it affiliated with the Atlanta Federation of Trades, which was composed of representatives from the various craft union AFL affiliates of the area, most of which were of an artisan nature.[55] In October, the AFL volunteer organizers in the Atlanta federation reported that the local textile union was in good shape and would soon become a member of the NUTW.[56]

In early December, the local charged Elsas with violating his pledge not to discriminate against union workers by firing several leaders of the August strike. The charge was supported by the Atlanta federation, which ordered a general strike against Fulton Mills on December 7. The next day over 1,000 operatives were out and Greene wired them his support. At first, Elsas refused to talk to any representatives of an "outside organization," but, finally, he received a committee of operatives. However, he refused to acknowledge them as union representatives. The committee demanded that the recently discharged hands be reinstated. Their demands were refused. On December 9, after feeding lunch to the 200 or so operatives who remained inside the mill for supposed fear that the strikers would harm them if they left the factory, Elsas locked out the nonstrikers. However, he reopened the mill the next day.[57]

Faced with Elsas' stubborn resistance, the strikers appealed to the AFL convention for aid. The convention responded by voting to "give all possible aid" and to send a special envoy to help the strikers.[58] By this time, the company had managed to reopen its mills successfully, using the original nonstrikers, a few strikebreakers from surrounding towns, and an ever-increasing number of capitulating strikers. In late December, Greene and an AFL legal representative came to Atlanta and were received by Elsas. Although Elsas admitted that the inexperienced hands hired to replace the strikers were damaging his machinery, he obviously held all the trumps. He still refused to meet the union's demands.[59] By early January 1898, Elsas' unyielding policy had broken the strike.[60] But the local, although never recognized by Elsas, rather than being destroyed, had grown considerably during the strike. Interested primarily in reopening his factory, Elsas evidently did not attempt to force his employees out of the union. He probably took this position because, at this time, the NUTW did not seem to represent a real threat.

Although union membership was growing in some areas, toward the end of 1897, the future of the NUTW as a whole looked promising only to the optimist. The union's overall progress in the South had been slow in 1896–1897. It was short of funds, lacked experienced leadership, and was rent by sectional strife. The Northern craft unions had renounced their affiliation with the NUTW during the period of Socialists' dominance. When the Southern operatives gained control of the union from the Socialists, the Northern locals refused to reaffiliate. The rank-and-file Northern operatives believed their financial resources would be siphoned off by the national to further unsuccessful Southern organizational activity. They felt these funds could be more productively employed at home. They also resented the South's control over a union which they had created. The departure of the large majority of Northern mill workers from the ranks of the NUTW deprived the union of its major source of funds, experienced organizers, and proven leadership.

It proved extremely difficult to convince the Southern mill hands of the need for a strong union treasury. Most of the NUTW's Southern members were without trade union experience. This included former members of the Knights of Labor, for that organization had emphasized education and cooperation, not the building of economically strong trade locals. In addition, the wages of even the skilled Southern operative were so low as to make prompt payment of dues difficult. The NUTW's financial difficulties were revealed by the assertion of the national treasurer at the 1900 convention that, for the first time in three years, the union was in sound financial condition. This by no means indicated that the union had by this time obtained what it considered adequate financial resources. It simply evidenced a balanced budget. At the same convention, Greene pleaded for further financial improvements, asking especially that the NUTW increase its strike fund. He urged the convention to increase the national monthly per capita dues from five cents to six cents.[61] Greene realized that if the union was to succeed in the South, it must have financial resources adequate both to support organizational work and give strength to the strike threat as a means of obtaining concessions from management.

The lack of experienced organizers within the ranks of the Southern NUTW locals alone probably would have been an insurmountable handicap in the union's organizational efforts had the AFL not furnished organizers from the ranks of union artisan laborers in the South. Only a handful of the NUTW's members were experienced union men, and even fewer of these had had any organizational experience. Of the operatives who actively engaged in field work in the drive to organize Southern textiles, Greene, C. P. Davis of High Point, North Carolina, G. B. McCracken of Augusta, and G. R. Webb of Langley, South Carolina, were the most prominent.[62] The members of the AFL's nontextile craft unions furnished many of the more effective organizers. These men often represented both the AFL and their local federation of trades, which usually included at least one textile local. Among such men were Will Winn of Columbus, a printer; Jerome Jones, of the Atlanta Federation of Trades; William Gredig of the Augusta Federation of Trades; and L. F. McGruder, a member of a Georgia Iron Molders' local.[63] By supplying organizers, the urban trade federation acted as a coordinator for the organizational activities of the NUTW and the AFL representatives.

Despite the NUTW's problems, by early 1898 it was preparing a vigorous organizational campaign in the South. The optimism of its leadership was not totally without foundation. The activities of Greene, Winn, and Robert Howard had provided the union a base of operations in Georgia's urban areas, especially in Atlanta and Columbus. This was underscored in May 1898 when Greene, after being elected president of the NUTW at the national convention, moved the union's headquarters from Massachusetts to Columbus, Georgia.[64] The threat of further internal wrangles with the Socialists no longer existed. And the AFL had promised to render "all possible aid and sympathy," a phrase the significance of which the NUTW's leadership could have easily overestimated.

The NUTW's plans to organize the South were somewhat complemented by action by the AFL. In 1898, the Federation decided to send several special, paid organizers into the South. They were not, however, to work exclusively in the textile field. However, the composition of the delegation appointed revealed the Federation's marked interest in Southern textile organization, for two of the four appointed organizers were members of the NUTW. Gompers appointed Winn for a ten-month term, McGruder for nine months, Greene for nine months, W. E. Couch of Atlanta for four months, and Webb for a one-month term.[65] Robert Howard also made another Southern organizational tour in the spring of 1898.[66] The NUTW was unable to place its own paid organizers into the field until 1900. Greene appointed C. P. Davis of High Point, North Carolina, and G. R. Webb of Langley, South Carolina, in the textile field as the NUTW's special Southern organizers, reflecting the South's continued dominance within the union.[67] Volunteer organizers in the various AFL nontextile locals of the mill towns of the South aided their professional counterparts in bringing the Southern operative into the folds of the NUTW.

During the years from 1898 to 1900, the AFL and NUTW organizers worked at a furious pace. In June 1899, Greene reported holding organizational meetings in Danville, Virginia; Salisbury, Spray, Haw River, and McAdamsville, North Carolina; Greenville, South Carolina; and Phoenix, Alabama, the mill town just across the Chattahoochee River from Columbus, which was actually Greene's base of operations.[68] Other organizers held meetings in High Point, Durham, Raleigh, Goldsboro, Charlotte, and Wilmington, North Carolina; Spartanburg, Rock Hill, Bath, Graniteville, Columbia, Greenwood, Abbeville, Bamburg, Vaucluse, and Charleston, South Carolina; Brunswick, Savannah, Augusta, and Macon, Georgia; and in other Southern textile towns.[69] In 1899, the NUTW issued charters to fifty-four newly formed locals, nearly all of them in the four Southern states of Georgia, Alabama, North Carolina, and South Carolina.[70] In 1900 alone, NUTW locals were established in the following North Carolina mill towns: Burlington, Altamahaw, Melville, Haw River, King's Mountain, Lexington, Charlotte, Spray, Salisbury, and Gastonia.[71]

Many of these newly organized locals comprised only a handful of members, and locals were not successfully established in all the towns in which organizational meetings were held. But, in the major urban areas, organizational efforts were usually effective and the unions established had surprisingly large memberships. With over 500 members, the Columbia, South Carolina, local was called by the Southern labor press, "the largest textile union in the world," and the Rock Hill local had 150 charter members.[72] Of the 6,000 operatives in Columbus and Augusta, the two cities' several NUTW locals claimed 3,000 members by 1900. More of the state's remaining 12,000 operatives in other cities were members of their local unions.[73] A Greensboro, North Carolina, local claimed 225 members.[74] The NUTW treasurer reported that the union's records showed 5,000 paid-up members as of May 1900, the vast majority of whom were in the South.[75] This was some four months before the union reached its peak strength in the fall of 1900.

If the union's figures were anywhere near correct, by the fall of 1900 the South should have had well over 5,000 operatives in the NUTW.[76] The vast majority of them were in Georgia and the Carolinas, with a few large concentrations in Alabama and Virginia. Although there were 90,085 operatives within these five states, the number of operatives who supported the union's goals but feared to make the commitment of joining can only be surmised.[77] Furthermore, it is difficult to get an accurate account of the number of operatives who joined the union some time between 1896 and 1903, although it was certainly well above 5,000, perhaps even twice that number.

With such a large membership, the NUTW naturally began to make itself felt in the Southern Piedmont, especially through its press. Labor papers established in Augusta, Atlanta, Charlotte, and Columbus criticized mill management.[78] Columbus had two labor papers: the *Columbus Herald,* edited by Winn, and the *Southern Unionist,* edited by Greene. Neither the *Herald* nor the *Journal of Labor,* the Atlanta paper, were exclusively textile union journals. Although no copies of Greene's paper exist, it was probably more an organ for the textile locals. However, it could hardly have been more critical of management than the *Columbus Herald.* In an editorial dated February 19, 1899, the *Herald* roasted the "mill barons." Criticizing the eviction orders of Augusta's management in a textile strike then occurring in that city, Winn journalistically quoted the "barons" as saying, "There shall be no homes among this rabble! and behold, there were none."[79] He severely criticized management's "speed-up" system, called for an eight-hour day, factory inspection laws, nationalized transportation and utilities, and campaigned vigorously for child labor legislation.[80]

Child labor legislation quickly became the AFL's major objective in the South and the NUTW, as a member of the Federation directly affected by the practice, entered wholeheartedly into the fray. In both Georgia and South Carolina, the NUTW petitioned the state legislature, sent operatives to legislative hearings to support child labor bills, and elected union members to the state house, at least four in Georgia alone, in an effort to obtain their bills' passage. In North Carolina, NUTW locals were also connected with child labor bills, but did not support them as actively as did the Georgia and South Carolina operatives. North Carolina owners escaped child labor legislation by agreeing to observe a sixty-six-hour week, to refuse to hire children under twelve during the school term (except children of widows and the disabled), and to refuse employment at all times to children under ten. The agreement was self-imposed and never kept, and, thus, served management's purpose.[81] In Georgia, child labor bills were defeated in 1897, 1899, 1901, and 1902. Their defeat came in the face of strong support from the operatives of Georgia's major industrial centers, especially Augusta, and in the face of the efforts of AFL lobbyist, Irene Ashby McFayden. South Carolina's legislature killed child labor bills backed by the AFL-NUTW in 1899, 1900, 1901, and 1902. Management often succeeded in obtaining operatives' signatures on petitions against the bills by suggesting that they would destroy the operatives' control over their families. Child labor legislation, they argued, would prevent the children of widows, disabled parents, and families in serious economic difficulty from aiding the family unit—even if both parents and children felt it necessary for the children to work. Petitions signed in opposition numbered 5,200, whereas only 830 operatives signed in favor of the 1901 bill. Most of the 830 were from the Horse Creek Valley area where the NUTW was fairly strong.[82]

Victims of the South's xenophobia and management's unrelenting resistance, and lacking political power, the unions failed in their attempts to get child labor bills passed. Yet, their efforts, by giving the issue so much publicity, probably helped prepare the ground for the native Southern, middle-class progressives who would be successful in their campaign soon after the turn of the century, when the union's threat to management had become practically nonexistent. Their association with attempts to enact child labor laws, of course, earned the AFL and the NUTW the undying hatred of Southern mill management.

As the North Carolina owners' agreement to voluntarily cease the employment of children demonstrated, management continued to view child labor as more important to their success than reduced hours.

The NUTW was also able to begin to exert pressure directly on management in specific disputes, especially in cases which involved disputes between management and locals composed of the more skilled operatives. Weavers at Langley in Horse Creek Valley successfully demanded a 5 percent increase in 1899, and loom fixers received a 20 percent pay raise at the same time. At Bath, also in Horse Creek Valley, organized card room hands obtained a 12 percent wage increase.[83] A one-day strike of loom fixers in the Muscogee Mills of Columbus in September 1899 resulted in management ending a recently instituted "speed-up" system.[84]

Although management did not take the growth of the NUTW seriously until 1900, its ever-increasing numbers and influence among the operatives did not go completely unchallenged before then. Management did not, however, make any concerted effort to crush the union in the late 1890s, but relied on more subtle methods of discouraging unionization among the operatives. The old charges that union organizers were the paid emissaries of New England manufacturers jealous of the South's rapid rise to prominence in the textile industry were repeated.[85] The Southern drive to ensure white supremacy by denying the Negro the franchise, then at its peak, provided the owner an excellent opportunity to once more emphasize his role as special protector of the white race and to attempt to link the NUTW with efforts to aid the Negro. For instance, the *Charlotte Mill News,* a management organ, declared at the height of the North Carolina white supremacy campaign that nearly all NUTW organizers opposed the grandfather clause.[86] Earlier, a South Carolina paper had charged that organizer Robert Howard planned to mix races in the mills. Unsympathetic papers also sought to link the union with the Republican party.[87]

The labor press was damned for enabling organizers to "sewer [sic] forth their pestilential filth upon reputable people of the community."[88]

Management's attempts to retard the NUTW's growth were not always so subtle. G. B. McCracken asked the AFL to boycott various Southern cotton mills because of their "Viciousness . . . against organized labor" and the "unfair" methods they used to discourage it.[89] Greene reported strong opposition from management during his attempts to organize the operatives of Columbia, Greenville, and Charlotte.[90] In 1898, a mill superintendent forced an organizer to leave the town of Bath, South Carolina. Greene, however, successfully challenged the superintendent's actions in April of the next year by appearing at another meeting at Bath and daring the official to prevent it.[91] His success indicated the union's growing strength and prestige among the mill workers.

Because of their youth and lack of experience, underfinanced NUTW locals plunged, rather foolhardily, into at least four strikes before July 1900. By far the largest was the Augusta strike of 1898–1899. In October 1898, the Southern Cotton Manufacturers Association, composed of mill officials from Augusta and Horse Creek Valley, South Carolina, announced that a wage reduction of from 8 percent to 12 percent would become effective November 21. The operatives maintained that the cuts averaged 13 percent, with some as high as from 25 percent to 40 percent. Although some operatives were inclined to accept the reductions, the weavers immediately began to organize. They requested and received aid from the AFL in the person of Andrew Mulcay, a carriage painter who was drafted by the Federation for the task. Although not an experienced organizer, Mulcay quickly organized seven locals, including the weavers and loom fixers. The workers also sought aid from Greene and the NUTW, for they realized financial aid would be necessary in case of a protracted strike. On the day the cut became effective, the weavers led strikes at the King,

Sibley, and Enterprise mills after the city's merchants had unsuccessfully petitioned management not to initiate the reductions. The union members were joined by large numbers of unorganized mill hands. Mayor Patrick Walsh met the strikers outside the mills, assured them of his sympathy, and warned them that the strike was against their best interests. Nevertheless, nearly 3,000 hands struck. Some, however, remained at their positions.[92] The strike soon spread to the mills of Bath and Langley in Horse Creek Valley.

Hastily organized, without experienced leadership, and totally dependent upon outside sources for finances, the striking operatives had little hope of success. Mulcay was not even a member of the AFL until he was given an organizer's commission and sent to organize the Augusta operatives. The relief committee that was established was swamped by striking operatives who now flocked to join the union, and were admitted. By the end of November, some strikers, especially the skilled ones who could easily find new positions, were leaving the city. Others were openly questioning continued resistance.[93] Management refused to arbitrate, maintaining that the old wages were 18 percent above those paid in the Carolinas. They refused to acknowledge the local character of the dispute and, instead, blamed it on "Northern labor agitators."

Mill officials increased the pressure on the strikers late in December by locking out those operatives who had not struck. This closed the mills, but prevented the strikers from receiving any financial aid from nonstriking operatives. The town's wholesale grocers coincidentally instituted a policy of denying credit to retailers giving credit to strikers. Some aid trickled in from other Southern locals and from troops stationed just outside the city who had been called up for the Spanish-American War. Such aid, however, was pitifully inadequate to meet the local's financial obligations. Desperate for funds, the relief committee sent out a national appeal, directed especially at New England operatives. "Our gain is your gain," the committee argued;

unless Southern operatives could prevent wage reductions Northern mills would surely reduce wages.[94]

With the coming of the new year, management announced an eviction policy to begin on January 9, 1899. Hoping the strikers would panic at this news, some of the mills reopened. Remarkably, the workers held firm. The mills were forced to close because of a lack of laborers. Actual eviction brought different results. On the day after evictions began, four mills were able to resume operations, their operatives protected by the police. On January 18, management began importing strikebreakers from surrounding rural areas and small towns. Meanwhile, the strikers had learned that they could expect no aid from the NUTW national organization because their locals had not been chartered the required six months.[95] Taken together, these events dealt the strike a mortal blow.

Without the hope of financial aid, under eviction proceedings, aware that the mills were successfully recruiting strikebreakers, and faced with the impossibility of obtaining further supplies on credit from the city's retail grocers, the strikers had little choice but to concede defeat. However, in an effort to avoid total defeat, Greene and Winn came to Augusta on January 21 to attempt to negotiate a settlement. Surprisingly, they were received by officials of the Southern Cotton Manufacturers Association, who were evidently willing to make slight concessions to bring the strike to an immediate end.

Greene erred seriously by presenting management with an "ultimatum" which was a thinly disguised effort to obtain through negotiation what the strikers had no hope of winning. He demanded a 10 percent reduction in company housing rent, the sale of fuel to operatives at cost, and recognition of the NUTW. Greene agreed to accept the wage reduction if these things were done and management would reduce the salaries of mill officials proportionately. Although Greene's demands concerning wages were promptly and flatly refused, some of his other points were incorporated into management's response.

Realizing that further resistance was foolish and that his bluff had been called, Greene accepted management's proposals, which contained some small concessions, a further indication that management was anxious to end the strike. In a settlement adopted January 26, the mills "guaranteed" to keep wage scales in the Augusta area at least 6 percent above those in the Carolinas, to sell fuel to the operatives at cost, and to rehire union laborers without discrimination "so long as no effort is made to interfere with the management or control of said mills, or with their employees." The mills also agreed to raise wages as soon as business warranted it.[96] The strikers had lost their major objective, but had not been totally defeated. They had received one minor material concession, two promises, and management's tacit recognition of the newly formed locals. In view of future events, management's decision not to press for the destruction of the locals at that time was to prove a costly tactical error for them.

A minor strike occurred at the Fulton Bag and Cotton Mills of Atlanta in February 1899. Here, the weavers struck when one of their number was discharged and replaced by a non-union man at lower wages. The weavers were unable to obtain the support of fellow operatives and President Elsas refused to consider a settlement, despite Robert Howard's coming from Fall River to attempt to negotiate the issue. Within a week, the strike was broken.[97] In Columbus, the loom fixers engaged in a strike from October 1899 until April 1900. The strike originated over the refusal of loom fixers at the Muscogee Mills to accept extra work requirements. Loom fixers from the Muscogee, Swift, and Hamburger mills went out, but only twenty men left the mills. Management, in turn, locked out the striking loom fixers. Unsupported by the other operatives and unable to receive funds from the financially weak national, the loom fixers were forced to rely on aid from individual Southern NUTW locals. Under such circumstances, their defeat was unavoidable.[98] In July 1900, forty beamers struck a Columbus firm when new machinery was installed to allow for increased production. The operatives, who received piece wages, demanded a corresponding increase in their wages. Their demands were refused. Because the mill could not run without the forty strikers, some 1,500 people were thrown out of work. At this juncture, the Central Labor Union of Columbus, with which the beamers were affiliated, negotiated a settlement by inducing management to make slight wage increases and other minor concessions.[99]

The situations surrounding these early NUTW strikes strikingly portended the union's future. In each, the operatives either making the demands or leading the strike were highly skilled. In Augusta, the skilled operatives were supported by the unskilled, but elsewhere this was not the case. Each strike was a defensive measure taken to counter some specific action by management. In Augusta, the unskilled workers followed the weavers and loom fixers because they were affected by the wage reductions. In Columbus and Atlanta, the unskilled were not directly affected and did not support the better organized skilled laborers who were. The NUTW's lack of funds significantly lessened the operatives' chances of success in each strike. Although in two of the strikes the unions were clearly defeated, in each case those locals leading the strike survived it. In none of the four strikes did management attempt to destroy the locals by refusing to rehire union laborers once the strikes were defeated. In both the 1898–1899 Augusta strike and the 1900 Columbus strike, management offered the union implied recognition, but only with the understanding that no further trouble was to be expected. This indicates that management had not yet begun to take the fledgling NUTW seriously. It was considered a tolerable annoyance, perhaps even a means of placating the more restive members of the work force, but certainly not as a threat.

By 1900, however, the NUTW had grown to such proportions that management could no longer continue to ignore it. The union's convention of that year was held in Augusta. It was the first national convention of a textile union to be held in the South. At this landmark convention the young and inexperienced union flung an open challenge at Southern management by adopting a motion to request a ten-hour day, without wage reductions, in all Southern mills by May 1, 1901. Locals were advised to begin immediately "agitating and organizing for the accomplishment of the above object." After adopting the motion, the convention voted to have it printed in the local papers of Southern textile towns and to distribute 20,000 pamphlets explaining their goal.[100] For the first time confronted with the threat of a serious ten-hour-day movement, led by a native labor organization with strong advocates of child labor legislation, among whom the NUTW and the AFL were the most vocal, management could no longer continue to disregard the NUTW. The time had come for management to attempt a serious attack on the union.

In view of its situation in early 1900, the NUTW's decision to press for a ten-hour day was a serious blunder. Despite its phenomenal growth since 1896 and the all-too-optimistic reports from its organizers in the field, the NUTW was actually ill-prepared to engage in major struggles with management by 1900.[101] Among its many weaknesses, the lack of finances was perhaps most crippling. For the past three years, the national had been too weak financially to aid any of its striking locals except by endorsing appeals to other locals. Since many locals had adopted a policy of low dues, such appeals seldom brought satisfactory results. Although the national's finances were improved by 1900, that year's convention refused to adopt Greene's recommendation either to raise monthly national per capita dues from five cents to six cents or to increase initiation fees from 50 cents to $1.00. A resolution was adopted, however, which allowed the president to assess member unions five cents per week per member to aid striking and locked-out locals.[102] Such lax financial policies presaged ill fortunes for the union in any prolonged struggle for survival.

Numerically, the NUTW's membership represented only slightly less than 6 percent of the industry's operatives in the five leading Southern textile states. The percentage was a bit higher in the Carolinas and in Georgia. But, its membership was highly concentrated in the urban mills from Columbus to Danville. The NUTW's failure to penetrate the South's closely guarded rural mills left its urban members at the mercy of their fellow rural operatives, as was clearly demonstrated in the 1898–1899 Augusta strike. Since the leadership and most of the union's members came from the ranks of the skilled operatives, again demonstrated by organizational patterns in Augusta, locals had to rely on the support of the unskilled, many of whom were unorganized even in urban areas. If these unskilled workers acted as strikebreakers, no strike could succeed, as was evidenced at Columbus and Atlanta. Lack of experienced local leaders in strike situations and a tendency to strike without adequate preparations, both again woefully apparent in the Augusta strike, were to be serious handicaps. The national NUTW leadership was active in only two of the union's strikes before 1900, and, after 1898, it was headquartered in the South.

In addition to its weaknesses listed above, the NUTW in early 1900 was envisioning a drive for a ten-hour day in an area where the press was decidedly anti-labor. It had no strong moral, political, or economic support among any other segment of the South's population, a fact demonstrated by the actions of the Augusta merchants in 1898–1899. The union also had to overcome management's assertions that it favored the Negro and hoped to improve his political, economic, and social status at the expense of white workers. The people the union sought to mobilize were scorned by both the farmer and the urban professional and merchant groups. They were literally segregated from the rest of the white community and, thus, often prone to view management as their champion. At the same time, they were highly dependent on management for food, supplies, even homes, in addition to wages. Some deeply resented this condition, others thankfully accepted it as their only escape from rural poverty and isolation. Management, on the other hand, possessed overwhelming financial resources, enjoyed tremendous social prestige, was a potent political force, and was capable of quickly organizing to present labor with a solid, unyielding front.

In short, the 1898–1899 Augusta strike had shown all the NUTW's weaknesses—lack of finances, absence of adequate leadership, the threat of strikebreakers from rural areas and smaller towns, and the lack of support among the townspeople. Under such circumstances, there was little ground for the optimism displayed at the 1900 NUTW convention. The union's growth had been rapid, but it lacked a solid foundation. A house built upon sand, the NUTW was to collapse when the storm came. And by adopting their ten-hour resolution, they had stirred up a storm.

6

The National Union
of Textile Workers
at High Tide

The 1900 NUTW convention's adoption of a resolution to agitate for the ten-hour day in Southern mills changed the tenor of labor-management disputes in Southern textiles. Prior to 1900, the NUTW had engaged in several strikes, most of which were lost. But, in each case, the locals involved came through the strike intact; in some cases, such as the 1898–1899 Augusta strike, the locals actually enlarged membership. Also, though refusing to recognize the locals officially by talking to their local and national leaders, management implied tacit recognition of the operatives' right to organize. In none of the early NUTW strikes did management deliberately attempt to eradicate the offending local. After the 1900 NUTW convention's ten-hour-day resolution, however, management throughout the South began to mobilize its forces in an attempt to eradicate the union. In the industrial warfare that followed, the NUTW's rapid growth was checked and its stronghold in Virginia and the Carolinas broken in the short period of eighteen months.

The NUTW's timing in presenting management with such an obvious and direct challenge could not have been worse. The South's mills had been making handsome profits since 1896, largely because of their penetration of the enormous market for coarse cotton goods in the Far East. But the Boxer Rebellion of 1900 drastically disrupted the Eastern flow of cotton goods momentarily. Exports of American cotton goods dropped from 5.7 million pieces in 1899 to 3.2 million pieces in 1900. Most of this was coarse cotton goods produced in Southern mills. Such tremendous losses forced the mills to reduce production.[1] Faced with tightening markets, management refused to entertain any union demands for a reduction of hours without a corresponding reduction of wages. Furthermore, Southern management was not without means to combat the NUTW.

Ranged against the union was the powerful Southern Cotton Spinners Association. (SCSA). Organized in 1897, the SCSA embraced nearly all the textile manufacturers of the South.[2] Its May 1900 convention at Charlotte was attended by over 500 mill men whose combined assets were valued at more than $500 million.[3] This organization, bolstered by such regional associations as the Southern Cotton Manufacturers Association of the Augusta and Horse Creek Valley area, gave management the coordination necessary to eliminate the NUTW from the South.[4]

During the crucial years of 1900 and 1901, NUTW officials directed much of their vital time and effort toward attempts to consolidate a national textile union which would include the New England craft unions. The efforts spent on these attempts, in addition to the NUTW's many handicaps discussed in the previous chapter, considerably aided management in its struggle with the union. Yet, the NUTW felt that the attempts toward consolidation had to be made at this time. Its leaders hoped that a strong national could use New England money and experience to organize the South. This, NUTW officials argued, would remove the constantly growing threat to wages in New England that cheap Southern labor posed. The Boxer Rebellion reinforced their argument. Faced with market losses because of the Rebellion and growing Southern competition, New England owners were determined to reduce labor costs. Thus, New England locals began to consider seriously the need for consolidation.

Under the guidance and pressure of the AFL, a consolidation movement began in 1900. That year, the NUTW elected Peter Oulman of North Adams, Massachusetts, to the presidency, while retaining Greene in the administration as secretary-treasurer.[5] Oulman's election was obviously designed to appeal to New England unions. But, bitter disputes between the NUTW, which was still dominated by Southern locals, and the New England unions had to be quelled before consolidation was accomplished.[6] Therefore, the NUTW began its drive for the ten-hour day as the industry was entering a period of depression and while occupied with a power struggle among the nation's various textile unions for a major voice in a proposed national textile union.

The first struggle between management and the NUTW came in North Carolina. Of the South's three leading textile states, North Carolina was perhaps least penetrated by the NUTW, primarily because it lacked urban textile centers. The union's difficulties there actually began before the May 1900 convention. In April, the AFL had commissioned C. P. Davis of High Point as a special part-time Southern organizer. Davis immediately began to organize the operatives of the North Carolina Piedmont, many of whom responded eagerly to his efforts. Yet, the NUTW feared management would suppress the new locals and Davis' organizational activities were evidently somewhat clandestine, for he had organized several locals before management became aware of his activities.[7]

Davis' efforts could not go undetected forever, and in early May, Moses and Caesar Cone, owners of the Proximity Mill outside Greensboro, learned that over 150 of their more than 1,000 operatives had joined a recently organized local.[8] The Cones, who had moved from Baltimore partially to escape unions, reacted swiftly to the NUTW's presence. Threatening to tear down the mill rather than run it with union labor, they locked out their entire labor force. Using the paternal system to destroy the local, the Cones then closed the company store, which also contained the post office. The operatives were thus forced to walk the two-mile distance to Greensboro to obtain supplies and mail. Though there was no violence associated with the lockout, the company employed twelve watchmen to protect the mill's property and the county sheriff made an appearance at the mill every day.[9]

The operatives found themselves without cash, credit, or supplies. James Long, an officer of the Proximity local, wired the NUTW convention, advising them of the lockout, which he insisted the Cones had instituted "without threat or demand from us." Long requested the aid of the national in breaking the lockout. The convention responded by sending Davis to Proximity to investigate the situation.[10] But, Davis achieved nothing, and the Cones maintained the pressure by beginning to evict any household that contained a union member. This action aroused much resentment among the operatives, many of whom helped to expand the union's membership rapidly to 250. As the additional members were as financially weak as the union's older members, their presence simply further depleted the local's meager strike fund. Within a week after beginning their eviction policy, the Cones felt confident enough of victory to reopen the mill. Only nonunion help was hired, and only after they had signed a pledge never to become union members. Resenting such treatment, the more ardent unionists tried to keep the local alive by holding secret meetings in the nearby woods, but the local soon began to disintegrate. Some of its hard-core members left to seek positions elsewhere, but the less zealous simply signed the required pledge and returned to work.[11] The Cones' complete control of a rural mill had defeated the union.

During the lockout, some of the Proximity operatives moved to Durham, where they obtained positions at the Erwin Mills. When management discovered their connections with the Proximity lockout, they were immediately discharged. Using as an excuse the actions of a union operative who left the mill on union business without his overseer's permission, President William Erwin posted a two-week notice for any of his operatives with union connections. The company store was closed to all who continued to support the union.[12]

The reaction of the operatives was pitifully divided. Some struck immediately, others refused to leave the union and were fired after two weeks; still others, largely nonunion, remained at work. Within a week after the enforcement of the decree, the union members appealed to Erwin for food. Playing well management's role of friend of the operative and foe of the union, Erwin issued a statement claiming that his quarrel was with "unwarranted interference" in his business, not individual operatives. He then authorized the company store to issue food to all mill hands, including the striking union members. This enlightened action seriously hurt the union's cause, even though 150 members were still out in late August. Erwin, unyielding in his refusal to hire union personnel, ultimately won the contest and the Durham local disbanded.[13]

Other strikes and lockouts occurred across North Carolina during the summer of 1900, perhaps as many as thirty all together.[14] In the spring of that year, twenty-eight Gaston County mills blacklisted union operatives in an evidently successful effort to break incipient NUTW locals in the area.[15] A lockout at Fayetteville, in which management used eviction, strikebreakers, and the blacklist, destroyed a fledgling local in that town.[16]

Management in Alamance County moved with the greatest force of all to crush the NUTW in the state. The center of cotton textile manufacturing in North Carolina, with a long history of cotton goods production, Alamance County was to become a symbol to both union and management. If the unions could be broken there, even if they continued to exist in a few scattered textile communities, the NUTW's thrust into the state would be effectively repelled.

The NUTW first came to Alamance County early in 1900 when some South Carolina operatives out on strike came north and obtained positions, bringing their union ideals with them.[17] They soon established a local in the county with headquarters at the little town of Graham. By August, Davis' organizational activities had resulted in the establishment of at least five other locals, encompassing the majority of the operatives in most of the county's mills.[18] The organization of the Alamance mills was viewed with alarm by the press as far south as Columbus. Basing an attack against the union on the South's xenophobia, the *Columbus Enquirer-Sun* charged that Northern mill men were behind the organization. The *Rock Hill* (S. C.) *Herald* noted that the Alamance situation represented the third recent labor-management dispute in the mills of North Carolina.[19]

Trouble between the union and the mills developed at Haw River, a small Alamance County textile community, in September 1900. A superintendent discharged a union weaver, Anna Whitsell, for taking unnecessary time to fill her loom and offered her position to Miss Johnnie Pope. No evidence exists that suggests she was fired for her union membership. Probably to avoid criticism from union operatives, Miss Pope refused the position when she learned the circumstances of Miss Whitsell's dismissal. The superintendent then instructed Miss Pope to accept the position or leave the mill. The girl, an orphan, chose to work. That night, September 27, the local met and decided to strike if Miss Pope was forced to accept Miss Whitsell's position the next day. The following morning the superintendent again demanded that Miss Pope accept the discharged weaver's position, and the operatives struck. Within an hour, two other Haw River mills struck and approximately 800 operatives had left their positions, although a few remained in the mills.[20]

The union was determined to obtain the discharge of the offending superintendent, who was accused of unjustly and rudely treating Miss Whitsell. A committee was sent to the management, requesting the superintendent's dismissal. "Believing that to yield to such demands on the part of the Labor Union would be to give up the entire control of the management of the mill on the part of the owners," management not only refused to recognize the union's committee, but supported the superintendent's actions.[21] As union-management relations grew even more tense, rumors began to circulate that the union operatives were plotting to blow up the mill from which Miss Whitsell had been discharged. Owners responded to the rumors by putting on extra guards carrying Winchester rifles.[22]

By striking, the workers turned a rather minor incident, evidently unrelated to the right to organize from management's point of view, into a direct challenge to management. Mill officials realized the basic instability of the locals and determined to use the strike as a vehicle for eliminating the NUTW in Alamance. On October 3, all but two of the county's mills posted the following notice:

> Whereas, recent developments have shown that this mill cannot be operated with that harmony between the owners and the operatives thereof that is essential success [sic], and to the interest of all concerned, so long as the operatives are subject to interference by outside parties; this is to give
>
> Notice, that on and after the 15th day of October, 1900, this mill will not employ any operative who belongs to a Labor Union, but will be run by Non-Union Labor only.
>
> All operatives who object to the above, and will not withdraw from Labor Unions, will please consider this as Notice, and vacate any house and premises belonging to us which they may now occupy, on or before the 15th day of October, 1900.[23]

By October 10, some 900 operatives had already left the mills and the three Haw River mills had been forced to halt production. Six days later, the NUTW held a large rally at Graham attended by over 1,000 operatives, with Davis as the principal speaker. On the same day, mills not involved in the strike polled their mill hands to determine how many were affiliated with the NUTW locals. All who admitted membership were immediately discharged. Only the two mills who had not posted the notice were now operating full time. One of the Holt family's plaid mills had only four remaining operatives. Several of the mills joining the lockout of union laborers were forced to close; others staggered along with only a handful of operatives. Nearly 4,000 operatives refused to return to work under the conditions imposed by management. By the middle of October, management had attempted to import strikebreakers from surrounding towns with little success.[24]

Management's lockout policy, which had thrown both union and nonunion operatives out of the mills, was considered unjust by many not directly involved in the strike, and public opinion began to favor the workers. Trying to counter growing public sympathy for the operatives, the owners explained that they had not been opposed to the union per se until it started making demands. These demands made it "difficult to maintain discipline among the operatives while at work and consequently the production was reduced and its cost increased." Seeking to discredit the union, management charged that union members had threatened the lives of strikebreakers and operatives who accepted the company's terms. Management did not, however, waver in its announced goal of destroying the union. "We are determined," Alf W. Haywood, Vice-president of the Holt Manufacturing Company, stated, "to run with nonunion labor or not run at all." Armed guards were placed around the mills at night and Winchesters were provided for the "protection" of those who returned to work under the owners' terms. Yet, the superintendent of a Holt mill declared that management did not actually expect any violence. Union leadership also denied threatening either the strikebreakers or those laborers who chose to return to work.[25]

By late October, it was apparent that things were going poorly for the strikers. Some operatives had begun to desert the union and return to their jobs, alleging that the strike was badly managed by the local's leadership. Others deserted the union because "they [the company] have been my friend and now I'm going to stand by them." Union operatives leaving the area to seek jobs elsewhere were stunned to find that they had been blacklisted in such mill towns as Fayetteville, Durham, Raleigh, and Gibsonville. Meanwhile, management was becoming more successful in their efforts to recruit strikebreakers. At this point, union leaders took pains to deny that the operatives' solidarity was beginning to crumble, but it was becoming increasingly obvious that their cause was weakening. Noting the union's weakness, on October 30, management used its most efficient weapon: it sent vacate notices to all union members remaining in company housing.[26]

On October 31, Greene came to Alamance to bring funds from the national organization, which had endorsed the Alamance locals' appeals to other Southern locals. Greene, in a show of defiance, vowed that the NUTW would support the Alamance strikers even if the struggle continued all winter. He also threatened the owners with a boycott of their products, a rather puny threat.[27] Unfortunately for the operatives, the NUTW had little money with which to back up their assertions. The financial support of the NUTW was embarrassingly small, and the appeals of the Alamance locals had brought only meager funds from other Southern textile locals. There was little hope that further financial aid would arrive from either source. Yet, the vast majority of the mill hands refused to yield.

At this juncture, management moved to terminate the struggle. At the beginning of November, eighteen of the county's twenty mills were either idle or running with greatly reduced labor forces. Management instituted their threatened eviction policy on November 9. Some of the evicted operatives obtained tents from the NUTW; others left the state seeking work.[28] As management continued to vacate union members and more and more operatives left the area, the locals began to realize that their situation was hopeless. They found neither support in their communities nor adequate aid from the NUTW. Their ranks began to disintegrate rapidly.[29]

Late in November, the national organization acknowledged the hopelessness of continuing the struggle and withdrew its support from the strike. Thoroughly defeated, the Alamance locals were forced to surrender on management's terms.[30] Despite later claims made by NUTW members that so many operatives left the county that management was forced to rehire union members to obtain a sufficient labor force, the Alamance strike completely broke the power of the NUTW in North Carolina. Never again able to challenge management in North Carolina seriously, the NUTW became a mere nuisance, a nuisance so insignificant that some mill owners tolerated the existence of a few impotent locals.

Unlike the Alamance strike, which was a result of the NUTW locals' defensive efforts, the 1901 Danville, Virginia, strike-lockout was caused by the demands of militant textile locals who had the announced support of both the NUTW and the AFL from the beginning. These demands involved the 1900 NUTW resolution to obtain a ten-hour work day without wage reductions in all Southern mills. Unionization had begun in Danville, a town completely controlled by the gigantic Riverside Mill, in January 1900. Once organized, the Danville locals began to agitate for the ten-hour day, a goal of no mean significance, as the Danville mills ran twelve hours, an hour more than the mills of Georgia and the Carolinas.[31]

Management met the laborers' request with a typical response. They refused to entertain union spokesmen to discuss a possible reduction of hours. Instead, they charged that the union was trying to "control or dictate to the management." As usual, management cited outside forces as the reasons for their trouble with the mill workers. They blamed the union's appearance on efforts to obtain child labor legislation and local attorneys with "political aspirations." As the union continued to grow, however, management decided to make some concessions, probably to avoid a time-consuming strike. On January 1, 1901, management announced that, henceforward, Danville mills would operate on an eleven-hour schedule from April through September and a ten-hour schedule from October through March, thus making the ten-and-one-half-hour day the yearly average, without wage reductions. The plan was immediately instituted.[32]

This was a major victory for the locals, one that had cost them nothing and could only have served to increase the influence of the NUTW in the upper South. The locals would have done well to have accepted the better than half a loaf that management offered. But both the NUTW and the AFL saw Danville as a test case in their drive to obtain a ten-hour day throughout the South, and they were determined that Danville would become the first victory in this campaign. The rapid growth of the Danville NUTW locals in early 1901 reinforced their determination to force management to retain the ten-hour day year round. Union leaders either conveniently ignored the fate of the Alamance laborers, who had been well organized in a major textile center, or reasoned that because of the Alamance defeat, they had to gamble on obtaining a total victory in Danville. At any rate, by March the NUTW and the AFL had decided to strike if necessary to see that the winter work schedule was retained after April 1.[33]

Local organizers whipped the union members into a fighting mood to prepare them for the coming struggle. Management, which had adopted a work day shorter than the Southern standard of eleven hours, was just as determined not to yield to the year-round ten-hour day. By the end of March, Danville was a tense, divided city, waiting for the inevitable.

The collision that everyone anticipated came on March 30 when Samuel Gompers arrived in town at 4:35 A.M. to be greeted by a band and an enthusiastic crowd of mill hands. That morning, Gompers met with local union leaders. They accompanied him to an afternoon meeting with R. A. Schoolfield, Secretary-Treasurer, and D. A. Overby, overseer of the Riverside Mill. Gompers demanded that the ten-hour day be continued; management refused. By this time, nearly all the major Southern textile union leaders, including Greene, had converged upon Danville.[34]

Gompers addressed a mass rally of the textile operatives that evening. In his address, Gompers flayed Southern textile mill management, saying that unions had temporized on the ten-hour issue for the past three months and that the time for action had finally arrived. He then read a list of resolutions that had been adopted by the locals' executive committee that afternoon. The resolutions stated that (1) at the present state of the industry, a ten-hour day was sufficient for progress, economy, and humanity, (2) having experienced the benefits of the ten-hour day, the locals were "unalterably opposed to the inauguration of the eleven-hour day in the Riverside Cotton Mills," (3) the operatives would refuse to enter the mills on April 1 while a five-man committee, appointed by the executive council, spoke to management and then reported to the operatives that afternoon, and (4) the operatives pledged on their honor to stay out until the ten-hour day was achieved, "come sunshine or storm." The audience, composed of both union and nonunion operatives, unanimously adopted the resolutions. Gompers then expressed his reluctance to use the strike, but noted that "only in civilized countries do they have strikes, and the more highly civilized they are the more strikes." By adopting the resolutions, he assured the operatives that they had not decided to strike; rather, they had given management a chance to avert one.[35]

After Gompers' speech, a strike could not have been prevented unless management had agreed to the union's demands. And faced with such an obvious challenge, management was determined not to yield, whatever the cost. On April 1, the locals sent a five-man committee composed of Greene, AFL organizer M. S. Belk, and three local union members to deliver the adopted resolutions to Schoolfield. The company successfully delayed action, claiming it needed time to assemble board members who resided out of town to discuss the resolutions before delivering an answer.[36]

The company's answer was swift and blunt. On April 2, President F. H. Burton refused the operatives' demands, noting that the mills had reduced the average working day from twelve to ten and one-half hours, which was shorter than the eleven-hour day of other Southern mills. The Danville strike began. The executive committee of the locals, headed by Harry Walker of Local 150 and AFL representative Belk, appealed to all NUTW locals, the national organization, and the AFL for aid. Gompers called Belk back to AFL headquarters to review the situation before finally officially committing the AFL to the support of the strike.[37] By so doing, he indicated that the AFL had some doubts about supporting the strikers "come sunshine or storm."

Faced with a determined opponent in the Riverside management and the responsibility of caring for over 2,000 idled operatives, the Danville locals had only a slim chance of success without complete solidarity and large amounts of outside financial aid. They received neither. By mid-April, Walker was frantically wiring Greene to come to Danville to settle quarrels within the executive committee. A dispute had developed between Belk, who was adhering to a strike policy outlined by Gompers and Greene, and a local lawyer named Cabel, who was urging the unions to use their political influence against management by supporting certain candidates in the upcoming municipal elections. On April 15, Belk wired Greene that the executive committee had voted to put the strike entirely under Cabel's direction and had actually made Cabel the head of the committee, replacing Walker. He also advised Greene that money was urgently needed. In his reply, Greene protested Cabel's involvement in the strike; Belk answered with an urgent request for Greene's presence. Greene arrived in Danville on April 29 to find Cabel in complete control of the strike; no financial aid from the national had yet arrived.[38]

All efforts to settle the locals' internal feuding and obtain adequate financial aid failed. On May 2, Greene left Danville for the NUTW convention in Massachusetts. He had not succeeded in his efforts to have Cabel removed from the chairmanship of the executive committee. Belk also left the city to go to Washington to report to Gompers, at the latter's request. At the convention, Greene pleaded for financial support of the Danville strikers, stressing the fact that Danville stood between ten- and eleven-hour country. A victory in Danville, reasoned Greene, would be a major step in forcing the mills further South to adopt the ten-hour standard. The convention voted to send a delegate to Danville to attempt to settle the strike and to aid the workers to victory in any possible way, but no financial assistance was provided. Meanwhile, Gompers was able to convince the AFL to declare its official support of the Danville strike, and the Federation eventually sent approximately $4,000 to the strikers. But his protests to the Danville executive committee about Cabel's involvement in the strike were unable to force his removal from the executive committee.[39]

Despite their lack of unity, leadership, and finances, the Danville strikers severely frightened the textile manufacturers across the border in North Carolina, setting the rumor mills grinding. Owners believed that Gompers intended to call a general strike throughout the South if the demands of the Danville operatives were not met. Other rumors had Gompers appearing in various North Carolina mill towns to organize the operatives for the planned general strike. Manufacturers began to make plans for a "concert of action among the mills" if such a general strike was called. One North Carolina owner declared, "The minute the [general] strike goes into effect, just that minute will every striker be notified to vacate the company house that he occupies. The shut-out on our side will be as complete as theirs."[40] Some owners, including SCSA President J. H. McAden, noting the decline in the textile market and the high cost of raw cotton, believed such a strike would do little harm to Southern mills. He claimed many were making no profit and continued to run solely to keep their labor force intact. McAden believed the NUTW was strong in Burlington, Raleigh, Greensboro, Concord, Gastonia, and Charlotte, but noted that most of these unions had been formed since the Alamance strike and were therefore relatively inexperienced and without financial resources. He also observed the weakness of the union in the rural mills, although other mill men believed "secret" unions existed in them. On the other hand, he maintained that the mills had done well in 1900 and could easily face even a pro-longed strike.[41]

Nevertheless, it was obvious that North Carolina owners were extremely worried about the Danville strike and the operatives' chances of victory. They, like Greene, realized that a victory for the strikers at Danville would have tremendous repercussions in Alamance and other northern Piedmont North Carolina textile centers.[42] This was especially true since a victory in Danville would mean that Carolina operatives would be working longer than their Virginia counterparts who had achieved shorter hours through the power of organization.

The Danville strikers struggled doggedly along as their situation steadily worsened. Crippled by its policy of low dues, the NUTW was unable to send them any significant financial aid.

The locals, many recently organized, had only $2,700 in their combined treasuries when the strike began, not nearly enough, even with the AFL contributions and funds from other NUTW locals, to support the over 2,000 idle workers. By the end of April, the Danville assemblies had representatives traveling to other NUTW locals to make personal appeals for additional contributions. These appeals, which met with little success, coupled with the poor financial showing of the national, exposed the desperate condition of the operatives to management.[43]

At the same time, Cabel continued to control the strike policy and evidently delivered the operatives' votes to his friends. As Gompers and Belk had warned, after the election, the political "friends" of the union advised the locals to accept the eleven-hour day. Betrayed by their political allies and without the financial means to continue the strike, the operatives began to break ranks and return to work in the late spring. By the middle of the summer, the strike was broken and the unions disorganized.[44]

In assessing the Danville defeat, Belk placed the blame squarely on the strikers' involvement in politics. Had they followed the plan of Gompers and Greene, he believed they could have won,

> but they allowed outsiders to influence them to dabble in politics. After the politicians used them on election day and told them to return to work under the eleven-hour system they realized who their real friends were, but it was too late.[45]

Only partially accurate, Belk's conclusions failed to take into account the union's meager finances, the strike's obviously bad timing, and management's determination not to yield, especially strong in this case since they felt they had already granted reasonable concessions.

The failure of the Danville strike not only stopped NUTW

agitation for the ten-hour day in the South; it broke the power of the union in the upper Piedmont. Had the operatives won at Danville, the unions defeated at Alamance, which were attempting to reorganize, would certainly have been strengthened by the knowledge that management had been beaten just a few miles to the north. Also, the Danville locals could have aided the locals to the south in organizational efforts and with finances in case major strikes developed. But, together, Alamance and Danville destroyed the effective existence and the promise of the NUTW north of South Carolina.

In South Carolina, the NUTW possessed some strength in two major areas. The union had organized operatives of the mills of the Horse Creek Valley area, but the valley mills were in many aspects simply an extension of the Augusta textile complex that lay to the south just across the South Carolina border. The other area in which the NUTW demonstrated some strength was Columbia, an urban area, which since 1895 had witnessed the construction of several large, modern textile mills. In addition, the union had established a few scattered assemblies in some of the mills of the state's upper Piedmont region.

In Horse Creek Valley, the locals organized during the 1898–1899 Augusta strike continued to function with some success. In the spring of 1900, the Warrenville Manufacturing Company installed new looms. The looms allowed the weavers, who were paid piece wages, to increase their production. Wages, however, were adjusted so that they remained at the same level. The weavers, who had an NUTW local, complained to Greene that their wages had been cut. Greene wired President Eugene Verdery, requesting that he not reduce wages. Verdery assured Greene that he would not, but he held that the refusal to allow the extra production made possible by the new looms to count in determining wages did not constitute a wage reduction. Thus, his assurances amounted only to mere semantics. After Verdery's reply, the NUTW dispatched a representative to settle the Warrenville dispute. The representative evidently was successful, for the matter was not mentioned again in the NUTW proceedings or in the state press.[46]

Locals farther north in the Piedmont were not so fortunate. In April 1900, the sixty members of a local in Abbeville were locked out "without any cause whatever." Determined "to carry our case to the Supreme Court," if necessary, they appealed without success to the national for financial aid. Despite the backing of some townspeople who resented management's lockout policy, the union there was crushed.[47] That same spring, members of a newly organized Greenwood local were locked out. NUTW organizer G. R. Webb was sent to Greenwood to attempt a settlement. He failed and the union was annihilated.[48]

Despite the failures of the NUTW in the state's rural areas, organizational activities continued. The *Columbia* (S. C.) *State* noted this and advised the newly formed locals to "accept responsibility with power" and not to work so rapidly for progress as to leave public opinion behind. The title of the editorial, "Menace to the Mills," revealed more than the ambiguous contents. In short, the editor hoped out loud that the operatives were not organizing to demand higher wages or shorter hours, but were, rather, preparing "against possible [and unspecified] contingencies of years to come." The press labeled such organizations good, and upheld the operatives' right to them, so long as they made no demands.[49]

Outside Horse Creek Valley, Columbia's gigantic textile union was proving to be a serious threat to management. The city's Labor Day parade in 1900 featured the textile local, whose members, led by fifty women, formed a double-file line over a block long. On the same day, the local had been instrumental in the founding of the South Carolina State Federation of Labor. The Federation, composed of various unions throughout the state, most of which represented skilled artisans, demanded from the state legislature a child labor law, a state bureau of labor with inspection powers, and a reduction of hours.[50] Child labor was given top priority largely because the employment of children necessarily reduced the adult labor force.

Any one of the three demands would have angered mill management; the three combined aroused their ire to the point of determining to destroy the Columbia local. Such a policy had already been attempted in the summer of 1900. W. B. Smith Whaley, President of Gramby Mills and a major stockholder in Columbia's other cotton factories, had then discharged all his union employees. Since the union made no demands, the relatively moderate *Columbia* (S. C.) *State* opposed this move. Threatened with a major strike, Whaley chose to abandon his position.[51] It is also very probable that Whaley had been unable to get other mill owners in the state to support his stand. However, the NUTW's continued growth and the adoption of the state Federation's legislative goals prompted management to launch another effort against the Columbia local in 1901.

In March 1901, under Whaley's guidance, the Columbia mills evidently decided to attempt to kill the union with kindness. The management of three of the city's larger mills, Gramby, Richland, and Olympia, voted to cooperate in providing a public hall, a library, and a school for the operatives and their children. They also agreed to contribute $2,550 and as much as a half-acre of land for the construction of a church. As usual, management failed to consider a raise in wages or a reduction of hours in lieu of the social services they planned to give to their operatives.[52] But, the generosity of the mills failed to deter the growth of the Columbia local and also failed to make union members more receptive to management's policies.

In late August 1901, the growing tension between union and management reached a crisis point, the result of a deliberate attempt by management to intimidate the local. Knowing that their operatives planned to participate in the Labor Day parade, the management of the Capitol City, Richland, and

Olympia mills ordered their hands to work six hours overtime on the Saturdays of August 24 and August 31 to make up the time that they would lose on Labor Day. Management, aware that such orders would arouse the resentment of the operatives, sought to stifle opposition by declaring that operatives who failed to work the required overtime would be suspended for a week, beginning Monday, August 26.[53]

Because the operatives believed Labor Day to be a legitimate holiday, they paid no attention to management's threats. Several hundred operatives, union and nonunion, refused to work on August 24. As a result, they were informed that they would be suspended the following Monday. The local's executive committee continued to treat the suspension as a bluff and advised all union members to return to work on Monday morning. They did, and were denied admittance to the mills. At noon, the suspended operatives conferred with those who had been allowed to work. Later that afternoon, the union held a rally, which was also attended by nonunion operatives. A local minister assured the operatives that the mill officials were their best friends and that any trouble was merely the result of a misunderstanding. By then, however, both union officials and management were well aware that this was no misunderstanding; so were the rank and file, who were in no mood for conciliatory words. Management sent extra police to the mills to quell expected disturbances which never occurred.[54] Although union leaders advised caution, they agreed to accept 100 new members. This was a disastrous decision, demonstrating the inexperience of the union officials, for the local's treasury could have hardly supported its old members, even in a short lockout.

At this juncture, Whaley revealed the real reason for the overtime demand and declared war on the union. He asserted that the Columbia mills provided more services for the operatives than other mills of the state, and did so at the risk of displeasing less generous mill owners. His assertion contained some truth, for only a few mills did more for their operatives. Whaley also sought to portray management as the reasonable party in the dispute. Management, he said, was "approachable" on the subject of the Labor Day parade. But, he continued, perhaps unconscious of his paternalistic overtones,

> this matter of unionism . . . that is another thing. We are the owners of our mills and we propose to run them. We do all we can for our help, and propose to do much more [a reference to the mill's social welfare plans]. We do not propose, however, to have any of this unionism business.[55]

Operatives who had refused to work overtime would be re-employed only when they signed pledges to leave the union permanently. Those choosing not to sign would be unable to find positions in any of the state's mills, for the owners had reached an "ironclad agreement" not to hire union help. As much as he personally regretted to see the operatives lose $25,000 per week in wages, Whaley maintained, he was prepared to close the mills rather than allow management to be dictated to by the union. Besides, he added, the mills could easily survive a month's layoff, or more.

Whaley's statement was a brilliant tactical maneuver in which he had simultaneously made a bid for public sympathy, attempted to separate the issue of the overtime demand and unionization, and threatened the union operatives with financial ruin. It was also a carefully worded exaggeration of fact. There was no "ironclad agreement" with other mill owners, although he almost certainly had the support of many of them. He entirely ignored the fact that the union had made no attempt to "dictate" to management, indeed, had made no demands concerning wages or hours. Quite obviously, he was forcing a confrontation with the Columbia local by making the very existence of the local the central issue, despite Senator Benjamin Tillman's warning that such a policy was potentially extremely dangerous.[56]

Local 211, led by its president, S. J. Thompson, a weaver, desperately attempted to avoid a strike which they realized they were in no position to wage. In what amounted to a slightly qualified surrender, the operatives agreed to all of management's demands, with the simple exception of the yellow dog contracts. Union officers explained to the *State* that no strike had been called, but that union operatives had been locked out, first for refusing to work overtime and then for refusing to leave the union. Meanwhile, management had met with several operatives, but recognized them only as individuals, not as union representatives. Determined to destroy the local, management refused all terms the operatives suggested.[57]

Faced with management's unyielding opposition, the local had no choice but to fight for its life. On August 28, it called a strike, bringing all its members and supporters out of the mills, whether or not they had been locked out. Operatives again flocked to join the union and, mistakenly, were admitted. Over 1,000 operatives were out, yet the city's larger mills continued to run with greatly reduced labor forces, although Whaley claimed over three-fourths of the operatives had remained on the job. Actually, the mills' labor forces were reduced as much as three-fourths by actual count of reporters of the *State,* whose thorough coverage of the strike Whaley vehemently resented.[58]

Whaley, who coupled his lockout with a refusal to talk to the press, had thus incurred the wrath of the *State* and the *Herald* of Rock Hill. Even owners outside Columbia criticized Whaley's arrogance, accusing him of being "drunk with power." Such criticism caused Whaley to deny that he had made the "ironclad agreement" statement to avoid public opinion from swinging too heavily behind the operatives.[59] Otherwise, his policies and objectives remained the same. On August 28, he increased the pressure on the striking operatives by serving them eviction notices.[60] He also successfully countered the efforts of Narciso Gener Gonzales, editor of the *State,* to settle the strike.[61]

By the end of August, it was apparent that the local's only hope lay in receiving substantial aid from the national. The small treasury of Local 211 was simply not adequate to support the union's greatly expanded membership. At this time, however, the NUTW was deeply involved in an attempt to merge with independent Northern locals to create a new national and was hampered by an empty treasury. It could give the Columbia strikers little aid. Faced with inevitable defeat, increasingly larger numbers of operatives left Columbia in search of jobs, many going to the Augusta area. Others yielded to Whaley's demands, left the union, and returned to work.[62]

By the end of September, the strike was broken and so was the local, once the largest textile local in the world. The completeness of Whaley's victory was dramatized by the operatives on Christmas Day, 1901, when they presented him with a gold watch and chain. There would be no textile local represented in Columbia's Labor Day parade of 1902.[63]

To consolidate their position, the victorious owners called a meeting of the state's mill men for September 10, 1901, in Greenville. James L. Orr, who replaced the late Henry Hammett as president of Piedmont Mills, denied the *State*'s charge that the meeting had been called to discuss methods of defeating future organizational efforts. Rather, he maintained, the owners planned to consider possible child labor legislation and the reduction of freight rates. He said, however, that if management wished to discuss the unions, it might do so. Encouraged by Whaley's victory, the owners now seemingly wished to prepare for the complete suppression of the NUTW within the state.[64] Thus, the Columbia defeat dealt the NUTW in South Carolina a staggering blow by consolidating management behind Whaley's approach to labor problems. The remaining South Carolina locals found their hopes and enthusiasm seriously dampened by the defeat of the Columbia strike and the apparent unity of the state's mill owners against the threat of organized labor, which it had engendered. The Columbia defeat, along with those of Alamance and Danville, had dealt the NUTW three staggering blows. They did not, however, prove to be mortal.

Despite the major defeats suffered in the Carolinas and Virginia, the NUTW continued to attempt to organize the mill workers of the three states. Most of this organizational activity was financed by the AFL, which in 1901 spent nearly $2,000 for organizational efforts in the South, a large proportion of which was expended on efforts among textile workers.[65] In North Carolina, after the Alamance strike, locals were established in Concord, Gastonia, Bessemer City, Harden, Dallas, Stanley Creek, Charlotte, and Salisbury.[66] Locals in Durham and Alamance County tried to recover, but experienced difficulty in doing so.[67] In December 1901, G. R. Webb claimed he had organized fifteen locals in South Carolina, all but one of which were prospering, and requested a general textile organizer for the state.[68] Other AFL local organizers were active among the operatives of Spartanburg and Rock Hill.[69] Vastly over-emphasized by Webb's unrealistically optimistic reports, the work of these organizers did not represent a resurgence of the NUTW in the Carolinas. Many of these locals, especially in North Carolina, survived only because they existed in secrecy.[70] Most of the South Carolina locals were situated in Horse Creek Valley or the vicinity and were actually adjuncts of the Augusta textile industry.

By the fall of 1901, it was painfully obvious, even to NUTW leaders, that the union had failed in its attempt to organize the operatives of the upper Southern Piedmont mills. Although a Durham, North Carolina, operative declared late in 1901 that "the principle of organized labor still burns in the bosom of the mill operative," principle had proven no match for the power of management.[71]

The defeats suffered by the NUTW in 1900 and 1901 revealed the same patterns that had occurred in the earlier strikes of 1898 and 1899. Again, lack of finances was a vital factor in the defeats. Since the unions involved in strike situations were often newly organized, they lacked the necessary time to build strong financial resources. The operatives' low wages prevented them from contributing heavily to build strong treasuries. Furthermore, the average Southern operative did not see the need for financial reserves until actually engaged in a strike. The newly organized locals sadly lacked experienced leadership. This deficiency was a serious handicap in Alamance, Columbia, and, especially, in Danville.

At Alamance, more experienced leadership might have avoided a strike, since management did not appear to have decided to provoke a confrontation, as was the case in Columbia. At Danville, Gompers simply made a gross error in judgment in not urging the union to accept management's offer. The NUTW was in no position to fight a major battle after having made major gains without doing so. This was especially true in view of what had happened to the Alamance unions. In Danville and elsewhere, once actually involved in strikes, locals continued to admit nonunion operatives, a policy which weakened already feeble treasuries to the point of uselessness. Although self-defeating, this policy was probably adopted in an effort to insure the support of operatives who otherwise might not have supported the union. Finally, the workers continued to exhibit a tendency to seek political solutions for their troubles, despite advice against involvement in local politics from national leaders. This tendency seriously weakened the Danville strikers' chances for success.

The most significant factors in the union's defeat, however, lay beyond the control of the mill workers. Geographically separated and completely controlled by management, the small rural mills had proved to be practically impossible to organize. As a result, the NUTW's strength lay almost solely in urban areas. Alamance County, the exception, was, in reality, a cluster of mill towns with something of an industrial heritage. Organized urban operatives could only hope for success if management was unable to obtain labor from outside the city. But the struck mills invariably managed to recruit strikebreakers from surrounding areas. Management used the paternalistic mill village system very effectively, especially their control of housing. The adoption of an eviction policy erased the union's slim chance for victory at Columbia and Alamance. The decline of the Chinese market because of the Boxer Rebellion undoubtedly stiffened management's determination to resist the NUTW.

Management's determination to break the NUTW completely, regardless of the costs incurred by such a policy, was the overriding factor in the defeat of the union's locals in the upper South. This was clearly evident at Alamance and Columbia. In Columbia, the decision was evidently made in advance, whereas in Alamance it appears that management decided to move to destroy the union only after the strike had begun. In any case, once this decision was made, management was able to execute it with dispatch.

7

Merger
and Final Defeat

The optimism with which the NUTW had entered upon its ten-hour-day campaign in the spring of 1900 had turned to bitter disappointment by the late fall of 1901. The defeats suffered in Virginia and the Carolinas had driven the union back into its urban Georgia strongholds. The length of the three major strikes in which the union had engaged had resulted in the total depletion of its meager treasury, incurring a large outstanding debt. All hopes of the NUTW's becoming a strong national organization under continued Southern control had been crushed, for Northern textile locals could hardly be expected to affiliate with a union whose track record contained so many serious defeats. Even those few NUTW locals that remained in Augusta and Columbus faced the possibility of extinction at any moment management should choose to force the issue of their operatives' right to organize. More than ever, Southern union operatives realized that, if the mills of the South were to be organized, the backing of a strong national organization that included the New England laborers was essential.

178

Events at the turn of the century caused the various New England textile unions to reconsider the possibilities of combining with one another and the NUTW to form a stronger national union of textile workers. Most of the New England craft unions had deserted the NUTW in 1895–1896 when the union was controlled by Socialists, and by so doing had also disaffiliated with the AFL. They demonstrated little desire to return to the national once it came under the control of the Southerners. However, by 1900, Northern management began to hint that continued Southern competition might force them to reduce wage schedules. And, although the finer products of Northern mills were less affected by the Boxer Rebellion than were the coarse goods of the South, they did not escape entirely.

Realizing the seriousness of the situation, the splintered Northern unions demonstrated some interest in creating a strong national which might include the NUTW, although it was still dominated by Southerners. But, personal ambition and sectional animosity hampered efforts to create such a national union. Northern textile union leaders directed their attention toward first creating a united Northern union, whereas the NUTW primarily sought to create an intersectional national in which the South would have a major voice. Finally, after a long series of negotiations, the NUTW and the Northern craft unions combined late in 1901 to create the United Textile Workers of America (UTWA).

Well before the launching of the 1900 ten-hour-day campaign, the Southern leaders of the NUTW had realized that the support of a truly national union would have enhanced their chances for success. As early as 1898, they had begun to take measures to create a strong, unified national, but one in which Southerners might retain their rather disproportionate powers. Hoping to force the Northern craft unions to reaffiliate, the NUTW had moved to protect its status as the official AFL affiliate in the textile industry, with the exception of the Mule Spinners Union, which had received a charter from the AFL prior to the chartering of the NUTW. This action was apparently prompted by requests of several Northern unions for separate charters from the AFL. At the 1898 AFL convention, Henry S. Mills, a delegate from one of the few NUTW Massachusetts locals, introduced a resolution asking

> that all applicants for affiliation with the American Federation of Labor coming from any branch or department of the textile industry be referred to the NUTWA for final disposition [with the NUTW to] be the proper source to determine what branch or department of the textile industry is within the jurisdiction of said NUTWA.

The convention adopted the resolution, after amending it to read as follows:

> that all applicants for affiliation with the American Federation of Labor coming from any branch or department of the textile industry, providing they do not properly come under the jurisdiction of other national organizations, be referred to the NUTWA for final disposition.[1]

The amendment was adopted primarily to protect the Mule Spinners. The Mills resolution had placed the Northern unions in the position of joining the NUTW or remaining permanently outside the AFL.

During the following year, Greene and other members of the NUTW hierarchy continued their unsuccessful attempts to obtain the reaffiliation of the Northern locals. Meetings with the Northern unions were held at Boston in September 1899. Peter Oulman of North Adams, Massachusetts, and John Morrison of New York City represented the NUTW. Both Northerners, they were obviously chosen to allay the Northern unions' suspicion of the NUTW's Southern orientation. Thomas Connolly and James Tansey of Fall River, Massachusetts, represented the Carders Union; Matthew Hart and Albert Hibbert of New Hampshire represented the weavers' National Federation of Textile Operatives (NFTO); John McCarthy and Richard Shevelton attended for the National Loom Fixers; Samuel Ross and Michael Duggan represented the Mule Spinners; and Joseph Jackson and Jonathan Hulis negotiated for the National Slasher Tenders Association. Oulman acted as chairman of the meeting and pleaded for a strong, aggressive national, affiliated with the AFL, which would emphasize Southern organization. His principal argument was that wages and hours could not be improved elsewhere unless they were first improved in the South. Indeed, unless Southern wages were raised, Northern manufacturers would be forced to lower wages to meet the competition of Southern mills. Although all agreed that the creation of one body was urgently needed, the politics of such a merger caused difficulties. The Northern locals feared the South would control the product of such a merger and that they might lose their autonomy within a strong national. Some Northern locals were also hesitant to commit themselves to affiliation with the AFL, a commitment that Oulman demanded as the first basis for negotiation. However, the group did manage to agree to support one another's strikes.[2]

As a result of this failure to merge in 1899, Greene requested the aid of the AFL Executive Council in bringing about an amalgamation of the NUTW, the Mule Spinners, the weavers' NFTO, the Carders Union, and the National Loom Fixers Association. Such a merger, he argued, would be in the best interests of the laborers of the entire industry. The AFL adopted Greene's resolution.[3] As all of the above unions were located in the North, with the exception of the NUTW, which had some Northern locals, such an amalgamation would necessarily mean a considerable weakening of Southern influence within the product of the proposed merger. Greene undoubtedly realized this. But, he also realized that Southern unionization efforts were doomed unless a strong national could be created.

The financial and leadership resources of the Southern operatives alone were simply inadequate for such a task.

Delegates to the NUTW's May 1900 convention thoroughly
considered the amalgamation issue. They realized that a national containing the New England unions could provide considerable financial support and organizational experience in
their upcoming campaign for the ten-hour day in Southern
mills. Delegates also reasoned that a strong national would
prove a boon to the Northern textile workers, for, once organized, Southern operatives could obtain wage increases and hour
reductions, thus removing Northern management's favorite argument for reducing wages and lengthening hours. When presented with a decision on whether to merge with the Northern
unions or remain a separate unit, the NUTW convention
heeded Greene's advice and voted overwhelmingly in favor of
the proposed merger. To smooth the road toward amalgamation, Peter Oulman, a representative from one of the NUTW's
few Massachusetts locals, was elected to the presidency. Greene,
elected secretary-treasurer, remained a key administrative figure. The convention also elected Greene, Oulman, and John
Morrison to a committee to represent the NUTW at further
merger negotiations.[4]

In short, the NUTW hoped to create a strong national that
could support a massive Southern organizational campaign,
obtain a uniform national work day within the industry, force
the mills to adopt a national wage scale, and better the working conditions encountered by all of the nation's textile workers. NUTW members obviously thought that a truly national
union in which their power was diminished could serve them
better than continued control of a supposedly national union
that possessed little strength outside the South. Yet, they continued to hope that Northern unions could be persuaded to enter
the existing NUTW structure.

A second major attempt to create a single textile national
floundered in the fall of 1900. Despite the NUTW's election

of Oulman to the presidency, Northern unions remained leery of affiliating with a weak national which was still controlled primarily by Southerners. Rather, the various Northern unions decided to create their own national and invite the NUTW to affiliate with it. Northern union officials began a series of meetings to determine the details of such a proposal. The first of these amalgamation meetings was held August 5, in Boston. All the Northern unions sent delegates. Though Oulman had been invited, he maintained that he had not been given adequate notice and failed to attend. At a second meeting in Boston on September 9, however, Oulman was in attendance. His presence had little effect on the events that transpired. At the meeting, the NFTO, carders, loom fixers, mule spinners, and slasher tenders merged to form the American Federation of Textile Operatives (AFTO). The new union made no immediate decision on the possibility of seeking AFL affiliation, although one of its member groups, the mule spinners, belonged to the Federation. Under the guidance of Albert Hibbert, the delegates voted to decide the question of affiliating with the AFL at the first AFTO convention, which was scheduled for December 1900. Refusing to join the new union, the NUTW explained that since it owed its very existence to the AFL, it could hardly become part of a national that might not affiliate with that organization.[5]

With the creation of the AFTO, the NUTW was faced with a powerful rival for national supremacy in the textile industry, a rival that was composed of the best-organized and best-financed locals in the country. Based in New England, the AFTO posed a clear threat to the NUTW's control over its few locals in that area. Its formation also virtually eliminated any possibility that other New England locals would join the NUTW. Unless a merger could be negotiated, organized labor in the textile industry faced a serious sectional split.

In December 1900, the AFTO held its first convention at

Washington, D.C., as scheduled. The NUTW refused to send representatives, but did request a copy of the constitution adopted by its new rival. At the convention, the delegates voted to seek affiliation with the AFL, thus removing the NUTW's supposed reason for refusing to merge. However, when the AFTO applied for an AFL charter in February 1901, Greene immediately protested and was able to convince the AFL to oppose the granting of such a charter on the grounds of dual unionism. In seeking AFL affiliation, the AFTO charged that the NUTW was strictly a Southern union. The NUTW easily refuted the charge since Oulman, a Northerner, was the union's president, and Greene was successful in his bid to block the granting of the AFL charter. But the AFL realized the need for a viable textile national, and, by this time, had become alarmed by the continuing North-South feud between the NUTW and AFTO. The Federation began to pressure both unions to work out terms for a merger. Gompers forced them to send representatives to a meeting scheduled to be held in Boston on May 11, 1901.[6] Unwilling to risk a conference run solely by the participating unions, Gompers arranged for AFL First Vice-president James Duncan to chair the meeting.[7]

At the time the meeting was held, the NUTW was in an almost untenable position to demand a major voice in the councils of the proposed national union. It had been defeated at Alamance and incurred a large debt in the process. The Danville strike was then in progress, and not going very well for the union. Gompers had made it clear that he favored the creation of a new national, not just the refurbishing of the NUTW.

These were the circumstances that faced the NUTW's representatives to the conference: Greene, Oulman, Morrison, M. J. Connors of Connecticut, and G. B. McCraken of Augusta, Georgia. Each of the individual unions comprising the AFTO sent representatives. Albert Hibbert and James Whitehead of Fall River, Massachusetts represented the weavers; J. C. Jackson of Fall River, the slasher tenders; and Thomas O'Donnell of Lowell, the mule spinners. AFTO President James Tansey of Fall River represented the organization as a whole.[8]

Bargaining from such a seriously compromised position, the NUTW had little choice but to agree to an amalgamation with the AFTO under the name of the United Textile Workers of America (UTWA). The delegates decided that the new national should seek to become an affiliate of the AFL, a foregone conclusion. A conference between the presidents and secretaries of the NUTW and the AFTO to facilitate the merger was planned for August 31, 1901. To guard against any mishaps, the meeting was to be chaired by James Duncan or some other AFL representative. A national UTWA convention was to be held no later than November 19, 1901. Two days before the planned UTWA convention, the NUTW and AFTO were to turn over their records and cash to an AFL representative, who would, in turn, present them to the officers of the UTWA elected by the convention.[9] On August 18, 1901, the NUTW's executive council met in New York and called for a special NUTW convention for November 18, 1901, in Washington, D.C., to disband the union and formally surrender its charter to the AFL.[10]

The August 31 final meeting, chaired by Duncan, proceeded smoothly, and the first UTWA convention was set for November 19, 1901. Each local within the NUTW and the AFTO was allowed one delegate for every 200 members, or any fractional part thereof. At the meeting, Greene and Oulman pledged their support to the operatives of Fall River in case management in Massachusetts carried out current threats to reduce wages before the November convention.[11] Thus, the NUTW came to its end, losing its identity in the newly created national.

As Greene and other Southerners had foreseen, the New Englanders dominated the UTWA convention, effectively ending the South's control of the AFL's national textile affiliate. James Tansey of Fall River, Massachusetts, was elected president, Albert Hibbert of New Hampshire became secretary, and

James Whitehead of Fall River was chosen as treasurer. Headquarters were established at Fall River. Yet, even with the New Englanders controlling the UTWA's administration, the various Northern unions refused to create a strong national. Instead, each union clung to the autonomy it enjoyed in the past. National per capita dues were set at five cents per quarter, largely because the New England delegates felt that local union treasuries should be kept strong, even at the expense of the national.[12] This less-than-enlightened policy infuriated Gompers, who had hoped that the national would be given the strong financial support of its member unions. Such a policy, said Gompers, made it impossible for the UTWA "to provide for raising sufficient funds for the successful propagation of organization or to carry out in full its necessary duties." Nevertheless, Gompers gave the newly created union his blessing.[13]

Other member unions also failed to surrender their funds to the UTWA as they had promised; the NUTW was as guilty of this offense as were the parochial New England locals.[14] The situation did not improve with time. For several years after the 1901 convention, delegates from Fall River and New Bedford dictated the policy of the UTWA. And, fearing a loss of their autonomy in a strong national, they continued to keep the UTWA a weak, very loose national federation.[15]

The UTWA could hardly have been expected to launch a vast new organizational campaign in the South. It was controlled by Northern members who were primarily concerned about wages and conditions in the New England mills. And by the time of the UTWA's first convention in 1901, investing money in efforts to organize Southern mill hands seemed to be a very bad risk. The NUTW just that year had lost two major strikes at Danville and Columbia and evidenced few signs of recovering from these defeats. Even so, the UTWA was not prepared to abandon completely its existing Southern locals, although it was to spend very little in the way of money or effort to create others. In the South, Augusta, Georgia, was the center of UTWA activity. In 1902 the city had four textile locals —the weavers, spinners, carders, and doffers. Some 35 percent of the city's adult male operatives were avowed members of the union. Perhaps another 20 percent secretly belonged to the four locals.[16] It was here that the UTWA would wage its first major strike, here that it would first encounter defeat, and here that the decision to abandon meaningful efforts to organize the Southern mill hands would be made.

Under the prevailing circumstances in the South, the UTWA had no chance of reversing the NUTW's record of defeats and winning in Augusta. At the moment the UTWA decided to support the Augusta strike, it was saddled with internal tensions, a disastrous financial policy, and a $1,700 debt inherited from the NUTW's unsuccessful Alamance strike.[17] As usual, the union encountered staunch opposition from the solidly united ranks of Southern mill management. In this case, management's opposition was the stronger because they realized Augusta was the union's last substantial foothold in the South. The failure of the UTWA in Augusta in 1902 eradicated effective textile union activities in the South for nearly a quarter of a century.

The Augusta strike resulted from a demand for a 10 percent wage increase by the workers at the King Mill. Charging that their wages were lower than those paid by other Augusta mills, the workers threatened to strike on March 17 if the increase was not granted. The Augusta Cotton Manufacturers Association opposed their demands, insisting that the operatives had no legitimate complaint and were merely "slaves at the beck and call" of the Fall River officers of the UTWA. Management's use of the "outside agitator" ruse was prompted by the fact that UTWA locals in New England were then involved in an eventually successful attempt to obtain a general 10 percent wage increase. The owners of the King Mill also explained that the firm had lost money in 1901, and that the market was just beginning to improve. Maintaining that present earnings did not justify wage increases, they refused to use accumulated capital to finance them.

This statement was certainly partially true, for 1901 was the year in which the full impact of the Boxer Rebellion was felt by the Southern mills. Possibly, the entire statement was true. The *Augusta Chronicle,* never an extremely anti-labor paper, warned the operatives that they were going into a strike with a false sense of security. The company had suffered in 1901, it said, and, contrary to rumors in the mill villages, the newly formed UTWA simply could not support Augusta's operatives in a prolonged strike.[18]

Determined to close the city's mills rather than meet the demands of the King Mill operatives, the manufacturers association waited to see if the strike would develop. Meanwhile, the Augusta operatives had requested aid from the UTWA only to find that body too concerned with a threatened strike in Lowell, Massachusetts, to respond. As a result, the Augusta strike was postponed. By the end of March, however, the New England unions had won a general 10 percent wage increase, and the Lowell strike had been postponed. Thus, on March 29, the King Mill operatives presented management with a new deadline, April 7.[19]

President Landon A. Thomas of King Mill refused the demand, noting that it "applies ultimately to every mill in the Augusta district . . . and will be so treated." Although the operatives denied the charge, on April 2 all the Augusta mills posted notices that if the King operatives struck, they would close. And, in what was certainly intended to be an intimidating show of power, the Augusta owners hosted a conference of fifty of the South's leading cotton manufacturers beginning April 3. Attended by such men as H. H. Hickman, Ellison A. Smyth, James L. Orr, W. B. Smith Whaley, Stewart Phinizy, D. Gunby Jordan, and others, the meeting evidently resulted in a decision to exterminate the Augusta locals. Although statements to the press from the owners denied that the threatened

strike was even mentioned, few believed that only labor legislation, shipping rates, possible markets, and "eastern hostility"
were discussed. Realizing that a clash between the locals and
management was imminent, the city's chamber of commerce
desperately tried to prevent a strike. Both sides spurned these
conciliatory efforts.[20]

On April 7, the King Mill operatives struck as scheduled
when President Landon Thomas again refused to meet their
demands. Management placed extra guards at the mill to prevent any violence, but none occurred. The only thing exchanged
between the operatives and the guards was some good-natured
taunting. True to their word, the next day, the other Augusta
mills initiated a lockout, throwing over 7,000 operatives out
of work. Only a few, well-trusted hands were allowed to remain in the mills. Again, the Augusta operatives appealed to
the UTWA for aid. By this time, the threatened Lowell, Massachusetts, strike had been averted. But the UTWA, with almost
no treasury, could not officially endorse the strike, which
would have entailed paying specific strike benefits to the strikers. But rather than attempt to prevent the strike, the UTWA
extended it quasi-recognition by levying an assessment of five
cents per member on its member locals to aid the Augusta
strikers and by sending Secretary Albert Hibbert to Augusta to
attempt to settle the dispute. Why the UTWA chose to react
to the Augusta strike in this manner is not clear. Perhaps the
union believed success under such adverse conditions was possible—or feared that completely abandoning the Augusta workers would eliminate any hope of organizing the South in the
foreseeable future. Whatever the UTWA's motives, its policy
quickly proved unlikely to succeed. Hibbert and a delegation
of local union leaders were received by management, but no
concessions were granted the striking operatives.[21]

The strikers struggled through April, but by May the strike
began to run into serious trouble. Many of the idle operatives,
especially nonunion members, were growing restless. Funds

were running short and chances of receiving further aid were poor. On May 14, the nonunion operatives revealed a plan to sue the locals for breach of promise, insisting that the locals had agreed to aid them just as they aided union members, but had failed to keep this pledge. Many operatives, including some union members, began to leave Augusta in search for jobs elsewhere.[22] The desertion of the unorganized operatives demoralized the strikers, but failed to break their determination to remain out.

On May 20, operatives from the Horse Creek Valley area of South Carolina dealt the cause of the Augusta workers a staggering blow, revealing the serious erosion of union strength in that area in the past year. Delegations from the valley area asked to see the King Mill's record books to determine if the operatives, who claimed that the mill's wages were below those paid by other Augusta firms, were justified in their demand for an increase. Management was more than delighted to show their records to the operatives, who were far from experienced in bookkeeping. On May 21, the South Carolina operatives announced at a mass rally that, in their opinion, the King operatives had no just complaint and advised the strikers to return to work.[23] Management, now confident of victory, reopened the King Mill on May 22, and as expected, large numbers returned to work, their ranks further swelled by strikebreakers imported from South Carolina. By May 26, all the Augusta mills had successfully reopened, although some were shorthanded.[24]

Still, the union, rather unrealistically, refused to yield. Its hard-core members established a tent city, using tents left by Spanish-American War troops purchased with UTWA funds. Residents of the tents lived by fishing and hunting. Large numbers, however, began to search for new positions. Financed by UTWA money, some left for jobs as far away as New Jersey.[25] As the hard-core members disappeared and the mills continued to augment their labor forces with South Carolina operatives, it became apparent even to the most adamant members that further resistance was folly. Finally, on August 6, 1902, the UTWA executive council at Fall River, Massachusetts, officially called off the strike, admitting that the Augusta mills had been so successful in recruiting workers that the strike had become a farce.[26] The UTWA had spent $10,000 of the special assessment funds in Augusta, only to see its last stronghold in the South fall because of the determined resistance of Southern management and the willingness of South Carolina operatives to condemn the strike and act as strikebreakers.[27]

Alamance, Danville, Columbia, and Augusta: four major defeats in a period of less than a year and a half ended all attempts to organize the South. For the Northern locals the defeat at Augusta, despite the expenditure of such large sums, ended any remaining hope of unionizing the Southern operatives. Northern workers felt, with good reason, that continued efforts in the South would only produce an unbearable drain on the financial resources of their locals. As a result of the Augusta defeat, the rank and file laborers who controlled the New England locals turned their backs on the South. Henceforth, the New England craft unions used their resources in an attempt to build strong organizations in the northeast before returning to organize the South's unskilled laborers. Besides, the four major Southern defeats had practically destroyed all locals in the South. Those that remained were small, secretive bodies, unable to contribute to the national organization in any manner.[28] New England operatives understandably refused to provide these remaining locals with "the sinews of a war which bade fair to drag on indefinitely."[29]

Yet, since scattered locals remained in the South, some UTWA leaders stubbornly believed the struggle to organize the region should not be abandoned completely. In 1902, Albert Hibbert urged the UTWA to do most of its organizing in the South, using the time-worn argument that it was useless to attempt to improve the conditions of the Northern operative until the situation that existed in Southern mills was remedied.[30] However, the UTWA's 1902 convention defeated a motion to place a full-time organizer in the Southern textile field. But, the executive council was empowered to appoint "missionaries" for one-month terms at a salary the council deemed adequate.[31] In December 1902, the AFL voted to put an organizer exclusively in the Southern textile field.[32] This was merely a gesture. John Golden of Fall River, the organizer put in the field, received $442.94 for his efforts in 1903. That same year, the AFL spent $1,958.95 in Louisiana and Mississippi to organize skilled laborers, or about the total sum that the Federation expended on organization in the major Southern textile states in 1901.[33] Obviously, the AFL, too, had given up hope of organizing the Southern operatives after the Augusta defeat.

After his appointment by the AFL, Golden was also commissioned by the UTWA to be their Southern organizer for a two-month period. In 1903, Golden toured the South, hoping to rekindle the flame of the few smoldering embers of unionism. His report to the UTWA's 1903 convention, at which he was elected to the presidency, read like a eulogy to the dying Southern locals. Golden began his tour in Augusta where he found that the locals there had faded into near oblivion. He attempted to pump some vigor into the operatives by holding several mass rallies, and he left hoping the Augusta locals would revive and grow, an ill-founded hope at best. In the Horse Creek Valley area, he found several weak locals, which he advised to merge into one unit. He held meetings in Warrenville and Langley to encourage locals to reorganize. The meetings were well attended, but produced few results.[34]

Elsewhere, Golden discovered much the same conditions. At Graniteville he encountered "one of the best locals in the South," but at Macon, Georgia, he found that no textile union existed, although all the town's skilled artisan laborers were organized. At Vineville, Georgia, operatives told him any attempt to establish a local would be futile, as the company owned all the property "for miles around" and would surely fight such attempts. In Columbia, Golden failed to reorganize the operatives, despite recent wage cuts. In Laurens, South Carolina, he met S. J. Thompson, President of the Columbia local during the 1901 strike. Thompson had been forced to leave Columbia because of his involvement with the union. His dedication to the concept of organization led him to assist Golden in an attempt to organize the weavers of Laurens; he and his wife were discharged for their efforts. The Thompsons' fate completely cowed the other operatives, and Golden sadly abandoned his efforts. Moving northward into North Carolina, Golden discovered small locals with rapidly dwindling memberships in both Charlotte and Salisbury, and nothing more. In short, Golden saw little in the South to encourage either the UTWA or the AFL to spend large sums in an attempt to organize the operatives of the area.[35]

Golden concluded his report by summarizing the obstacles to organization in the South. "The chief obstacle I had to contend with was ignorance of the mill people in regard to trade unionism. They have no conception of the great progress that has been made during the past few years by the trade unions of this country."[36] He called for an intense propaganda campaign to educate the Southern operatives in the principles, goals, and methods of trade unionism. The UTWA could begin such a program by circulating as much labor literature as possible in the South. Despite the dreary facts contained in his report, Golden also recommended that an aggressive organizational campaign be waged in the South, arguing once again that no further progress could be made in the North until the South was organized. The UTWA rejected his advice and, for the second time, voted not to send a full-time organizer to the South. Their reasoning was simple. As one delegate expressed it, "after all that money that was sent to Augusta, Georgia, during the strike last year, there is not today a union in that city worthy of the name."[37]

In 1903, the UTWA also adopted more stringent financial policies, voting to expel member locals that had failed to pay assessments. This policy practically eliminated the remainder of the union's Southern locals, as they lacked the financial means to meet the new requirements. Of the forty-one locals that lost their charters because of this policy, twenty were former NUTW members, most of them located in the South.[38] As a result of the implementation of this policy, the attendance of a delegate from a Salisbury, North Carolina, local at the 1903 convention was the last representative of a Southern local to be found at the UTWA's national convention until 1913, with the exception of 1908.[39] In 1903, the UTWA issued a charter to a Columbus local, and in 1904 locals in Columbus, Augusta, and Salisbury were in good standing, although the number of members they contained was not revealed. But, the following year the Columbus and Augusta locals seceded from the national, and the Salisbury local was suspended for not paying its per capita dues.[40] Unionism in the textile mills of the South was dead and its rejuvenation lay far in the future.

The New England locals can hardly be blamed for refusing to continue to finance organizational campaigns in the South. They had seen large Southern locals methodically defeated in clashes with management at Alamance, Danville, and Columbia. They realized that the NUTW's attempts to create a strong national were largely motivated by the desire to obtain their resources to finance the operatives' battles in the South. Therefore, they resisted a merger until the AFL had practically forced them to accept it. Once in control of the UTWA's policies, they had not immediately abandoned the Southern assemblies, but neither had they spent large sums in an effort to recoup the NUTW's losses. The Augusta strike confirmed their worst fears and reduced the union's Southern membership to a handful of pathetically weak locals. The Golden report even more firmly convinced the Northern members that Southern mill hands were an undesirable liability. Dismayed by the lack of positive results in the South, the UTWA decided to write off the region and concentrate on struggles with management in New England where the union possessed more strength. The argument that the competition from Southern mills run by cheap, unorganized labor was directly related to their own economic problems was no longer effective on the rank and file of the UTWA's Northern members.

8

Conclusions

The New South, like the Old South, has often been shrouded in myth. According to many Southern spokesmen, the stately plantations, benevolent planters, and contented slaves typified the Old South. In the same vein, virtually unbroken harmony, benevolent employers, and docile, appreciative laborers supposedly characterized the mill village of the New South. Textile union activity clearly demonstrates this picture of the New South's labor force to be false. There were serious attempts to organize the Southern cotton textile operative in the late nineteenth and early twentieth centuries by both the Knights of Labor and the NUTW-UTWA. These attempts, especially those of the NUTW-UTWA, elicited the response of thousands of discontented operatives who opposed the paternalistic mill village system of that era. However, the organizational efforts of both unions ended in eventual failure, despite a promising beginning. They failed for approximately the same reasons, and their failure deterred any further strenuous Southern organizational efforts by a national textile union for nearly a quarter of a century. The appearance and failure of both the Knights and the NUTW-UTWA followed certain clearly discernible patterns, many of which reappeared in the unionization struggles of the late 1920s and early 1930s, and, indeed, some of which still survive in Southern cotton factories and communities.

In their brief period of existence in the Southern mills, both the Knights and the NUTW-UTWA were largely an urban phenomenon. The more rural areas in which they gained strength were traditional textile centers with something of an industrial heritage, as in Alamance, or an extension of a nearby urban textile complex such as Horse Creek Valley, which also was an old textile center. The Knights were unquestionably strongest in the mills of the Augusta and the Horse Creek Valley areas. The NUTW-UTWA exhibited an even more definite urban orientation, with Atlanta, Columbus, Augusta, Columbia, Alamance County, and Danville as their major Southern strongholds. This increased emphasis on urban mills by the NUTW-UTWA is explained by the development of the large urban mills after 1880. Columbia, Atlanta, and Danville became major cotton textile centers after that date, and new mills were erected in the older centers such as Augusta. Many of these new mills housed thousands of spindles and hundreds of looms and employed well over a thousand operatives.

For the unions, the emphasis on urban organization was also a tactical necessity. An urban mill was necessarily less subject to the owner's paternalism than was a mill several miles from the nearest town where management was the only practical source of the very necessities of life. The urban worker, cut off from the land, his traditional source of income, tended to view his position as permanent and was more concerned with obtaining the highest possible return for his labor. The rural operative, however, not only often supplemented his income by cultivating a garden plot provided by management, but could reenter the old agrarian economy more easily than his urban counterpart. Reluctant to regard himself as a permanent industrial laborer, he was less likely to respond to the unions.

The control management exercised over these isolated fiefs played the most important role in limiting the unions' ability to penetrate the rural mills. Organizers from both the Knights and the NUTW-UTWA found that, in such well policed mills, efforts to organize openly were futile and secret organization was impossible. But, had the rural mills, most of which were small spinning plants, been accessible to organizers, the unions still would have concentrated on the cities where large numbers of operatives existed in small areas.

This was especially true of the NUTW-UTWA, for by 1896 the Piedmont's cities, with their gigantic modern mills, had become the centers of cotton textile production. It was simply easier to organize the thousands of operatives who manned the numerous mills of the urban textile centers. And, since these mills usually had a large number of looms and often produced better grades of yarn, a larger percentage of the urban operatives were skilled workers. Possessing industrial skills, they were harder to replace and more inclined toward organization than were the few hundred, largely unskilled, operatives of the isolated rural mills.

The importance of the skilled laborer in the efforts of the unions is borne out by the percentage of both members and leaders who came from the ranks of the skilled operatives. However, the role of the skilled laborer in the NUTW-UTWA was especially significant, as woven goods and the production of fine yarns had become more important parts of the total production of the South's mills by the turn of the century. The weavers, who were by far the most aggressive group of operatives in the nineteenth century, were also the industry's most skilled laborers and the most difficult to obtain. The weavers were the first operatives who responded to the Knights in South Carolina, and the weavers precipitated the 1886 Augusta strike. Disputes between weavers and management triggered the 1896 Columbus strike, the Augusta strike of 1898–1899, the Atlanta strike of 1899, the 1900 Alamance strike, the 1900 Warrenville, South Carolina, dispute, and the 1902 Augusta strike. Prince W. Greene, President of the NUTW from 1898 to 1900, was a weaver, as was S. J. Thompson, the leader of the 1901 Columbia strike. The loom fixers, another highly skilled group but smaller in number than the weavers, had separate locals in Columbus, Augusta, Langley, and probably in other towns. They led the 1899–1900 Columbus strike. Possessing skills well beyond those of the average mill hand, the loom fixer and the weaver could more easily afford to adopt a militant position than could the more expendable spinner and other unskilled operatives who made up the majority of the Southern labor force.

Surprisingly, though they operated in a region of reputed and real violence, the Southern unions rarely resorted to violence in their strikes, even in strikes as bitter as those in Alamance, Danville, and Augusta. Union members rarely turned to violence unless the racial issue was involved, even when evicted from their homes. Strikers occasionally hurled epithets at scabs, guards, and police and, at times, gathered in angry groups about struck mills. But they never damaged mill property, and they seldom harmed strikebreakers or nonunion operatives, despite management's tendency to see threatened violence in every dispute and to place extra armed guards around mills to prevent anticipated disorder. What use of force or threat of force that did occur was management's responsibility. On more than one occasion, management used violence or threats of violence to discourage organization and force prominent union leaders either to abandon their projects or flee a specific town.

This lack of violence in Southern textile strikes seems all the more strange when contrasted with the pattern of violence evidenced in the relationships between whites and Negroes, and, indeed, in personal relationships among whites. Since extralegal force often settled personal and racial disputes in the South, it may be assumed that the worker evidently valued his racial integrity and his honor more than his means of obtaining a livelihood. At least, he feared the Negro more than he feared and resented management's nearly absolute power over him. The operatives' threats of violence in the 1898 Atlanta strike, which was prompted by the hiring of black mill hands, and their actual use of violence in similar cases further supports this assumption. The conservative influence of his agrarian background and the strong Southern sense of sacredness of property also contributed to his respect for management's property, even in the midst of a bitter strike. Violence in the South traditionally has been directed at persons, and this was true of the few violent incidents involving strikers.

Yet it can hardly be argued that this lack of violence indicates docility, since neither the Knights nor the AFL advocated violent measures. Furthermore, docile laborers do not remain on strike for two and three months when, by signing a yellow dog contract, they could return to their jobs at any time. In addition, strike situations usually resulted in management rushing armed men to the mills or obtaining the aid of the local police. What management's response to physical provocation from the strikers would have been is hardly a matter of conjecture; it was more or less known at the time. The possibility of such a violent response from management probably helped to deter acts of violence on the part of the strikers.

Both the Knights and the NUTW relied on organizers who were not operatives, but craftsmen, artisan laborers, or professional people. The Knights' loose membership policy and the close relationship between the NUTW and the AFL insured the availability of such organizers. J. Simmions Meynardie, organizer of the 1886 Augusta strike, was a minister, not a mill hand. The available evidence indicates that the Augusta Knights were welded together by the sheer force of Meynardie's personality and the intense dedication he brought to what he considered a holy cause. Since organizers' commissions were all too easily come by until well into 1886, many of the textile assemblies in North Carolina and South Carolina were organized by nonoperatives. This conclusion is also supported by the fact that the organization of Knights in these states began in the artisans' ranks and then spread to the mills.

The list of craftsmen members of the AFL who acted as organizers for the NUTW is a long one, including, in Georgia alone, Will Winn, Jerome Jones, William Gredig, and Andrew Mulcay. Organizers from other occupations were used out of necessity, and their use again underscores the mill hands' lack of experience with organized labor. Many realized the need for organization of some sort, but had no idea how to go about it. The organization of the Columbus mill hands in 1896 clearly illustrates this fact. Faced with wage reductions, they attempted to organize. But it was Winn, a printer, who organized the Columbus textile locals that soon became so active in the NUTW.

Another highly significant feature of both the Knights and the NUTW-UTWA was their basically defensive nature. Both appeared as a somewhat spontaneous protest by Southern operatives against wage cuts, the Knights after the wage reductions in 1884 and the NUTW because of the wage reductions in 1896. The individual strikes of both unions demonstrate essentially the same defensive pattern. The Knights' big Augusta strike, although for increased wages, was actually an attempt to restore wages to their pre-1884 levels. Of the four major NUTW-UTWA strikes, only one was really an offensive strike, the Danville strike of 1901. And even there the operatives were trying to extend a privilege they had partially achieved, the ten-hour day. The Alamance strike and the Columbus strike were definitely defensive measures, the latter actually provoked by management. And the Augusta strike, since it centered around the King Mill operatives' contention that they were paid less than other Augusta operatives, must also be considered a defensive act. In short, in origin and in most specific disputes, Southern unions constantly responded to management's actions. Faced with a powerful adversary, mill hands were willing to fight to protect a previously attained position, but less willing to do so for desired improvements.

The attempt of the NUTW to take the offensive in 1900 by demanding the ten-hour day without wage reductions failed for a number of reasons, but does indicate the willingness of some operatives to adopt a more aggressive policy. Management's implacable resistance proved the most important deterrent by far. But, the union's timing hardly could have been worse. The effects of the Boxer Rebellion, which the NUTW had no way of predicting, on the Far East market for coarse goods shored up management's determination to resist the union's demands. The NUTW also badly mismanaged their only important offensive strike, the 1901 Danville strike. Indeed, the calling of the Danville strike, although done at Gompers' suggestion, was questionable. The NUTW had recently lost a major strike in the upper South at Alamance. By that time, the union's leadership should have realized that the declining profits of the past year, resulting from the partial closing of the markets of Asia, had stiffened management's will to resist what they regarded as increased expenditures. The company had already tacitly recognized the union and come halfway in meeting its demands, to the point of accepting a half-hour disadvantage when compared with Carolina mills. The Danville operatives worked less hours than workers in either the Carolinas or Georgia. Had they accepted the major gains won rather than striking to force further concessions from management, the union's efforts in other textile centers would have been bolstered. The NUTW would have been in a better position to reorganize the North Carolina locals, using the Danville gains as a lever. The union's entire planned Southern offensive could have been altered so as to demand the same hours in the rest of the South that had been obtained in Danville without a strike. Choosing to gamble in Danville and losing, the NUTW-UTWA was thrown back on the defensive and was never again in a position to take positive steps to improve the operatives' conditions. As a result, the union in the upper Southern Piedmont was nearly obliterated.

The defensive nature of Southern unions should not be allowed to obscure a most important fact: the mill hands actively sought organization. They were not coaxed or coerced into the ranks of organized labor by "outside agitators." The Knights and the NUTW both obtained operative members primarily because they provided a means through which the operatives hoped to obtain certain ends. Operatives joined the Knights because they saw the order as a means to obtain immediate, tangible benefits. They joined even though the Knights had focused primarily on the artisan before 1886 and did not have a full-time textile organizer in the field. In Columbus, in 1896, workers first organized and then joined the NUTW. As late as 1898, Augusta mill hands, threatened by wage reductions, literally sought out an AFL organizer and prevailed upon him to organize them into NUTW assemblies. And, although largely as a result of their naïveté, rank-and-file members of both the Knights and the NUTW frequently demonstrated considerably more aggressiveness than did their national leadership. The inability of the unions to obtain desired immediate benefits was a factor in their decline, especially that of the Knights.

The failure of the Knights and the NUTW-UTWA not only discouraged further serious organizational attempts in the South until well after World War I, it also established yet more firmly the misconception of the Southern operative's docility and proved the effectiveness of management's anti-union tactics. The reasons for the failure of these unions, therefore, do merit close scrutiny.

Management's power and adamant resistance, above all other factors, accounted for the defeat of the unions. Supplying the operatives with housing, food, education, churches and other social services, as well as wages through the paternalistic mill village system, management dominated the operative econom-ically and socially. The often used and always successful evic-tion policy most forcefully demonstrated this overwhelming power. Used when striking unions began to evidence a slight weakness, eviction proceedings never failed to break a strike. Management's political power resulted in the defeat of all efforts to create labor bureaus, except in North Carolina, pass factory inspection laws, or enact meaningful child labor or maximum hours legislation. Replacing the planter as the Southern demigod and dominant figure in the region's power structure, the mill owner was virtually above criticism. What little criticism management drew came from the press when nonunion operatives were locked out in an attempt to curb unionization.

Although they opposed organization for the operatives, man-agement effectively used their own organizations against labor, beginning with the 1886 Augusta strike. Management's success against the NUTW-UTWA at Alamance, Danville, Columbia, and Augusta within less than eighteen months strongly indi-cates a concerted effort to destroy the union. As the Southern Cotton Spinners Association's records are not available to scholars, this can be neither proved nor disproved. But the events of the Columbia and Augusta strikes and manage-ment's response to rumors sparked by the Danville strike indi-cate that such was the case. To assume that mill owners gath-ered in textile centers while mills in those centers were being struck without discussing means to combat unionization would be a rather ludicrous assumption, although one which man-agement asked the public to make at that time.

Another major factor in the unions' defeat was the operatives' lack of trade union experience, indeed, their lack of a knowledge of the fundamental concepts of unionism. Failure to build and maintain strong treasuries, too liberal admission policies, espe-cially during strikes, and a tendency to become involved in local politics, to their detriment, were traits demonstrated by both the Knights and the NUTW-UTWA. The lack of a strong financial policy, caused by the operatives' inability to pay high dues as well as their refusal to do so, was particularly damaging to the NUTW, which admittedly was forced to rely heavily on the resources and talents of the AFL just to remain in existence. Realizing the potential of organization to improve their condition, but basically unaware of their duties to the union, Southern operatives were too ready to strike and often struck when they had no reasonable hope for victory. Leaders of both the Knights and the NUTW-UTWA, aware of their unions' weaknesses, often advised caution, only to be ignored. The Alamance strike was sheer folly, given the disturbances in the textile market at the time, and the decision to initiate the Danville strike was an unpardonable miscalculation.

The average Southern operative's almost total lack of an industrial heritage further hindered his efforts to organize, as did his dismal lack of formal education. Both of these factors retarded the development of an economic class consciousness among the operatives. This was especially true in regard to the operatives' lack of education, for the organizer was forced to rely on mass rallies, personal appearances, and the educated local union advocates to introduce unionism to the worker. The individualism that the operative retained from his agrarian background even further complicated this task. And the South's social mores, to which the mill hands subscribed, emphasized social and racial, rather than economic classes. In such an atmosphere, management was always ideologically ahead of union labor. The organizer based his appeals on concepts alien to the Southern laborer. Management requested loyalty because they were Southern, and because they shared the heritage and blood of the laborer.

In a less tradition-bound society, labor's appeals might have been heeded. But few societies are completely rational, and the New South, like the Old South, was gripped by racial fears and agrarian traditions. Periods of immediate crisis, especially in urban mills, brought workers to the union. But such crises did not instantly instill within the Southern laborers either the values of an industrial society or an understanding of organized labor.

The Negro played a major role in the failure of the Southern worker to develop a strong economic class consciousness, for fear of economic and social competition with the Negro both reinforced and was reinforced by the political turmoil surrounding the South in the 1890s. Management bitterly and consciously attacked both the Knights and the NUTW-UTWA for supposedly trying to improve the lot of the Negro at the expense of the white operative. In effect, management used the Negro to channel off the operatives' hostile feelings that might otherwise have been directed at them. The Negro was also a very real economic threat to the operative, and this fact was readily understood by management. Mill officials were perfectly willing to employ the Negro if, in their judgement, it became necessary, and they financed experiments to determine the feasibility of the use of black laborers. Such experiments, combined with the avowals of some owners that blacks could be trained as operatives as easily as could whites, were not without effect on the white laborers. They realized that the vast pool of potential Negro mill hands would become an actuality if management believed circumstances warranted its use. Operatives who joined the union and struck for improved wages had second thoughts when faced with rumors of Negro employment. Indeed, in Atlanta the NUTW was born of protests against the employment of blacks.

Not only did a large potential Negro labor supply hinder organized labor's efforts in the South, but competition among whites for mill positions was also a very real obstacle to unionization. During most of the period under study, an abundant supply of white labor existed. When the supply in the immediate Piedmont was exhausted, mountaineers were brought into the mills. Thus, management avoided the explosive racial issue, which would have touched off violent reactions by the white mill hands, while continuing to maintain a surplus labor force. Mountaineer laborers also enabled management to continue to pose as the defender of white mill workers against economic competition with blacks.

Although it became somewhat more difficult to obtain good skilled workers, especially weavers, with the rapid expansion of the mills in the late 1890s, unskilled hands were always available. This is a major reason why the unions seldom penetrated the ranks of the unskilled except in urban areas. And even in urban areas, the unions drew their strongest support from the more skilled laborers. Moreover, the training and, therefore, the replacement of weavers was not a prohibitively difficult task, although management naturally wished to keep personnel rotation to a minimum. Such conditions severely handicapped strikes from the start. In most of the South's major strikes, management was always able to produce enough strikebreakers from the surrounding areas to augment nonstriking operatives and keep the mills running during the strikes. This tended to demoralize those workers on strike, who constantly had to face the possibility that the next strikebreakers hired might be assigned to and then retain their jobs. Management usually abandoned lockouts the moment it realized that enough strikebreakers and nonstrikers could be obtained to reopen the mills. The 1902 Augusta strike, perhaps, best illustrates this. The dispute was started by weavers, but broken, in part, by unskilled strikebreakers from South Carolina.

The agrarian nature of the Southern economy at this time practically predetermined the failure of the Knights and the NUTW-UTWA. Even had the operatives been thoroughly organized, it is doubtful that they could have commanded widespread popular support in political or industrial conflicts. The political failure of the Knights, the refusal of the agrarian reform groups to champion labor's cause effectively, the repeated defeat of labor legislation before 1903, and the failure of every major strike demonstrate the truth of this statement. Labor could elect an occasional state legislator, but such political success was temporary and reflected only the aspirations of the operatives of a small area, a tiny minority of the South's total population. And when elected, such labor spokesmen were ineffective in legislative bodies dominated by agrarians and industrialists. The agrarians were powerful enough to gain political control of most of the South in the 1890s, but the laborers did not constitute a large enough element of the South's population to arouse the interest or sympathy of the general public.

The unions also failed to gain any substantial aid from the South's non-agrarian populace. In specific strikes, the strikers nearly always rallied the moral support of some of the townspeople. But, the support of these few was not enough, and it was seldom based on a genuine concern for the operatives. Merchants, for example, supported strikers only so long as they could pay for supplies obtained. The unions could expect the acquiescence of the Southern press only when they made no trouble for management. Strong, aggressive locals invariably received only censure from the forces that controlled public opinion.

The failure of the Southern organizational efforts reflects, to a large extent, the society of which the operative was a part. In many respects, the Southern operative faced the same problems as did his Northern counterpart, only in a more intensified form. The Northern operative faced competition from the newly arrived immigrant; the Southern operative faced actual competition from others seeking to leave the farm and the potential competition of the Negro. In the North, management clung to its concepts of laissez-faire economics and Social Darwinism, but Southern owners further supported their economic doctrines with their version of Reconstruction. The Northern laborer, although often scorned by the middle class, at least labored in a society that had accepted the industrial system. The Southern operative was regarded as a traitor to the Southern way of life by the farmers, who comprised the majority of the South's population, and was disliked by professional groups as well.

In other respects, the problems of the Southern operative were unique. He lacked the industrial experience of the Northern worker. In the Northeast, leaders such as Gompers welded continental trade union theory and American experience into a successful labor movement. The South sadly lacked such leadership. The New South's industry, like the Old South's agriculture, shackled itself to the production of one product, whereas the Northern industrial system was highly diversified. Lacking in real economic alternatives, the unorganized Southern operative could only accept the terms management offered or return to the farm. His unsuccessful organizational efforts underscored the factors that would continue to prevent unionization of the Southern mills: continuing movement of the farmer to the factory, the Negro question, management's unrelenting resistance, and the lack of meaningful economic alternatives.

The defeat of the Knights and the NUTW-UTWA has been interpreted as a failure of organized labor to enter seriously the Southern textile fields or as proof of the docility of the native operative. Neither view, however, fully represents the events of the era. Rather, they reflect the lack of a close examination of organized labor in the South's early textile industry. The evidence presented in this study indicates that both the Knights and the NUTW-UTWA, the latter with encouragement, finances, and leadership provided by the AFL, did make significant efforts to organize the Southern cotton textile operative. Despite the power of management and the social forces that made a response to unionism difficult, it is clear that large numbers of native operatives did respond to these efforts, especially those of the NUTW-UTWA. It is also clear that large numbers of operatives, rather than submitting docilely to management, chose to engage in strikes, many of which were prolonged and bitter. Indeed, the very tenacity with which management opposed both the Knights and the NUTW-UTWA indicates the strength of the challenge with which they were presented.

It should also be noted that the unsuccessful struggle of the Knights and the NUTW-UTWA in the South occurred in an era of general economic depression which saw a decline in the ranks of organized labor throughout the nation. Although the Southern mills were relatively untouched by the era's depression, the Southern operatives received little aid from national organizations because no strong textile national, or for that matter, no other strong national, existed. Rather, the unsuccessful struggle to create and control a strong textile national, which led to the establishment of the UTWA, sapped much of the energy of the NUTW's leadership. And after it was created, the UTWA remained for years a weak regional federation, largely because its controlling New England locals jealously guarded their autonomy and, in view of the failure of the NUTW in the South, turned their backs on the Southern operatives.

The large number of Southern cotton textile workers who responded to both the Knights and the NUTW-UTWA, despite the agrarian traditions and economic realities which militated against organization, certainly provides adequate grounds for revising former conceptions about the docility of the Southern laborer and the extent of organized labor in the region's cotton mills prior to World War I. Southern mill hands were neither inherently docile nor satisfied with the status quo. They were dissatisfied with their hours, wages, working conditions, and the employment of their children. It is impossible to determine the number who joined the Knights, although from 2,000 to 3,000 would seem a reasonable estimate. Well over 5,000 operatives joined the NUTW. Thousands more who failed to join either union sympathized with their ideals. The fact that the operatives at times actually sought out a union through which to express their grievances underscores their dissatisfaction with the status quo. And once organized, they were not docile. Thousands engaged in five major strikes in the four leading textile states of the region.

Organized labor did not fail to develop in Southern textile mills because the operatives were satisfied, or uneducated, or subservient to mill management. Organized labor failed because management took the offensive against it and destroyed it. The blacklist, the lockout, eviction proceedings, and the conscious use of racial fears prevented the growth of union labor in the South's mills. Economic realities of the region, a surplus pool of laborers, black and white, a lack of industrial alternatives, and a depressed agrarian economy allowed management to use such tactics with impunity. Pragmatic businessmen that they were, mill officials adopted and retained these policies because they were effective. Their application of these tactics in a more truly urban industrial society resulted in the violent labor-management clashes within the industry during the Great Depression and the era of the New Deal.

Notes

INTRODUCTION

1. For major secondary works concerning the Southern mill worker, see Bibliography.

2. August Kohn, *The Cotton Mills of South Carolina* (Charleston: Daggett Printing, 1907), 151.

3. Philip A. Bruce, *The Rise of the New South* (Philadelphia: G. Barrie and Sons, 1905), 187.

4. Norman J. Ware, *The Labor Movement in the United States, 1860–1895* (New York: Appleton, 1929), chaps. 4–7.

5. Broadus Mitchell, *The Rise of Cotton Mills in the South,* Johns Hopkins University Studies in Historical and Political Science, vol. 39, no. 2 (Baltimore: Johns Hopkins University Press, 1921), 231.

6. George Sinclair Mitchell, *Textile Unionism and the South* (Chapel Hill: University of North Carolina Press, 1931), 23–26. (For a thorough discussion of the founding of the NUTW, see chap. 5, this volume.)

7. Selig Perlman and Philip Taft, *Labor Movements,* vol. 4, in *History of Labor in the United States: 1896–1936,* ed. John R. Commons (New York: Macmillan, 1918–1935), 603.

8. Robert W. Dunn and Jack Hardy, *Labor and Textiles* (New York: International Publishers, 1931), 178–182.

9. Herbert J. Lahne, *The Cotton Mill Worker* (New York: Farrar and Rinehart, 1944), 183–187.

10. C. Vann Woodward, *Origins of the New South: 1877–1913,* vol. 9,

in *A History of the South,* ed. Wendell H. Stephenson and E. Merton Coulter (Baton Rouge: Louisiana State University Press, 1947–   ), 228, 421–422.

11. F. Ray Marshall, *Labor in the South* (Cambridge, Mass.: Harvard University Press, 1967), 80–83.

CHAPTER 1

1. Glenn Gilman, *Human Relations in the Industrial Southeast* (Chapel Hill: University of North Carolina Press, 1956), 87.

2. Marjorie Young, ed., *Textile Leaders of the South* (Columbia, S.C.: R. L. Bryan, 1963), 191–193.

3. Ibid., 466; William P. Jacobs, *The Pioneer: Biographical Sketches of North and South Carolina Textile Manufacturers* (Clinton, S.C.: Jacobs, 1935), 56–59.

4. Broadus Mitchell, *William Gregg: Factory Master of the Old South* (Chapel Hill: University of North Carolina Press, 1928), 1–34.

5. South Carolina Department of Agriculture, Commerce, and Industries, *The Cotton Mills of South Carolina: Their Names, Location, Capacity, and History* (Charleston: News and Courier Book Presses, 1880), 5 (hereafter cited as S.C. Dept. of Agric., *Cotton Mills of S.C.*).

6. Holland Thompson, "The Civil War and Social and Economic Changes," *The Annals of the American Academy of Political and Social Science* 153 (Jan. 1931), 18.

7. Gilman, *Human Relations,* 68.

8. Holland Thompson, *From the Cotton Field to the Cotton Mill* (New York: Macmillan, 1906), 58.

9. Ibid., 59; Mitchell, *William Gregg,* 235–236.

10. U.S. Bureau of the Census, Twelfth Census of the United States: 1900, Manufacturing, vol. 9, *Special Reports on Selected Industries* (Washington, D.C.: Government Printing Office, 1902), 56–57.

11. Ibid.

12. S.C. Dept. of Agric., *Cotton Mills of S.C.,* 16; B. Mitchell, *Rise of Mills,* 143.

13. S.C. Dept. of Agric., *Cotton Mills of S.C.,* 5–11; Jacobs, *Pioneer,* 35–36.

14. *Charleston News and Courier,* Feb. 10, 1880.

15. U.S. Bureau of the Census, *Census of Manufactures: 1905,* pt. 3, *Special Reports on Selected Industries* (Washington, D.C.: Government Printing Office, 1908), 40–50 (hereafter cited as *U.S. Census, Manufactures, 1905).*

16. Ibid.

17. This interpretation is perhaps best presented in B. Mitchell, *Rise of Mills,* chap. 2.

18. Gerald W. Johnson as quoted in Wilbur J. Cash, *The Mind of the South* (New York: Knopf, 1941), 178.

19. B. Mitchell, *Rise of Mills*, chap. 2.

20. *Columbia* (S.C.) *State*, Sept. 6, 1899; North Carolina Bureau of Labor, *Fifth Annual Report, 1891*, 130–131 (hereafter all such reports are cited as *N.C. Labor Report*); Daniel A. Tompkins, *Cotton Mill, Commercial Features: A Textbook for the Use of Textile Schools and Investors* (Charlotte, N.C.: By the author, 1899), 109.

21. David Duncan Wallace, "One Hundred Years of Gregg and Graniteville" (typed manuscript), William Gregg Foundation, Graniteville, S.C., 1954, 214–215; Gustavus G. Williamson, "Cotton Manufacturing in South Carolina, 1865–1892" (Ph.D. diss., Johns Hopkins University, 1954), 155–156 (hereafter cited as "S.C. Cotton Manufacturing").

22. S.C. Dept. of Agric., *Cotton Mills of S.C.*, 5–11; Thompson, "Civil War and Changes," 18; Samuel B. Lincoln, *Lockwood Greene: The History of an Engineering Business, 1832–1958* (Brattleboro, Vt.: Stephen Greene Press, 1960), 122, 157.

23. John Lowndes McLaurin, "The Commercial Democracy of the South," *North American Review* 173 (Nov. 1901), 657–662; Ben F. Lemert, *The Cotton Textile Industry of the Southern Appalachian Piedmont* (Chapel Hill: University of North Carolina Press, 1933), 31–32.

24. For a thorough discussion of the role of South Carolina mill men in determining the United States' Asian policy, see Richard H. Davis, Jr., "The Role of South Carolina's Cotton Manufacturers in the United States' Far Eastern Policy, 1897–1902" (Master's thesis, University of South Carolina, 1966). [Hereafter cited as "Cotton Manufacturers and the Far East."] Also see Charles S. Campbell, *Special Business Interests and the Open Door Policy*, Yale Historical Publications, vol. 53 (New Haven, Conn.: Yale University Press, 1951), 17–21, 60; *U.S. Census, 1900, Manufacturing* 20–21.

25. Lemert, *Cotton Textile Industry*, 32–33; B. Mitchell, *Rise of Mills*, 62, 151–152; Wallace, "Gregg and Graniteville," 214–215; John Wilbur Jenkins, *James B. Duke, Master Builder* (New York: George H. Doran, 1927), 179–181.

26. Melvin T. Copeland, *The Cotton Manufacturing Industry in the United States*, Harvard Economic Studies, vol. 8 (Cambridge, Mass.: Harvard University Press, 1912), 39 (hereafter cited as *U.S. Cotton Manufacturing*).

27. S.C. Dept. of Agric., *Cotton Mills of S.C.*, 5–16; *N.C. Labor Report, 1897*, 15; *Columbia* (S.C.) *State*, Sept. 6, 1899; Williamson, "S.C. Cotton Manufacturing," 155–156; Robert S. Smith, *Mill on the Dan* (Durham, N.C.: Duke University Press, 1960), 9.

28. Williamson, "S.C. Cotton Manufacturing," 155–156; Rupert B. Vance, *Human Geography of the South* (Chapel Hill: University of North Carolina Press, 1932), 189. Vance's study, though done in a later

era, vividly demonstrates the extent of tenancy in the Southern Piedmont, especially in South Carolina and Georgia.

29. Stephen J. Kennedy, *Profits and Losses in Textiles: Cotton Textile Financing Since the War* (New York: Harper Bros., 1936), 6.

30. Lahne, *Cotton Mill Worker,* 177–181.

31. National Union of Textile Workers, *Proceedings of the Eleventh Annual Convention, 1900,* 17–18, 30, 32 (all such proceedings hereafter cited as *NUTW Convention Proceedings*).

32. Lemert, *Cotton Textile Industry,* 32–33.

33. Williamson, "S.C. Cotton Manufacturing," 155–156.

34. Wallace, "Gregg and Graniteville," 214–215.

35. S.C. Dept. of Agric., *Cotton Mills of S.C.,* 1–15; B. Mitchell, *Rise of Mills,* 77–160; Williamson, "S.C. Cotton Manufacturing," chaps. 1–4.

CHAPTER 2

1. Cash, *Mind of the South,* 200.

2. C. V. Woodward, *Origins,* 223.

3. Charles B. Spahr, "The New Factory Towns of the South," *Outlook* 61 (Mar. 4, 1899), 510–517; S.C. Dept. of Agric., *Cotton Mills of S.C.,* 5–17.

4. Lawrence B. Graves, "The Beginning of the Cotton Textile Industry in Newberry County" (Master's thesis, University of South Carolina, 1947), 49; Thompson, *From the Cotton Field,* 109.

5. Vance, *Human Geography,* 73–74; Cash, *Mind of the South,* 22–23; Thompson, *From the Cotton Field,* 103, 109.

6. For discussions of the term "poor white," see Thompson, *From the Cotton Field,* 113–114; Vance, *Human Geography,* 75–76; Cash, *Mind of the South,* 21–28; and especially Shields McIlwaine, *The Southern Poor White from Lubberland to Tobacco Road* (Norman, Okla.: University of Oklahoma Press, 1939), xii–xxv.

7. S.C. Dept. of Agric., *Cotton Mills of S.C.,* 1–16; B. Mitchell, *Rise of Mills,* 172–190. Also, any of the North Carolina Bureau of Labor reports attest to this fact, as do the editorials in any Southern paper of the era.

8. "J. M. O'Dell Manufacturing Company Time and Wage Book," *Chatham County Miscellaneous Books,* vol. 19, June 1899, Southern Historical Collection, University of North Carolina, Chapel Hill, N.C.

9. Edward Porritt, "Cotton Mills in the South," *New England Magazine* 12 (July 1895), 575–586; Kohn, *Cotton Mills,* 21–26.

10. Kohn, *Cotton Mills,* 22–26; B. Mitchell, *Rise of Mills,* 190–199. Kohn's *Cotton Mills* is especially valuable. However, Kohn, a reporter and investor in cotton mills, was something of a self-appointed publicist for Southern mills and must be read with care.

11. Sam Patterson to his mother, Sept. 23, 1897, Patterson Papers, North Carolina Department of Archives and History, Raleigh, N.C.

12. William W. Thompson, Jr., "A Managerial History of a Cotton Textile Firm: Spartan Mills, 1888–1958" (Ph.D. diss., University of Alabama, 1962), 80–86 (hereafter cited as "Spartan Mills"); B. Mitchell, *Rise of Mills,* 190–91; H. Thompson, *From the Cotton Field,* 160.

13. *Columbia* (S.C.) *State,* Oct. 23, 1904.

14. Daniel A. Tompkins to C. H. Dale, Feb. 16, 1905, Daniel A. Tompkins Papers, Southern Historical Collection, University of North Carolina, Chapel Hill, N.C.

15. Kohn, *Cotton Mills,* 24, 199–207.

16. Ibid., 23–24; Lahne, *Cotton Mill Worker,* 77; B. Mitchell, *Rise of Mills,* 189–191.

17. Lahne, *Cotton Mill Worker,* 289.

18. "Minutes of the Richland Cotton Mills," June 21, 1897, 62–65 (Now in the possession of S.C. Electric and Gas Co., Columbia, S.C.). [Hereafter cited as "Richland Mills Minutes"]; B. Mitchell, *Rise of Mills,* 171.

19. Clare de Graffenried, "The Georgia Cracker in the Cotton Mill," *Century Magazine* 41 (Feb. 1891), 495.

20. *N.C. Labor Report, 1905,* 228.

21. Ibid.; *N.C. Labor Report, 1901,* 422.

22. Bruce, *Rise of South,* 185–86; Thompson, *From the Cotton Field,* 109–111; Mrs. John Van Vorst and Marie Van Vorst, *The Woman Who Toils* (New York: Doubleday, Page, 1903), 300.

23. Patterson to his mother, Sept. 23, 1897, Patterson Papers.

24. *Columbia* [S.C.] *State,* Sept. 6, 1899.

25. Thomas R. Smith, *The Cotton Textile Industry of Fall River, Massachusetts* (New York: King's Crown Press, 1944), 80–86.

26. *U.S. Bureau of the Census, Census of Manufactures: 1905,* pt. 2, *States and Territories* (Washington, D.C.: Government Printing Office, 1907), 172, 882, 1022 (hereafter cited as *U.S. Census, 1905, Manufactures—States*).

27. S.C. Dept. of Agric., *Cotton Mills of S.C.,* 6–15.

28. *N.C. Labor Report, 1895,* 123. North Carolina was the first Southern state to establish a bureau of labor, and, with the exception of Virginia, which established a labor bureau in 1897, it was the only Southern state to do so in the nineteenth century. The reports of the North Carolina Bureau of Labor are invaluable to the student of Southern labor.

29. *U.S. Census, 1905, Manufactures—States,* 172, 882, 1022.

30. *N.C. Labor Report, 1890,* 23; ibid., *1905,* 229.

31. Graves, "Textile Industry in Newberry," 85; Bruce, *Rise of South,* 189.

32. Edgar G. Murphy, *Problems of the Present South* (New York: Macmillan, 1904), 107.

33. J. W. McPherson to Mark Morgan, Nov. 20, 1897, Mark Morgan Papers, Morgan-Malloy Papers, Duke University Library, Durham, N.C.; Wallace, "Gregg and Graniteville," 202–203.

34. Lahne, *Cotton Mill Worker*, 103.

35. For details see chaps. 4, 5, and 6, this volume.

36. B. Mitchell, *Rise of Mills*, 230; Thompson, *From the Cotton Field*, 114–117.

37. M. Raphael, "Child Labor," *American Federationist* 3 (Oct. 1896), 157–158. The role of unions in child labor reform efforts is discussed further in chap. 5, this volume.

38. de Graffenried, "Georgia Cracker," 438–487; Thompson, *From the Cotton Field*, 133–135.

39. *N.C. Labor Report, 1900,* 182; Thompson, *From the Cotton Field,* 133–135.

40. Van Vorst and Van Vorst, *Woman Who Toils,* 227; de Graffenried, "Georgia Cracker," 483–487; John Montgomery to Ellison A. Smyth, Apr. 9, 1900, Letter Book, John Montgomery Papers, South Caroliniana Library, University of South Carolina, Columbia, S.C.

41. Ben Robertson, *Red Hills and Cotton: An Upcountry Memory* (Columbia: University of South Carolina Press, 1960), 274.

42. For specific strikes caused by disputes over hours, see chaps. 5 and 6, this volume.

43. S.C. Dept. of Agric., *Cotton Mills of S.C.,* 12–13; *N.C. Labor Report, 1887,* 142–143.

44. U.S. Commissioner of Labor, *1904 Report,* 480; *N.C. Labor Report, 1895,* 24.

45. Bruce, *Rise of South,* 186–187; Kohn, *Cotton Mills,* 136; B. Mitchell, *Rise of Mills,* 225.

46. Thompson, *From the Cotton Field,* 281–283; Lahne, *Cotton Mill Worker,* 167–172; B. Mitchell admits as much in *Rise of Mills,* 229–230.

47. U.S. Bureau of Labor, *Eleventh Annual Report of the Commissioner of Labor, 1895–1896: Work and Wages of Men, Women, and Children* (Washington, D.C.: Government Printing Office, 1897), 193, 210–211, 227, 254.

48. *N.C. Labor Report, 1887,* 143; ibid., *1895,* 23; ibid., *1905,* 229.

49. Leonora Beck Ellis, "A Model Factory Town," *Forum* 32 (Sept. 1901), 64.

50. Jerome Dowd, "Strikes and Lockouts in North Carolina," *Gunton's Magazine* 20 (Feb. 1901), 136–138; *N.C. Labor Report, 1890,* 70–89.

51. *Augusta Chronicle,* June 11–20, 1886.

52. *N.C. Labor Report, 1887,* 143; ibid., *1895,* 23; ibid., *1905,* 229.

53. B. Mitchell, *Rise of Mills,* 226.

54. S.C. Dept. of Agric., *Cotton Mills of S.C.,* 5–11.

55. B. Mitchell, *Rise of Mills,* 274, 264.

56. *U.S. Census, Manufactures,* 1905, 20–21.

57. Tompkins, *Cotton Mill,* 51. Tompkins, perhaps the entrepreneur most knowledgeable about the industry from all aspects, wrote numerous long works on Southern mills. He owned several mills in both North and South Carolina. A native of Edgefield, South Carolina, he was educated as an engineer and constructed many of the South's largest mills. As owner of the *Charlotte* [N.C.] *Observer,* he was also one of the industry's leading promoters. Of the works he authored, many of them highly technical, *Cotton Mill* is by far the most valuable to the historian.

58. "Minutes of the Board of Directors and Stockholders Meetings," Graniteville Manufacturing Company, Oct. 30, 1852–Oct. 30, 1918, William Gregg Foundation, Graniteville, S.C. (hereafter cited as "Graniteville Minutes").

59. Allen Stokes, "John H. Montgomery, A Pioneer Southern Industrialist" (Master's thesis, University of South Carolina, 1967), 69–70; W. W. Thompson, "Spartan Mills," 75.

60. Thompson, *From the Cotton Field,* 83–84.

61. Smith, *Mill on the Dan,* 29–30.

62. *Augusta Chronicle,* May 29–June 2–6, 1886; *Raleigh News and Observer,* Oct. 6, 1900; Wallace, "Gregg and Graniteville," 210–212.

63. John D. Jennings to Mark Morgan, Jan. 1, 1896, Mark Morgan Papers; *Augusta Chronicle,* May 29, 1886.

64. U.S. Industrial Commission, *Reports,* vol. 7, *On the Relations and Conditions of Capital and Labor Employed in Manufactures and General Business* (Washington, D.C.: Government Printing Office, 1901), 570–571, 557 (hereafter cited as U.S. Industrial Commission, *Reports, Labor and Capital).*

65. Several strikes originated in operative-overseer disputes, including the 1900 Alamance strike. See the *Raleigh News and Observer,* Oct. 1–10, 1900.

66. Dowd, "Strikes and Lockouts," 136–137; Tompkins, *Cotton Mill,* 34–35.

67. Tompkins, *Cotton Mill,* 34–35.

68. Ellis, "Model Factory Town," 60–65; Thomas M. Young, *The American Cotton Industry* (New York: Charles Scribner's Sons, 1903), 70.

69. de Graffenried "Georgia Cracker," 483; Van Vorst and Van Vorst, *Woman Who Toils,* 223–224.

70. U.S. Industrial Commission, *Reports, Labor and Capital,* 543, 558.

71. T. W. Uttley, *Cotton Spinning and Manufacturing in the United States of America* (Manchester, England: Manchester University Press, 1905), 48–49 (hereafter cited as *Cotton Spinning, USA).*

72. Harriet L. Herring, *Welfare Work in Mill Villages: The Story of Extra-Mill Activities in North Carolina* (Chapel Hill: University of North Carolina Press, 1929), 254–255.

73. For the views of contemporaries on both sides of the issue, see

U.S. Industrial Commission, *Reports, Labor and Capital,* 556–569, 569–570, 543–544, 483.

74. Ibid., 552.

75. de Graffenried, "Georgia Cracker," 490; Van Vorst and Van Vorst, *Woman Who Toils,* 232, 246.

76. Van Vorst and Van Vorst, *Woman Who Toils,* 223–234, 215; Ellis, "Model Factory Town," 60–62.

77. For details of the use of eviction proceedings in specific strikes, see chaps. 4, 6, and 7, this volume.

78. *N.C. Labor Report, 1887,* 143.

79. Ellis, "Model Factory Town," 60–62; de Graffenried, "Georgia Cracker," 490; U.S. Industrial Commission, *Reports, Labor and Capital,* 483.

80. *N.C. Labor Report, 1887,* 152; ibid., *1890,* 70–76.

81. Dowd, "Strikes and Lockouts," 136–137.

82. C. V. Woodward, *Origins,* 223; de Graffenried, "Georgia Cracker," 487–488; Kohn, *Cotton Mills,* 143–150; William E. Woodward, *The Gift of Life: An Autobiography* (New York: E. P. Dutton, 1947), 41–44. Also see chap. 3, this volume.

83. *N.C. Labor Report, 1894,* 73; ibid., *1901,* 419–421; Marjorie A. Potwin, *Cotton Mill People of the Piedmont: A Study in Social Change* (New York: Columbia University Press, 1927), 96–97.

84. *Columbia* (S.C.) *State,* Sept. 2, 1901.

85. Tompkins, *Cotton Mill,* 37; Kohn, *Cotton Mills,* 124–177.

86. Herring, *Welfare Work,* 38–43; William E. Woodward, *The Way Our People Lived: An Intimate American History* (New York: E. P. Dutton, 1944), 354–355.

87. Broadus Mitchell and George S. Mitchell, *The Industrial Revolution in the South* (Baltimore: Johns Hopkins University Press, 1930), 135–136.

88. Kohn, *Cotton Mills,* 150.

89. W. E. Woodward, *Gift of Life,* 36–41; B. Mitchell, *Rise of Mills,* 198.

90. *Columbus* (Ga.) *Enquirer-Sun,* June 25, 1899; Ellis, "Model Factory Town," 62; W. E. Woodward, *Way People Lived,* 326.

91. Thompson, *From the Cotton Field,* 111–114; B. Mitchell, *Rise of Mills,* 177–180.

92. *N.C. Labor Report, 1893,* 51.

93. Thompson, *From the Cotton Field,* 111–114.

94. Herring, *Welfare Work,* 42–43.

95. U.S. Industrial Commission, *Reports, Labor and Capital,* 482; Leonora Beck Ellis, "A New Class of Labor in the South," *Forum* 31 (May 1901), 306–311.

96. Robertson, *Red Hills,* 275–277.

CHAPTER 3

1. Cash, *Mind of the South,* 179–180.
2. Williamson, "S.C. Cotton Manufacturing," 180; Jacobs, *Pioneer,* 30–73; B. Mitchell, *Rise of Mills,* 106; Stokes, "John Montgomery," 11–16.
3. George T. Winston, *A Builder of the New South; Being the Story of the Life Work of Daniel A. Tompkins* (Garden City, N.Y.: Doubleday, Page, 1920), 237 (hereafter cited as *Tompkins*).
4. Gilman, *Human Relations,* 81; Gerald W. Johnson as quoted in Cash, *Mind of the South,* 178; B. Mitchell, *Rise of Mills,* 147–148.
5. S.C. Dept. of Agric., *Cotton Mills of S.C.,* 5, 11.
6. Tompkins, *Cotton Mill,* 51–63.
7. *Charleston News and Courier,* Feb. 10, 1880.
8. *Atlanta Constitution,* Jan. 20, 1898.
9. All as quoted in Cash, *Mind of the South,* 184.
10. Ibid.
11. Stokes, "John Montgomery," 11–16; Jacobs, *Pioneer,* 30–70; B. Mitchell, *Rise of Mills,* 106; Williamson, "S.C. Cotton Manufacturing," 180; also see Young, *Textile Leaders.*
12. The American businessmen's attempts to apply Darwin's theories to the social and economic world are ably discussed in any number of works. Two of the best are Richard Hofstadter, *Social Darwinism in American Thought,* 2d rev. ed. (Boston: Beacon Press, 1959) and Irvin G. Wyllie, *The Self-Made Man in America, the Myth of Rags to Riches* (New Brunswick, N.J.: Rutgers University Press, 1954).
13. Tompkins, *Cotton Mill,* 109; Mitchell and Mitchell, *Industrial Revolution,* 147–148; Winston, *Tompkins,* 182.
14. W. E. Woodward, *Way People Lived,* 334, 342.
15. Tompkins, *Cotton Mill,* 115.
16. *Columbus* (Ga.) *Enquirer-Sun,* June 25, 1899; Ellis, "Model Factory Town," 62.
17. *Raleigh News and Observer,* May 11, 1900.
18. *N.C. Labor Report, 1893,* 51; ibid., *1895,* 64–70; ibid., *1902,* 168; *Columbia* (S.C.) *State,* Sept. 11, 1901; Kohn, *Cotton Mills,* 125–132; Tompkins, *Cotton Mill,* 115; Southern Cotton Spinners Association, *Certificate of Incorporation, By Laws and Proceedings of the Seventh Annual Convention, 1903* (Raleigh, N.C.: Edwards and Broughton, Printers and Binders, 1903), 45–47 (hereafter cited as *SCSA Proceedings*).
19. Richard Spillane, "Striking Facts about Southern Cotton Mills and Cotton Mill Employees," *Manufacturer's Record* 86 (Dec. 11, 1924), 195–196. Emphasis added.
20. Cash, *Mind of the South,* 210.

21. "Minute Book Number 1, Gramby Cotton Mills," Mar. 1, 1901, 103 (now in the possession of S.C. Electric and Gas Co., Columbia, S.C.). [Hereafter cited as "Gramby Minutes."]

22. Tompkins, *Cotton Mill*, 113.

23. *SCSA Proceedings, 1903*, 45–47.

24. Ibid.; Graves, "Textile Industry in Newberry," 58; Winston, *Tompkins*, 188.

25. Spillane, "Striking Facts about Mills," 195–196.

26. Kohn, *Cotton Mills*, 21–23.

27. B. Mitchell, *Rise of Mills*, 172, 177, 185, 194.

28. *N.C. Labor Report, 1891*, 154; ibid., *1890*, 43; *SCSA Proceedings, 1903*, 151. It is interesting to compare this particular view of the operative with the planter's view of the slave.

29. *N.C. Labor Report, 1894*, 79.

30. *Columbia* (S.C.) *State*, Sept. 6, 1899.

31. Knights of Labor, *Records of the Proceedings of the General Assembly, 1885*, 33 (hereafter cited as *Knights Assembly Proceedings*). *Carolina Spartan* (Spartanburg, S.C.), Sept. 21, 1887; *N.C. Labor Report, 1898*, 398; Hartwell Ayer, ed., *The Resources and Manufacturing Industries of the State of South Carolina, Mountains to the Seaboard* (Charleston: Lucas and Richardson, 1895), 25.

32. *Columbus* (Ga.) *Herald*, Feb. 20, 1898; *Atlanta Constitution*, Feb. 18, 1898; *Greenville* (S.C.) *Daily News*, Jan. 8, 1899; Daniel A. Tompkins to J. C. Pritchard, August 1, 1898, Daniel A. Tompkins Letter Book, Feb. 25, 1898–Oct. 1, 1900, 111, Southern Historical Collection, University of North Carolina, Chapel Hill, N.C.

33. Daniel A. Tompkins, *Labor and Legislation* (Charlotte, N.C.: n.p., 1901), 2–7; Thompson, *From the Cotton Field*, 211.

34. S.C. Dept. of Agric., *Cotton Mills of S.C.*, 5–17; Southern Commercial Congress, *Proceedings, Third Annual Convention, 1911*, 605–606.

35. Thompson, *From the Cotton Field*, 197–198; *N.C. Labor Report, 1893*, 51; Winston, *Tompkins*, 259–260; *N.C. Labor Report, 1896*, 73.

36. A survey of Jacobs, *Pioneer*, and Young, *Textile Leaders*, vividly illustrates this phenomenon.

37. *N.C. Labor Report, 1894*, 51.

38. *Carolina Spartan* (Spartanburg, S.C.), Sept. 21, 1887; Tompkins, *Cotton Mill*, 111–112; Winston, *Tompkins*, 260–261.

39. Reports of such organizations begin in 1884 and continue throughout the period. The Southern Cotton Manufacturers was one such group. For examples of less formal groups, see H. H. Hickman to G. C. Goodrich, Aug. 17, 1886, Piedmont Letter Book, South Caroliniana Library, University of South Carolina, Columbia, S.C.; *Columbia* (S.C.) *State*, Sept. 6, 1901.

40. *N.C. Labor Report, 1901*, 212; Tompkins, *Cotton Mills*, 113; *N.C. Labor Report, 1902*, 227; ibid., *1903*, 129.

41. McLaurin, "Commercial Democracy of the South," 657–662; Davis, "Cotton Manufacturers and the Far East."

42. Tompkins, *Cotton Mill*, 109; Winston, *Tompkins*, 122–123.

43. *SCSA Proceedings, 1903*, 45–47.

44. U.S. Industrial Commission, *Reports, Labor and Capital*, 568; Robertson, *Red Hills*, 274–279.

45. Thompson, *From the Cotton Field*, 195–196; W. E. Woodward, *Gift of Life*, 71–73.

46. U.S. Bureau of Labor, *Report on Conditions of Woman and Child Wage Earners in the United States*, vol. 1, *Cotton Textile Industry* (Washington, D.C.: Government Printing Office, 1910), 611 (hereafter cited as U.S. Bureau of Labor, *Report on Wage Earners*).

47. United Textile Workers of America, *Proceedings of the Third Annual Convention, 1903*, 48 (all such proceedings hereafter cited as *UTWA Convention Proceedings*); *N.C. Labor Report, 1901*, 412, 416, 419–421; *American Federationist* 8 (Sept. 1901), 367–389.

48. *N.C. Labor Report, 1890*, 23–25; ibid., *1891*, 173–174; Van Vorst and Van Vorst, *Woman Who Toils*, 238; W. E. Woodward, *Way People Lived*, 341.

49. *N.C. Labor Report, 1887*, 143.

50. W. E. Woodward, *Way People Lived*, 326.

51. de Graffenried, "Georgia Cracker," 488.

52. J. A. Sizemore to Mark Morgan, Aug. 19, 1891, Mark Morgan Papers.

53. Ellis, "New Class of Labor," 306–310.

54. *Greenville* (S.C.) *Enterprise and Mountaineer*, Nov. 3, 1886; Potwin, *Cotton Mill People*, 102–103; U.S. Bureau of Labor, *Report on Wage Earners*, 608.

55. Robertson, *Red Hills*, 274–275.

56. Francis Butler Simkins, *Pitchfork Ben Tillman: South Carolinian* (Baton Rouge: Louisiana State University Press, 1944), 222.

57. Williamson, "S.C. Cotton Manufacturing," 56.

58. Cash, *Mind of the South*, 201–202.

59. *Columbia* (S.C.) *State*, Sept. 3, 1890.

60. W. E. Woodward, *Gift of Life*, 45.

61. Wallace, "Gregg and Graniteville," 231–232; *N.C. Labor Report, 1901*, 419–421.

62. See chap. 4 for the role of ministers in the Knights of Labor.

63. *Columbus* (Ga.) *Herald*, Jan. 27, 1900.

64. Ibid.; *N.C. Labor Report, 1901*, 425.

65. Robertson, *Red Hills*, 280–281.

66. *Journal of the House of Representatives of the General Assembly of the State of South Carolina, 1901* (Columbia: State Company, State Printers, 1901), 129–130.

67. Uttley, *Cotton Spinning, USA*, 48–49; *N.C. Labor Report, 1887*, 149; de Graffenried, "Georgia Cracker," 485.

68. *N.C. Labor Report, 1901,* 213; C. V. Woodward, *Origins,* 223.

69. Young, *American Cotton Industry,* 75–76.

70. Any general study will verify the Negro's position in the mills. For examples, see Kohn, *Cotton Mills,* 24; Tompkins, *Cotton Mill,* 109–110; Thompson, *From the Cotton Field,* 250–251; Sterling D. Spero and Abram L. Harris, *The Black Worker* (New York: Atheneum, 1968), 348–351.

71. S.C. Dept. of Agric., *Cotton Mills of S.C.,* 1–17.

72. *Atlanta Constitution,* July 17, 1896, Aug. 5–6, 1898; *Columbus* (Ga.) *Herald,* June 4, 1899.

73. Stokes, "John Montgomery," 84–126; B. Mitchell, *Rise of Mills,* 215–216; *Columbia* (S.C.) *State,* July 10, July 13, 1897.

74. Jerome Dowd, "Colored Men as Cotton Manufacturers," *Gunton's Magazine* 23 (Sept. 1902), 254–256; Tompkins, *Cotton Mill,* 110; Thompson, *From the Cotton Field,* 248–268; B. Mitchell, *Rise of Mills,* 213–221; George B. Tindall, *South Carolina Negroes: 1877–1900* (Columbia: University of South Carolina Press, 1952), 132–135 (hereafter cited as *S.C. Negroes).*

75. James L. Orr, "The Negro in the Mills," *Independent* 53 (Apr. 11, 1901), 845–846; Tompkins, *Cotton Mill,* 110; Stokes, "John Montgomery," 116.

76. South Carolina, State Board of Agriculture, *South Carolina Resources and Population, Institutions and Industries* (Charleston: Walker, Evans and Cogswell, Printers, 1883), 587–588 (hereafter cited as S.C. Dept. of Agric., *S.C. Resources).*

77. Daniel A. Tompkins, *Picking, Bailing and Manufacturing of Cotton, from a Southern Point of View* (By the author, 1895), 11–12.

78. U.S. Industrial Commission, *Reports, Labor and Capital,* 482, 485, 766, 790.

79. S.C. Dept. of Agric., *S.C. Resources,* 587–588; Daniel A. Tompkins, "The Future of Cotton Manufacturing in the South," *Transactions of the New England Cotton Manufacturers' Annual Meeting, April 29–30, 1896, Boston, Massachusetts* (Waltham, Mass.: Press of E. L. Barry, 1896), 243–244.

80. *Greenville* (S.C.) *Daily News,* Jan. 8, 1899.

81. *Charleston News and Courier,* Feb. 10, 1880.

82. Williamson, "S.C. Cotton Manufacturing," 178.

83. Tompkins, *Picking, Bailing, and Manufacturing of Cotton,* 12.

84. John H. Montgomery to Ellison A. Smyth, Nov. 26, 1899, Letter Book, John H. Montgomery Papers, South Caroliniana Library, University of South Carolina, Columbia, S.C.

85. U.S. Industrial Commission, *Reports, Labor and Capital,* 790–791.

86. *Charleston News and Courier,* July 27, 1900; Tindall, *S.C. Negroes,* 132–133.

87. *Atlanta Constitution,* July 17, 1896, Aug. 5–6, 1898; Marshall, *Labor in the South,* 81; Mercer G. Evans, "The History of the Organ-

ized Labor Movement in Georgia" (Ph.D. diss., University of Chicago, 1929), 89 (hereafter cited as "Labor in Georgia").

88. *Columbus* (Ga.) *Herald,* June 4, 1899; *Rock Hill* (S.C.) *Herald,* May 31, 1899.

89. Will H. Winn, "The Negro, His Relation to Southern Industry," *American Federationist* 4 (Feb. 1898), 269–271.

90. *Raleigh News and Observer,* Mar. 20, 1900.

91. Ibid., July 14, 1900; *Columbia* (S.C.) *State,* Aug. 12, 1897; *Truth Index* (Salisbury, N.C.), July 17, 1900.

92. The white mill hand's hatred for the Negro has proved as enduring as it was bitter. In 1964, while working in the presidential campaign, I encountered mill hands in Columbia, S.C., who favored Lyndon Johnson's economic policies, but intended to vote for Barry Goldwater because they feared Johnson, if elected, "would put niggers in our jobs." For further considerations of this topic, see Charles H. Wesley, *Negro Labor in the United States: 1850–1925* (New York: Vanguard Press, 1927), 238–245; Spero and Harris, *Black Worker,* 343–351; Murphy, *Problems of the South,* 103–104; Marshall, *Labor in the South,* 80–85, 112–120; F. Ray Marshall, *The Negro and Organized Labor* (New York: Wiley and Sons, 1965), 14–17, 190–191.

93. E. T. H. Shaffer, "Southern Mill People," *Yale Review* 19 (Dec. 1929), 325–340.

94. Thompson, *From the Cotton Field,* 196.

CHAPTER 4

1. G. S. Mitchell, *Textile Unionism,* 24.

2. "Graniteville Minutes," Oct. 30, 1875, Jan. 19, 1876; Wallace, "Gregg and Graniteville," 210–212.

3. Nathan Fine, *Labor and Farmer Parties in the United States: 1828–1928* (New York: Russell and Russell, 1961), 119. Gerald N. Grob, *Workers and Utopia* (Evanston, Ill.: Northwestern University Press, 1961), 35. Grob's study is the best work available on the Knights, and is relied on heavily in this work.

4. Frederick Meyers, "The Knights of Labor in the South," *Southern Economic Journal* 6 (Apr. 1940), 479–487; Grob, *Workers and Utopia,* 35–36; Norman J. Ware, *The Labor Movement in the United States, 1860–1895: A Study in Democracy* (New York: Appleton, 1929), 61–62. Although it is outdated, one should also consult John R. Commons, ed., *History of Labor in the United States,* vol. 2 (New York: Macmillan, 1921), 332–469.

5. Ware, *Labor Movement,* 60–61.

6. Ibid., 155–160; Grob, *Workers and Utopia,* 35–36, 119–138.

7. A survey of the reports of Southern locals in the *Journal of United Labor* will confirm this. Also see Meyers, "Knights of Labor," 485.

8. Terence Vincent Powderly, *The Path I Trod: An Autobiography*, ed. Harry J. Carman (New York: Columbia University Press, 1940), 161, 427; Grob, *Workers and Utopia*, 38, 187–188.

9. Philip S. Foner, *History of the Labor Movement in the United States*, II (New York: International Publishers, 1955), 81.

10. Ware, *Labor Movement*, 90; Grob, *Workers and Utopia*, 42.

11. *Journal of United Labor*, May 25, 1884, 706 (hereafter cited as *JUL*).

12. Grob, *Workers and Utopia*, 47.

13. Ware, *Labor Movement*, 82, 90; Fine, *Labor and Farmer Parties*, 125–126.

14. Grob, *Workers and Utopia*, 84–85; Ware, *Labor Movement*, 90.

15. C. A. Wright, "Historical Sketch of the Knights of Labor," *Quarterly Journal of Economics* 1 (Jan. 1887), 157–159.

16. Grob, *Workers and Utopia*, 86–87. A brief study of the Knights' local press in 1888 would also overwhelmingly confirm this.

17. Powderly as quoted in Fine, *Labor and Farmer Parties*, 121.

18. Fine, *Labor and Farmer Parties*, 120; *Knights Assembly Proceedings, 1884*, 780.

19. Grob, *Workers and Utopia*, 48–52; *Knights Assembly Proceedings, 1886*, 45–46, 62; *Knights Assembly Proceedings, 1887*, 1566.

20. *JUL*, June 10, 1886, 2090; Ware, *Labor Movement*, 116–154; Grob, *Workers and Utopia*, 48–52.

21. *JUL*, June 10, 1886, 2090.

22. Ware, *Labor Movement*, 117–127.

23. Powderly as quoted in Spero and Harris, *Black Worker*, 474.

24. For details of the Richmond assembly and the reaction it caused, see Terence Vincent Powderly, *Thirty Years of Labor: 1859–1889* (1890: reprint ed., New York: Augustus M. Kelley, Publishers, 1967), 347–353; "Knights of Labor and the Color Line," *Public Opinion* 2 (Oct. 16, 1886), 1.

25. *JUL*, June 11, 1887, 2422; *Fayetteville* (N.C.) *Messenger*, Mar. 16, Apr. 20, 1888; *Raleigh News and Observer*, July 15, 1886.

26. *Fayetteville* (N.C.) *Messenger*, Mar. 30, 1888, Oct. 21, 1887; *Alabama Sentinel* (Birmingham), June 11, 1887; George T. Starnes and John E. Hamm, *Some Phases of Labor Relations in Virginia* (New York: Appleton-Century, 1934), 72–80; Allen W. Moger, "Industrial and Urban Progress in Virginia from 1880 to 1900," *Virginia Magazine of History and Biography* 46 (July 1958), 324–325.

27. Meyers, "Knights of Labor," 479–487.

28. *Knights Assembly Proceedings, 1880*, 203, 209–210; ibid., *1883*, 527.

29. *JUL*, July 10, 1884, 741; *JUL*, Dec. 10, 1883, 605.

30. *Knights Assembly Proceedings, 1884,* 580, 690, 827–831.
31. *JUL,* July 10, 1884, 741; Harry M. Douty, "Early Labor Organizations in North Carolina, 1880–1890," *South Atlantic Quarterly* 34 (July 1935), 263.
32. *JUL,* Jan. 25, 1885, 895.
33. *JUL,* Feb. 25, 1886, 2009; *JUL,* May 7, 1887, 2380.
34. *Knights Assembly Proceedings, 1887,* 1847–1850.
35. *JUL,* Sept. 10, 1883, 560; *JUL,* Dec. 10, 1883, 613.
36. *JUL,* Oct. 10, 1885, 1099–1100; *JUL,* Nov. 10, 1885, 1123; *Knights Assembly Proceedings, 1885,* 219–223.
37. *JUL,* June 10, 1885, 1007; "Minute Book of the Raleigh Knights of Labor, Local Assembly 3606," North Carolina State Department of Archives and History, Raleigh, N.C., 10 (hereafter cited as "Raleigh Knights Minutes").
38. B. Mitchell, *Rise of Mills,* 274; Williamson, "S.C. Cotton Manufacturing," 97–99.
39. Lahne, *Cotton Mill Worker,* 183; Robert R. R. Brooks, "The United Textile Workers of America" (Ph.D. diss., Yale University, 1935), 33–34 (hereafter cited as "UTWA").
40. *Alabama Sentinel* (Birmingham), Jan. 21, May 12, 1888.
41. *JUL,* Dec. 10, 1883, 605; *JUL,* July 10, 1884, 741; *N.C. Labor Report, 1887,* 224.
42. *Raleigh News and Observer,* Nov. 9, 1886.
43. Douty, "Early Labor Organizations," 260–262.
44. Andrew W. Pierpont, "Development of the Textile Industry in Alamance County, North Carolina" (Ph.D. diss., University of North Carolina, 1953), 154 (hereafter cited as "Alamance Textiles"); G. S. Mitchell, *Textile Unionism,* 25.
45. W. A. Fogleman to Terence V. Powderly, Oct. 18, 1886, Letterbox 25, Powderly to Fogleman, Nov. 10, 1886, Letter Press Copy Book 23, 87, Terence V. Powderly Papers, Catholic University Library, Washington, D. C.
46. F. A. Watkins to Powderly, Nov. 24, 1886, Letterbox 26, Powderly Papers; Douty, "Early Labor Organizations," 256.
47. *JUL,* July 10, 1886, 2113; *JUL,* Aug. 10, 1886, 2142; *JUL,* Sept. 10, 1886, 2159; *JUL,* Dec. 10, 1886, 2226.
48. Meyers, "Knights of Labor," 486; Pierpont, "Alamance Textiles," 136; *Greensboro* (N.C.) *Morning News,* Feb. 2, 1887; *JUL,* Dec. 3, 1887, 2556; *JUL,* Mar. 3, 1888, 2588; G. S. Mitchell, *Textile Unionism,* 25.
49. Douty, "Early Labor Organizations," 260–262.
50. Pierpont, "Alamance Textiles," 136, 156.
51. Harley E. Jolley, "The Labor Movement in North Carolina: 1880–1922," *North Carolina Historical Review* 30 (July 1953), 360.
52. *JUL,* June 18, 1887, 2431; *Fayetteville* (N.C.) *Messenger,* Feb. 24, 1888.

53. *JUL*, June 18, 1887, 2431.

54. *Raleigh News and Observer*, Oct. 8, 1886; *Fayetteville* (N.C.) *Messenger*, Nov. 25, 1887, Jan. 6, Mar. 16, 1888.

55. Grob, *Workers and Utopia*, 86–87; Joseph G. Rayback, *A History of American Labor* (New York: The Free Press, 1966), 168–173.

56. *Raleigh News and Observer*, Sept. 12, 1886.

57. Ibid.

58. *JUL*, Apr. 2, 1887, 2339; Jolley, "Labor Movement," 360.

59. For this reason, its reports are invaluable to the student of Southern labor in the late nineteenth and early twentieth centuries. Virginia established a bureau of labor in 1897; other Southern states continued to postpone the task until well into the twentieth century.

60. *N.C. Labor Report, 1887*, 1.

61. *Fayetteville* (N.C.) *Messenger*, Apr. 20, 1888.

62. *JUL*, Feb. 11, 1888, 2576; *JUL*, May 19, 1888, 2632; *Fayetteville* (N.C.) *Messenger*, July 6, Sept. 16, 1888.

63. *Fayetteville* (N.C.) *Messenger*, June 15, Sept. 14, 1888.

64. Ibid., Mar. 16, Nov. 2, 1888; *Raleigh News and Observer*, Nov. 1–6, 1888.

65. *Fayetteville* (N.C.) *Messenger*, June 29, July 13, 1888.

66. Ibid., July 13, Aug. 31, Nov. 2, 1888.

67. Ibid., Sept. 28, Oct. 12, 1888.

68. *Raleigh News and Observer*, Nov. 8, 1888; *Fayetteville* (N.C.) *Messenger*, Nov. 9, 1888.

69. *Raleigh News and Observer*, Nov. 9, 1888; *Fayetteville* (N.C.) *Messenger*, Nov. 9, 1888.

70. *JUL*, Jan. 10, 1886, 1192–1193.

71. *Augusta Chronicle*, Aug. 15, 1886.

72. "Graniteville Minutes," Apr. 22, 1886.

73. Hammett to Dexter Converse, Mar. 30, 1886, Piedmont Letter Book, I, 252, South Caroliniana Library, University of South Carolina, Columbia, S.C. (hereafter cited as PLB); Hammett to Ellison Smyth, Apr. 23, 1886, PLB, I, 289.

74. Hammett to P. A. Montgomery, June 17, 1886, PLB, I, 409.

75. Hammett to William E. McCoy, June 1, Sept. 2, 1886, PLB, I, 415–416; II, 39.

76. *JUL*, May 10, 1886, 2067–2068; *Augusta Chronicle*, Aug. 10, 1886.

77. *Augusta Chronicle*, Aug. 15, 1886.

78. Ibid., July 20, 1886; *Carolina Spartan* (Spartanburg, S.C.), Aug. 4, 1886; Hammett to W. E. McCoy, June 23, 1886, PLB, I, 420.

79. Wallace, "Gregg and Graniteville," 224.

80. Hammett to James F. Iler, Oct. 12, 1886, PLB, II, 118; Hammett to James A. Brice, Oct. 14, 1886, PLB, II, 120.

81. Hammett to Converse, Nov. 18, 1886, PLB, II, 214; *JUL*, Nov. 10, 1886, 2201.

82. T. L. Bowers to Powderly, Oct. 18, 1886, Letterbox 25, Powderly Papers; Hammett to Francis J. Pelzer, Oct. 16, 1886, PLB, II, 126.

83. *JUL,* June 18, 1887, 2431.

84. *Carolina Spartan* (Spartanburg, S.C.), July 13, 1887.

85. *JUL,* Aug. 6, 1887, 2468; *JUL,* Sept. 10, 1887, 2487; *JUL,* Oct. 1, 1887, 2500.

86. *JUL,* Oct. 15, 1887, 2508; *Carolina Spartan* (Spartanburg, S.C.), Sept. 14, 19, 20, 1887.

87. *Fayetteville* (N.C.) *Messenger,* Nov. 18, Dec. 2, 1887.

88. *JUL,* Oct. 15, 1887, 2508; *JUL,* Dec. 3, 1887, 2536.

89. *Knights Assembly Proceedings, 1888,* 50; G. S. Mitchell, *Textile Unionism,* 25; Williamson, "S.C. Cotton Manufacturing," 198.

90. G. S. Mitchell, *Textile Unionism,* 25.

91. Evans, "Labor in Georgia," 24.

92. *Knights Assembly Proceedings, 1887,* 1847–1850.

93. *Augusta Chronicle,* Jan. 8, 1886.

94. *Atlanta Constitution,* Mar. 14, 1886; *JUL,* July 10, 1886, 2112; *Knights Assembly Proceedings, 1886,* 21.

95. Evans, "Labor in Georgia," 83; *Augusta Chronicle,* May 28, 1886; *JUL,* Nov. 10, 1886, 2201.

96. *JUL,* July 23, 1887, 2460; *JUL,* Nov. 10, 1886, 2201; *JUL,* July 10, 1886, 2112–2113.

97. Williamson, "S.C. Cotton Manufacturing," 97–99.

98. Evans, "Labor in Georgia," 83.

99. The manufacturers had not, however, abandoned plans to form a trade association. Prompted by the strike and depression, they again unsuccessfully tried to organize such an association in 1885. See Williamson, "S.C. Cotton Manufacturing," 100–102.

100. Gustavus G. Williamson, Jr., "Southern Cotton Manufacturers in a Year of Decision, 1886" (private manuscript in the author's possession; Dr. Williamson is currently in the Department of History, Virginia Polytechnic Institute, 1–8 (hereafter cited as "Year of Decision").

101. *Augusta Chronicle,* Apr. 1, 1886.

102. Ibid., Apr. 25, 1886.

103. Ibid., Mar. 21, 1886.

104. *Carolina Spartan* (Spartanburg, S.C.), Aug. 4, 1886; Hammett to W. E. McCoy, June 23, 1886, PLB, I, 420.

105. A good account of the 1886 Augusta strike is contained in Williamson, "Year of Decision." Especially good are the descriptions of the events leading to the strike and the account of the strike in its first two months. The following account relies heavily upon this paper, particularly up to mid-July 1886, in addition to the primary sources cited.

106. Meynardie to Powderly, Apr. 13, 1886, Letterbox 19, Powderly Papers.

107. *Augusta Chronicle,* Apr. 21, 25, 27, 1886.

108. Ibid., May 29, June 2, 1886.

109. Ibid., June 2, 6, 1886.

110. Ibid., June 12, 13, 15, 1886.

111. Ibid., June 19–20, 1886; *Charleston News and Courier,* June 18, 1886.

112. *Augusta Chronicle,* July 7–8, 1886; *Charleston News and Courier,* July 8, 1886.

113. *Augusta Chronicle,* July 8–14, 1886; *Charleston News and Courier,* July 8–14, 1886; Powderly to Mullen, July 12, 1886, Letter Press Copy Book 19, 235, Powderly Papers.

114. *Augusta Chronicle,* July 10–17, 1886.

115. Ibid., July 17, 20, 1886.

116. Hammett to W. E. McCoy, June 19, 1886, PLB, I, 415–416.

117. *Augusta Chronicle,* Aug. 8, 1886; Williamson, "Year of Decision," 14.

118. *Augusta Chronicle,* July 20–Aug. 1, 1886; *Charleston News and Courier,* July 21–31, 1886.

119. *Augusta Chronicle,* Aug. 8–12, 1886; Williamson, "Year of Decision," 13–14.

120. Meynardie to Powderly, Aug. 10, 1886, Letterbox 23, Powderly Papers.

121. Mullen to Powderly, Aug. 14, 1886, Letterbox 23, Powderly Papers.

122. *Augusta Chronicle,* Aug. 12–17, 1886; Turner to Powderly, Aug. 14, 1886, and John N. Hayes to Powderly, Aug. 14, 1886, Letterbox 23, Powderly Papers; Powderly to Meynardie, Aug. 13, 1886, Letter Press Copy Book 21, 91, Powderly Papers.

123. *Augusta Chronicle,* Aug. 14–20, 1886; *Charleston News and Courier,* Aug. 15–19, 1886.

124. *Augusta Chronicle,* Aug. 21–Sept. 11, 1886.

125. Hammett to W. E. McCoy, Aug. 14, 1886, PLB, I, 493–495.

126. Hammett to McCoy, Aug. 19, 1886, PLB, II, 5–6.

127. Hammett to McCoy, Sept. 2, 1886, PLB, II, 39.

128. Hammett to McCoy, Sept. 16, 1886, PLB, II, 49.

129. Meynardie to Powderly, Aug. 30, 1886, Letterbox 23, Powderly Papers.

130. *Knights Assembly Proceedings, 1886,* 102–103; *Knights Assembly Proceedings, 1887,* 1566; *Augusta Chronicle,* Sept. 15–Oct. 1, 1886.

131. *Augusta Chronicle,* Oct. 1–12, 1886.

132. Ibid.

133. Ibid., Oct. 1–13, 1886; Meynardie to Powderly, Dec. 12, 1886, Letterbox 26, Powderly Papers.

134. *Augusta Chronicle,* Oct. 12–26, 1886.

135. *Knights Assembly Proceedings, 1886,* 45–46; *Knights Assembly Proceedings, 1887,* 1566; Powderly to Meynardie, Dec. 23, 1886, Letter Press Copy Book 24, 21, Powderly Papers; Williamson, "Year of Decision," 15.

136. *Knights Assembly Proceedings, 1887,* 1412–1414; Powderly to Meynardie, Dec. 23, 1886, Letter Press Copy Book 24, 21, Powderly Papers.

137. *Augusta Chronicle,* Oct. 27–Nov. 8, 1886.

138. *Knights Assembly Proceedings, 1887,* 1413–1414.

139. Meynardie to Powderly, Dec. 12, 1886, Letterbox 26; Powderly to Meynardie, Dec. 23, 1886, Letter Press Copy Book 24, 21, Powderly Papers.

140. Connor to Powderly, Jan. 27, Feb. 4, 1887, Letterbox 29; Powderly to Connor, Feb. 19, 1887, Letterbox 29, Powderly Papers.

141. Mullen to Powderly, Jan. 22, 1887, Letterbox 28, Jan. 29 and Feb. 18, 1887, Letterbox 29; Powderly to Mullen, Jan. 18, 1887, Letter Press Copy Book 27, 3, Jan. 26, 1887, Letter Press Copy Book 27, 63, Powderly Papers.

142. Litchman to Powderly, Feb. 18, 1887, Letterbox 29, Powderly Papers.

143. Powderly to Turner, Feb. 21, 1887, Letter Press Copy Book 27, 255, Powderly Papers.

144. Levi B. Davis to Powderly, Mar. 15, 1887, Letterbox 30, Powderly Papers.

145. Evans, "Labor in Georgia," 410–412.

146. G. S. Mitchell, *Textile Unionism,* 25.

147. W. J. Benning and R. M. Sasser to Powderly, Aug. 12, 1886, Letterbox 23, Powderly Papers.

148. Powderly to Sasser, Aug. 16, 1886, Letter Press Copy Book 21, 108, Powderly Papers.

149. *Alabama Sentinel* (Birmingham), July 2, 1887; W. J. Benning to Powderly, Oct. 9, 1886, Letterbox 24, Powderly Papers.

150. *Alabama Sentinel* (Birmingham), Jan. 21, Feb. 11, May 12, 19, Oct. 6, 1888.

151. *JUL,* Aug. 16, 1888, 2687.

152. Hammett to Converse, Nov. 18, 1886, PLB, II, 214; W. E. Woodward, *Gift of Life,* 71–73.

153. Any number of such cases can be found in the Knights' national paper. For examples in textile assemblies, see *JUL* Sept. 10, 1886, 2162; *JUL,* Apr. 16, 1887, 2357.

154. *JUL,* May 26, 1888, 2336. This attitude can also be seen clearly in Robert R. Jackaway, *The Great Labor Question, or the Noble Mission of the Knights of Labor* (Savannah, Ga.: Press of Savannah Times Publishing, 1886).

155. *JUL,* Apr. 21, 1888, 2616.

156. While reading the correspondence to Powderly from all types of assemblies, I was struck by the almost worshipful attitude toward him expressed by Southern Knights. They believed Powderly and the national order had almost supernatural powers over capital, and they viewed Powderly as a deliverer or savior.

CHAPTER 5

1. For a contrary view of Populism, see Norman Pollack, *The Populist Response to Industrial America, Midwestern Populist Thought* (New York: W. W. Norton, 1966), especially the Introduction. Pollack acknowledged his omission of Southern sources, and maintained that by concentrating on midwestern Populism, one finds "a more crystallized form of the relation between industrialism and agrarian radicalism than might otherwise be possible." In view of the Southern Populist response to industrialism, a study of the entire Populist movement might change some of his conclusions.

2. Simpkins, *Pitchfork Ben Tillman*, 222.

3. Benjamin R. Tillman, "Introductory Address," *Laying of the Corner Stone of the Winthrop Normal and Industrial College of South Carolina at Rock Hill, S.C., May 12, 1894* (Lancaster, S.C.: Enterprise Publishing, 1894), 23.

4. Stuart Noblin, *Leonidas LaFayette Polk: Agrarian Crusader* (Chapel Hill: University of North Carolina Press, 1949), 266.

5. See chap. 3, this volume.

6. *JUL*, Aug. 2, 1888, 2676.

7. Orr to Robert McCaughrin, Sept. 29, 1892, as quoted in Gustavus G. Williamson, "South Carolina Cotton Mills and the Tillman Movement," *Proceedings of the South Carolina Historical Association, 1949*, 44.

8. *Columbia* (S.C.) *State,* Apr. 19, 1892; *Carolina Spartan* (Spartanburg, S.C.), Aug. 17, 1892.

9. Williamson, "South Carolina Cotton Mills," 44–47.

10. Noblin, *Leonidas Polk,* 73–147.

11. J. S. Ragsdale to Thomas Settle, Jan. 26, 1895, Thomas Settle Papers, Southern Historical Collection, University of North Carolina, Chapel Hill, N.C.

12. Williamson, "South Carolina Cotton Mills," 39–43.

13. C. Vann Woodward, *Tom Watson, Agrarian Rebel* (New York: Oxford University Press, 1963), 162–164.

14. Ibid., 270–271.

15. Williamson, "South Carolina Cotton Mills," 37–39.

16. *Columbia* (S.C.) *State,* Apr. 19, 1892; *Carolina Spartan* (Spartanburg, S.C.), Aug. 17, 1892.

17. Orr to Robert L. McCaughrin, Sept. 29, 1892, as quoted in Williamson, "South Carolina Cotton Mills," 42.

18. Williamson, "South Carolina Cotton Mills," 39–43.

19. *Columbia* (S.C.) *State,* Dec. 15, 1892.

20. Davidson, *Child Labor Legislation,* 107–109; Hugh T. Lefler and Albert T. Newsome, *North Carolina: The History of a Southern State* (Chapel Hill: University of North Carolina Press, 1954), 513–517.

21. *Columbia* (S.C.) *State*, Dec. 15, 1892; Davidson, *Child Labor Legislation*, 73.

22. James C. Bonner, "The Alliance Legislature of 1890," *Studies in Georgia History and Government*, ed. James C. Bonner and Lucien E. Roberts (Athens: University of Georgia Press, 1954), 513–517.

23. Alex M. Arnett, *The Populist Movement in Georgia* (New York: Longmans, Green, 1922), 114; C. V. Woodward, *Tom Watson*, 241–242.

24. Arnett, *Populist Movement in Georgia*, 154; C. V. Woodward, *Tom Watson*, 269–271.

25. As quoted in Grob, *Workers and Utopia*, 191.

26. Gompers' labor philosophy can be studied in two volumes of his speeches and writings, both edited by Hayes Robbins—*Labor and the General Welfare* (New York: E. P. Dutton, 1919) and *Labor and the Employer* (New York: E. P. Dutton, 1920).

27. A survey of the *American Federationist* revealed no evidence of AFL or NUTW activity in the South prior to 1895. See also Lahne, *Cotton Mill Worker*, 185.

28. Grob, *Workers and Utopia*, 179.

29. Samuel Gompers, *Seventy Years of Life and Labor: An Autobiography*, 2 vols. (New York: E. P. Dutton, 1925) 1: 418–419.

30. American Federation of Labor, *Proceedings of the Annual Convention, 1895,* 74 (hereafter cited as *AFL Convention Proceedings);* Herbert J. Lahne, "Labor in the Cotton Mill: 1865–1900" (Master's thesis, Columbia University, 1934), 181.

31. Gompers, *Seventy Years,* 1: 418–419; Fred Ester of Columbus was the second organizer, according to Lahne, "Labor in the Mill," 181. This does not tally with reports from Winn, who began organizational work early in 1896.

32. "Cotton Mills of the South," *Tradesman* 33 (Apr. 15, 1895), 61–72; Edward Porritt, "The Cotton Mills in the South," *New England Magazine* 12 (July 1895), 575–576.

33. As quoted in the *Columbus* (Ga.) *Herald*, Jan. 2, 1898; see also *Columbus* (Ga.) *Enquirer-Sun*, Dec. 17, 1897, Apr. 5, June 6, 1898; *Columbia* (S.C.) *State*, Dec. 20–22, 1897; George Gunton, "The South's Labor System," *Gunton's Magazine* 18 (Mar. 1900), 234–239.

34. *AFL Convention Proceedings, 1897,* 55; *AFL Convention Proceedings, 1898,* 18–19; *AFL Convention Proceedings, 1900,* 141.

35. *Columbus* (Ga.) *Herald,* Dec. 10, 1899.

36. *Columbus* (Ga.) *Enquirer-Sun,* Mar. 1, 1896; Ray Ginger, *The Bending Cross: A Biography of Eugene Victor Debs* (New Brunswick, N. J.: Rutgers University Press, 1949), 190–192; McAlister Coleman, *Eugene V. Debs: A Man Unafraid* (New York: Greenberg Publisher, 1930), 179–184.

37. *Columbus* (Ga.) *Enquirer-Sun,* Mar. 28–Apr. 1, 1896.

38. Ibid., Apr. 1–4, 1896.

39. Ibid., Apr. 5–May 5, 1896.

40. Ibid., May 6–14, 1896.

41. Ibid., May 17, 1896.

42. *Columbus* (Ga.) *Herald,* Sept. 4, 1898; Nov. 19, 1899.

43. "Organizers Report," *American Federationist* 3 (Aug. 1896), 130.

44. Lahne, "Labor in the Mill," 181; Williamson, "S.C. Cotton Manufacturing," 204.

45. The Bigby incident is one of the few cases of outright corruption in the Southern mills. For a detailed account of the legal battles which it engendered, see the *Columbus* (Ga.) *Enquirer-Sun,* June 14–Oct. 14, 1896; Dec. 24–29, 1896; Dec. 10, 1897; June 8, 1898.

46. Brooks, "UTWA," 37; Lahne, *Cotton Mill Worker,* 184.

47. Gompers, *Seventy Years,* 1: 418–419.

48. Ibid.; U.S. Industrial Commission, *Labor Organizations, Labor Disputes, and Arbitration, and on Railway Labor,* vol. 17 (Washington, D.C.: Government Printing Office, 1901), 76 (hereafter cited as U.S. Industrial Commission, *Reports, Labor Organizations).*

49. Lahne, *Cotton Mill Worker,* 181–182.

50. Gompers, *Seventy Years,* 1: 418–419; "Textile Workers' Convention," *American Federationist* 4 (July 1897), 93.

51. *Columbus* (Ga.) *Herald,* Apr. 3, 1899. George Mitchell mistakenly claimed that Greene came to power in 1898. Both Brooks and Lahne accepted Mitchell's account of Greene's rise, but both also spoke of a strike in Columbus in 1898 that propelled Greene to the forefront. Both gave Mitchell as a source, but Mitchell did not mention an 1898 Columbus strike, although one must read him very carefully to discover this. Rather, he cited the 1898 Augusta wage cuts as the reason for Greene's success. Unless the local press completely failed to cover an 1898 Columbus strike, there was none. There was a wage cut in Augusta in 1898, but by this time Greene had been acting president of the NUTW for over a year. See G. S. Mitchell, *Textile Unionism,* 26–27; Lahne, *Cotton Mill Worker,* 184–185; Brooks, "UTWA," 39–49.

52. The last serious threat from the Socialists in the South came in July and August 1897. See the *Atlanta Constitution,* July 7, 25, Aug. 4–6, 1897.

53. U.S. Industrial Commission, *Reports, Labor Organizations,* 76; *AFL Convention Proceedings, 1897,* 55.

54. *Atlanta Constitution,* Aug. 5–6, 1897.

55. Ibid., Sept. 1897.

56. "Notes and Doings," *American Federationist* 4 (Oct. 1897), 197–198.

57. *Atlanta Constitution,* Dec. 7–12, 1897.

58. *AFL Convention Proceedings, 1897,* 69–70; Philip Taft, *AFL in the Time of Gompers* (New York: Harper Bros., 1957), 131.

59. *Atlanta Constitution,* Dec. 21, 1897.

60. Evans, "Labor in Georgia," 86–87.

61. *NUTW Convention Proceedings, 1900,* 29. Because the NUTW

had acquired Canadian affiliates, at the 1900 convention it changed its name to the International Union of Textile Workers (IUTW). However, the union will be referred to as the NUTW throughout the remainder of this work.

62. *NUTW Convention Proceedings, 1900,* 33.

63. *AFL Convention Proceedings, 1900,* 11; "Special Organizers for the South," *American Federationist* 6 (Apr. 1899), 31.

64. *Columbus* (Ga.) *Herald,* Apr. 3, 1899; Brooks, "UTWA," 38–39; Lahne, *Cotton Mill Worker,* 184–185.

65. *AFL Convention Proceedings, 1899,* 56.

66. "Textiles Return Thanks," *American Federationist* 6 (July 1899), 115–116.

67. *NUTW Convention Proceedings, 1900,* 4, 34.

68. Prince W. Greene, "Organizing the South," *American Federationist* 6 (June 1899), 77.

69. "What Our Organizers Are Doing," *American Federationist* 6 (June 1899), 89; "Southern Organization," ibid. (May 1899), 61–66; "The New South," ibid. (May 1899), 57–59; "What Our Organizers Are Doing," ibid. (Nov. 1899), 223–229; *Rock Hill* (S.C.) *Herald,* June 27, 1900; Evans, "Labor in Georgia," 96; *NUTW Convention Proceedings, 1900,* 18–19; Dowd, "Strikes and Lockouts," 136–140.

70. *NUTW Convention Proceedings, 1900,* 10–11.

71. *N.C. Labor Report, 1901,* 388–391.

72. *Columbus* (Ga.) *Herald,* May 28, 1899; G. S. Mitchell, *Textile Unionism,* 26.

73. Evans, "Labor in Georgia," 96–97.

74. G. S. Mitchell, *Textile Unionism,* 26.

75. *NUTW Convention Proceedings, 1900,* 18–19.

76. George Mitchell says that the Southern NUTW membership was never much above 4,000, although he admits that "a much larger number than this passed through the union," G. S. Mitchell, *Textile Unionism,* 27. Lahne accepts Mitchell's figure of 4,000 Southern members at any given time, Lahne, *Cotton Mill Worker,* 185.

77. *U.S. Census, 1900, Manufacturing,* 56–57.

78. *NUTW Convention Proceedings, 1900,* 23; *Salisbury* (N.C.) *Truth Index,* June 18, 1901.

79. *Columbus* (Ga.) *Herald,* Feb. 19, 1899.

80. Ibid., Jan. 15, Apr. 16, July 9, 1899.

81. "Minutes of a Meeting of Cotton Mill Owners and Managers in Greensboro, N.C., January 16, 1901," Southern Historical Collection, University of North Carolina, Chapel Hill, N.C.; "Subterfuge and Greed in North Carolina," *American Federationist* 8 (May 1901), 163–164; Davidson, *Child Labor Legislation,* 114–116.

82. For a thorough discussion of the role of organized labor in the early fight for child labor laws in the South, see Davidson, *Child Labor Legislation,* chaps. 1–5. The work contains an excellent bibliography.

However, it must be noted that Davidson mistakenly credits the UTWA, not the NUTW, with early efforts in this area (see page 95).

83. "What Our Organizers Are Doing," *American Federationist* 6 (Oct. 1899), 119.

84. *Columbus* (Ga.) *Herald,* Sept. 24, 1899.

85. *Columbia* (S.C.) *State,* Nov. 22, 1898; *Raleigh News and Observer,* July 14, 1900; Williamson, "S.C. Cotton Manufacturing," 204.

86. As quoted in the *Raleigh News and Observer,* July 14, 1900. The grandfather clause was tacked on to bills making literacy a requirement for the franchise. However, persons who were direct lineal descendents of voters registered prior to the ratification of the Fourteenth Amendment were allowed to vote, even if illiterate. Few Negroes claimed such forebears, although many could have certainly met the clause's requirements.

87. *Raleigh News and Observer,* July 14, 1900; *Salisbury* (N.C.) *Truth Index,* July 17, 1900; Williamson, "S.C. Cotton Manufacturing," 204.

88. *Salisbury* (N.C.) *Truth Index,* June 18, 1901.

89. *AFL Convention Proceedings, 1900,* 110.

90. "What Our Organizers Are Doing" (May 1899), 61–63; "The New South," 57–59; Greene, "Organizing the South," 77.

91. "The New South," 57–59.

92. *Augusta Chronicle,* Oct. 24–Nov. 20, 1898; U.S. Industrial Commission, *Reports, Labor and Capital,* 564–565.

93. *Augusta Chronicle,* Nov. 20, 1898.

94. Ibid., Nov. 20–Dec. 31, 1898; *Columbia* (S.C.) *State,* Nov. 25–27, 1898.

95. *Augusta Chronicle,* Jan. 1–21, 1899.

96. Ibid., Jan. 19–28, 1899; U.S. Industrial Commission, *Reports, Labor and Capital,* 564–565.

97. U.S. Industrial Commission, *Reports, Labor and Capital,* 573.

98. *Columbus* (Ga.) *Enquirer-Sun,* Oct. 15, 1899; *Columbus* (Ga.) *Herald,* Dec. 17, 1899; *NUTW Convention Proceedings, 1900,* 7–8.

99. Evans, "Labor in Georgia," 88–89.

100. *NUTW Convention Proceedings, 1900,* 23–27.

101. Greene, "Organizing the South," 77; "The New South," 57–59; "What Our Organizers Are Doing," 223–229; ibid. (Oct. 1899), 201–202.

102. *NUTW Convention Proceedings, 1900,* 22, 29–31, 7–11.

CHAPTER 6

1. Davis, "Cotton Manufacturers and the Far East," 49. The Boxer Rebellion, an uprising of nationalistic Chinese against "foreign devils," was crushed by the combined military forces of several western nations,

including the United States. Beginning in the spring of 1900, the up-rising was not effectively curbed until late summer. During the revolt trade relations between China and the West were severely disrupted.

2. In 1903 the SCSA became the American Cotton Manufacturers Association (ACMA).

3. *Raleigh News and Observer,* May 11, 1900.

4. Although records exist for all the meetings of the SCSA at the ACMA offices in Charlotte, they are not available to scholars. This is extremely unfortunate, for they would, perhaps, shed considerable light on management's efforts to crush the NUTW. However, one year's records, *Certificate of Incorporation, By Laws and Proceedings of the Southern Cotton Spinners Association* (Raleigh, N.C.: Edwards and Broughton, Printers and Binders, 1903), was found in the North Carolina Room of the University of North Carolina Library, Chapel Hill, N.C.

5. *Columbus* (Ga.) *Herald,* May 12, 1900.

6. For a full account of the merger, see chap. 7, this volume.

7. Dowd, "Strikes and Lockouts," 136–137; Lahne, *Cotton Mill Worker,* 186–187.

8. Dowd, "Strikes and Lockouts," 136–138.

9. Ibid.

10. Ibid.; *NUTW Convention Proceedings, 1900,* 29.

11. Dowd, "Strikes and Lockouts," 137–138.

12. Ibid.; *N.C. Labor Report, 1901,* 416.

13. *Columbus* (Ga.) *Enquirer-Sun,* Aug. 22, 1900; Dowd, "Strikes and Lockouts," 136–138; Thompson, *From the Cotton Field,* 192.

14. Dowd, "Strikes and Lockouts," 136.

15. W. H. Winn to Samuel Gompers, June 12, 1900, as quoted in Davidson, *Child Labor Legislation,* 113.

16. G. S. Mitchell, *Textile Unionism,* 28; Lahne, *Cotton Mill Worker,* 187.

17. U.S. Industrial Commission, *Reports, Labor and Capital,* 497.

18. *Raleigh News and Observer,* Oct. 5, 1900; *N.C. Labor Report, 1901,* 230–232; Dowd, "Strikes and Lockouts," 138–139.

19. *Columbus* (Ga.) *Enquirer-Sun,* Aug. 22, 1900; *Rock Hill* (S.C.) *Herald,* Nov. 28, 1900.

20. Dowd, "Strikes and Lockouts," 138–139.

21. *Raleigh News and Observer,* Oct. 5, 1900.

22. Dowd, "Strikes and Lockouts," 138–139.

23. *Raleigh News and Observer,* Oct. 5, 1900.

24. Ibid., Oct. 5–18, 1900.

25. Ibid., Oct. 18–20, 1900.

26. Ibid., Oct. 20–31, 1900.

27. Ibid., Oct. 31, 1900; *NUTW Convention Proceedings, 1901,* 32–34.

28. Some moved to Columbus, Georgia, the NUTW's Southern head-quarters. Graham Clark to Walter Clark, Sept. 24, 1901, Walter Clark

Papers, Southern Historical Collection, University of North Carolina, Chapel Hill, N.C.

29. *Raleigh News and Observer,* Nov. 1–21, 1900.

30. Ibid., Nov. 21–28, 1900; *Rock Hill* (S.C.) *Herald,* Nov. 28, 1900.

31. Smith, *Mill on the Dan,* 51–52.

32. Ibid.

33. *NUTW Convention Proceedings, 1901,* 12–13; Smith, *Mill on the Dan,* 51–52.

34. "The Awakening of the South," *American Federationist* 8 (May 1901), 167; *NUTW Convention Proceedings, 1901,* 41–46.

35. "The Awakening of the South," 167–169; *NUTW Convention Proceedings, 1901,* 41–46.

36. *NUTW Convention Proceedings, 1901,* 41–49.

37. Ibid.

38. *NUTW Convention Proceedings, 1901,* 41–50, 60; M. S. Belk, "New Unions in Virginia," *American Federationist* 8 (July 1901), 244.

39. *NUTW Convention Proceedings, 1901,* 41–50, 60; *AFL Convention Proceedings, 1901,* 12; Belk, "New Unions in Virginia," 244.

40. *Raleigh News and Observer,* Apr. 21, 1901.

41. Ibid., Apr. 6–27, 1901.

42. *Rock Hill* (S.C.) *Herald,* Apr. 10–17, 1901.

43. *Raleigh News and Observer,* Apr. 23, 1901; *AFL Convention Proceedings, 1901,* 14.

44. Belk, "New Unions in Virginia," 244; *AFL Convention Proceedings, 1901,* 14; Smith, *Mill on the Dan,* 52–53.

45. Belk, "New Unions in Virginia," 244.

46. *NUTW Convention Proceedings, 1900,* 17–18, 30, 32.

47. Ibid., 8–9; *Columbia* (S.C.) *State,* Jan. 24, 1901.

48. *NUTW Convention Proceedings, 1900,* 30; *Columbia* (S.C.) *State,* Jan. 24, 1901.

49. *Columbia* (S.C.) *State,* June 23, Sept. 4, 1900.

50. Ibid., Sept. 4, 1900.

51. Ibid., Aug. 30, 1901.

52. "Gramby Minutes," Mar. 1, 1901, Book I, May 30, 1895–Nov. 13, 1903 (in the possession of the South Carolina Electric and Gas Company, Columbia, South Carolina).

53. *Columbia* (S.C.) *State,* Aug. 25–27, 1901.

54. Ibid.

55. Ibid., Aug. 27, 1901.

56. Ibid., Aug. 27–28, 1901; *Rock Hill* (S.C.) *Herald,* Aug. 31, 1901.

57. *Columbia* (S.C.) *State,* Aug. 27–29, 1901.

58. Ibid., Aug. 28–Sept. 2, 1901.

59. Ibid.; *Rock Hill* (S.C.) *Herald,* Aug. 31, 1901.

60. *Columbia* (S.C.) *State,* Aug. 29, 1901.

61. Ibid., Sept. 2–4, 1901; "Minutes of the Meetings of the Stockholders and Board of Directors of Richland Mills," Sept. 3, 1901 (pri-

vate manuscript in the possession of the South Carolina Electric and Gas Company, Columbia, South Carolina).

62. *Columbia* (S.C.) *State,* Sept. 6, 1901; Fenelon De Vere Smith, "The Economic Development of the Textile Industry in Columbia, South Carolina, Area from 1790 through 1916" (Ph.D. diss., University of Kentucky, 1952), 191–192.

63. *Columbia* (S.C.) *State,* Sept. 2, Jan. 29, 1902.

64. Ibid., Sept. 5–6, 1901; *Rock Hill* (S.C.) *Herald,* Sept. 7, 1901.

65. *AFL Convention Proceedings, 1901,* 52.

66. *N.C. Labor Report, 1901,* 230–232, 407–425; "What Our Organizers Are Doing," *American Federationist* 8 (Nov. 1901), 483–495.

67. *N.C. Labor Report, 1901,* 414.

68. "What Our Organizers Are Doing" (Dec. 1901), 566–574.

69. Ibid. (Sept. 1901), 367–389.

70. *Raleigh News and Observer,* Apr. 21, 1901.

71. *N.C. Labor Report, 1901,* 416.

CHAPTER 7

1. *AFL Convention Proceedings, 1898,* 16, 99.

2. *NUTW Convention Proceedings, 1900,* 15–16; U.S. Industrial Commission, *Reports, Labor Organizations,* 76–77; Lahne, *Cotton Mill Worker,* 186.

3. *AFL Convention Proceedings, 1899,* 109.

4. *NUTW Convention Proceedings, 1900,* 15–17, 35; *Columbus* (Ga.) *Herald,* May 12, 1900.

5. *NUTW Convention Proceedings, 1901,* 66–75; Brooks, "UTWA," 48–49; Lahne, *Cotton Mill Worker,* 185–186.

6. *NUTW Convention Proceedings, 1901,* 101–102.

7. James Duncan, "Textile Workers Conference at Boston," *American Federationist* 8 (June 1901), 203–205.

8. Ibid.

9. Ibid.

10. *Columbia* (S.C.) *State,* Aug. 20, 1901.

11. James Duncan, "Textile Workers' Amalgamation," *American Federationist* 8 (Oct. 1901), 410.

12. Brooks, "UTWA," 84–86, 117–119.

13. *AFL Convention Proceedings, 1901,* 14.

14. Brooks, "UTWA," 82.

15. Ibid., 128.

16. Young, *American Cotton Industry,* 78–80.

17. Brooks, "UTWA," 82.

18. *Augusta Chronicle,* Mar. 9–30, 1902; *AFL Convention Proceedings, 1902,* 38; Evans, "Labor in Georgia," 84.

19. *Augusta Chronicle,* Mar. 18–Apr. 7, 1902.
20. Ibid.
21. Ibid., Apr. 8–May 14, 1902.
22. Ibid., May 15, 1902.
23. Ibid., May 14–22, 1902.
24. Ibid., May 21–26, 1902.
25. Young, *American Cotton Industry,* 84–86.
26. *New York Times,* Aug. 7, 1902, 2.
27. Lahne, *Cotton Mill Worker,* 190.
28. Thompson, *From the Cotton Field,* 194–199; G. S. Mitchell, *Textile Unionism,* 27; Lahne, *Cotton Mill Worker,* 190.
29. *UTWA Convention Proceedings, 1903,* 33–34; Young, *American Cotton Industry,* 86.
30. Albert Hibbert, "Trade Union History, United Textile Workers," *American Federationist* 9 (Dec. 1902), 873–875.
31. Brooks, "UTWA," 133–134.
32. *AFL Convention Proceedings, 1902,* 17, 218.
33. *AFL Convention Proceedings, 1903,* 54.
34. *UTWA Convention Proceedings, 1903,* 44–48.
35. Ibid.
36. Ibid., 48, 34–35.
37. Ibid.
38. Ibid., 30.
39. Ibid., 2; Thompson, *From the Cotton Field,* 194–199; Lahne, *Cotton Mill Worker,* 190.
40. *UTWA Convention Proceedings, 1903,* 30; ibid., *1905,* 25–26, 34.

Bibliography

Unpublished Primary Sources

PRIVATE PAPERS

CLARK, WALTER. Private Papers. 1783–1920. 8,000 Items. North Carolina Department of Archives and History, Raleigh, N.C.

MONTGOMERY, JOHN HENRY. Private Papers. 1899–1901. South Caroliniana Library, University of South Carolina, Columbia, S.C., Microfilm.

Patterson Papers. 1765–1926. 1,150 Items. North Carolina Department of Archives and History, Raleigh, N.C.

POWDERLY, TERENCE VINCENT. Private Papers. 1871–1924. 193 Boxes and 50 Letter Press Copy Books. Department of Archives and Manuscripts, Catholic University, Washington, D.C.

SETTLE, THOMAS. Private Papers. 1850–1898. 10 Boxes. Southern Historical Collection, University of North Carolina, Chapel Hill, N.C.

TOMPKINS, DANIEL AUGUSTUS. Private Papers. 1838–1919. 30,000 Items. Southern Historical Collection, University of North Carolina, Chapel Hill, N.C.

241

MILL RECORDS, LETTER BOOKS, MISCELLANEOUS

Granby Cotton Mills. "Minutes of the Meetings of the Board of Directors and Stockholders, May 30, 1895–November 13, 1903." South Carolina Electric and Gas Company, Columbia, S.C.

Graniteville Manufacturing Company. "Minutes of the Board of Directors and Stockholders Meetings, October 30, 1852–October 30, 1918." William Gregg Foundation, Graniteville, S.C.

J. M. O'Dell Manufacturing Company. Chatham County Miscellaneous Books, vol. 19, June 1898–June 1900. Southern Historical Collection, University of North Carolina, Chapel Hill, N.C.

"Minute Book of the Raleigh Assembly of the Knights of Labor: 1886–1890." North Carolina Department of Archives and History, Raleigh, N.C.

"Minutes of a Meeting of Cotton Mill Owners and Managers in Greensboro, N.C., January 16, 1901." Southern Historical Collection, University of North Carolina, Chapel Hill, N.C.

Morgan-Malloy Mill. Correspondence. Duke University, Durham, N.C.

Olympia Cotton Mills. "Minute Book of the Meetings of the Board of Directors, August 4, 1899–November 24, 1911." South Carolina Electric and Gas Company, Columbia, S.C.

———. "Minute Book of the Meetings of the Stockholders, May 16, 1899–May 12, 1912." South Carolina Electric and Gas Company, Columbia, S.C.

Piedmont Manufacturing Company. Letter Books: 1886–1899. South Caroliniana Library, University of South Carolina, Columbia, S.C.

———. "Minute Book of the Stockholders and the Board of Directors Annual Meeting, Piedmont Mills, 1873–1933." South Caroliniana Library, University of South Carolina, Columbia, S.C.

Richland Cotton Mills. "Minutes of the Meetings of the Board of Directors and Stockholders, January 17, 1895–May 22, 1912." South Carolina Electric and Gas Company, Columbia, S.C.

Published Primary Sources

ARTICLES

BALDWIN, JESSE A. "Evils of Southern Factory Life." *Gunton's Magazine* 22 (April 1902), 326–37.

BELK, M. S. "New Unions in Virginia." *American Federationist* 8 (July 1901), 244.

"Cotton Mills of the South." *Tradesman* 33 (April 1895), 61–72.

DE GRAFFENRIED, CLARE. "The Georgia Cracker in the Cotton Mill." *Century Magazine* 41 (February 1891), 483–98.

DOWD, JEROME. "Colored Men as Cotton Manufacturers." *Gunton's Magazine* 23 (September 1902), 254–56.

———. "Strikes and Lockouts in North Carolina." *Gunton's Magazine* 20 (February 1901), 136–40.

ELLIS, LEONORA BECK. "A Model Factory Town." *Forum* 32 (September 1901), 60–65.

———. "A New Class of Labor in the South." *Forum* 31 (May 1901), 306–10.

———. "A Study of Southern Cotton Mill Communities." *American Journal of Sociology* 8 (March 1903), 623–30.

GOMPERS, SAMUEL. "Organized Labor's Attitude Toward Child Labor." *Annals of the American Academy of Political and Social Science* 27 (March 1906), 337–41.

GUNTON, GEORGE. "The South's Labor System." *Gunton's Magazine* 18 (March 1900), 234–39.

———. "What Can Be Done about It." *Gunton's Magazine* 18 (February 1900), 112–30.

"Knights of Labor and the Color Line." *Public Opinion* 2 (October 16, 1886), 1–5.

MCLAURIN, JOHN LOWNDES. "The Commercial Democracy of the South." *North American Review* 173 (November 1901), 657–62.

ORR, JAMES L. "The Negro in the Mills." *Independent* 53 (April 11, 1901), 845–46.

PORRITT, EDWARD. "The Cotton Mills in the South." *New England Magazine* 12 (July 1895), 575–86.

SPAHR, CHARLES B. "The New England Factory Towns of the South." *Outlook* 61 (March 4, 1899), 510–17.

TOMPKINS, DANIEL A. "The Future of Cotton Manufacturing in the South." *Transactions of the New England Cotton Manufacturers' Annual Meeting, April 29–30, 1896, Boston, Massachusetts.* Waltham, Mass.: Press of E. L. Barry, 1896, 243–44.

WRIGHT, CARROL D. "An Historical Sketch of the Knights of Labor." *Quarterly Journal of Economics* 1 (January 1887), 137–67.

BOOKS

AYER, HARTWELL M., ed. *The Resources and Manufacturing Industries of the State of South Carolina: Mountains to the Seaboard.* Charleston, S.C.: Lucas and Richardson Company, 1895.

GOMPERS, SAMUEL. *Labor and the General Welfare.* Edited by Hayes Robbins. New York: E. P. Dutton and Company, 1919.

———. *Labor and the Employer.* Edited by Hayes Robbins. New York: E. P. Dutton and Company, 1920.

———. *Seventy Years of Life and Labor: An Autobiography.* 2 vols. New York: E. P. Dutton and Company, 1925.

JACKAWAY, ROBERT R. *The Great Labor Question, or the Noble Mission of the Knights of Labor.* Savannah, Ga.: Savannah Times Publishing Company, 1886.

KOHN, AUGUST. *The Cotton Mills of South Carolina.* Charleston, S.C.: Daggett Press Company, 1907.

MURPHY, EDGAR GARDNER. *Problems of the Present South.* New York: Macmillan Company, 1904.

POWDERLY, TERENCE VINCENT. *The Path I Trod: An Autobiography.* Edited by Harry J. Carman. New York: Columbia University Press, 1940.

———. *Thirty Years of Labor: 1859–1889.* New York: Augustus M. Kelley, Publishers, 1967. Reprint of 1890 edition.

TILLMAN, BENJAMIN RYAN. "Introductory Address." *Laying of the Corner Stone of the Winthrop Normal and Industrial College of South Carolina at Rock Hill, S.C., May 12, 1894.* Lancaster, S.C.: Enterprise Publishing Company, 1894, 14–28.

TOMPKINS, DANIEL AUGUSTUS. *Cotton Mill, Commercial Features:*

A Text Book for the Use of Textile Schools and Investors. Charlotte, N.C.: By the author, 1899.

———. *Cotton Mill Process and Calculations.* Charlotte, N.C.: By the author, 1899.

———. *Labor and Legislation.* Charlotte, N.C.: By the author, 1905.

———. *The Cultivation, Picking, Bailing and Manufacturing of Cotton, from the Southern Standpoint.* By the author, 1895.

UTTLEY, T. W. *Cotton Spinning and Manufacturing in the United States of America.* Manchester, Eng.: Manchester University Press, 1905.

VAN VORST, MRS. JOHN AND VAN VORST, MARIE. *The Woman Who Toils: Being the Experiences of Two Ladies as Factory Girls.* New York: Doubleday, Page and Company, 1903.

WOODWARD, WILLIAM E. *The Gift of Life: An Autobiography.* New York: E. P. Dutton and Company, 1947.

———. *The Way Our People Lived: An Intimate American History.* New York: E. P. Dutton and Company, 1944.

YOUNG, THOMAS M. *The American Cotton Industry.* New York: Charles Scribner's Sons, 1903.

GOVERNMENT DOCUMENTS

Journal of the House of Representatives of the General Assembly of the State of South Carolina, 1901. Columbia: The State Printing Company, State Printers, 1901.

North Carolina Bureau of Labor and Printing. *Annual Reports: 1887–1905.* State Printer, 1887–1905.

South Carolina Department of Agriculture, Commerce, and Industries. *The Cotton Mills of South Carolina, Their Names, Location, Capacity, and History.* Charleston, S.C.: News and Courier Book Presses, 1880.

South Carolina State Board of Agriculture. *South Carolina Resources and Population, Institutions and Industries.* Charleston, S.C.: Walker, Evans and Capwell, Printers, 1883.

U.S. Bureau of Labor. *Annual Reports of the Commissioner of*

Labor, 1888–1905. Washington, D.C.: Government Printing Office, 1888–1905.

————. *Report on Conditions of Woman and Child Wage-Earners in the United States.* 19 vols. Washington, D.C.: Government Printing Office, 1910.

U.S. Bureau of Labor Statistics. *History of Wages in the United States from Colonial Times to 1928.* Bulletin No. 499. Washington, D.C.: Government Printing Office, 1929.

U.S. Bureau of the Census. *Ninth Census of the United States: 1870. The Statistics of the Wealth and Industry of the United States,* vol. 3. Washington, D.C.: Government Printing Office, 1872.

————. *Tenth Census of the United States: 1880. Report on the Manufacturers of the United States,* vol. 2. Washington, D.C.: Government Printing Office, 1883.

————. *Eleventh Census of the United States: 1890. Report on Manufacturing Industries in the United States,* pt. 3. *Selected Industries.* Washington, D.C.: Government Printing Office, 1895.

————. *Twelfth Census of the United States: 1900. Manufacturing,* vol. 9. *Special Reports on Selected Industries.* Washington, D.C.: Government Printing Office, 1902.

————. *Census of Manufactures: 1905,* pt. 2. *States and Territories.* Washington, D.C.: Government Printing Office, 1907.

————. *Census of Manufactures: 1905,* pt. 3. *Special Reports on Selected Industries.* Washington, D.C.: Government Printing Office, 1908.

U.S. Industrial Commission. *Reports.* 19 vols. Washington, D.C.: Government Printing Office, 1900–1902.

PROCEEDINGS

American Federation of Labor. *Proceedings of the Annual Convention, 1895–1903.* Washington, D.C.: American Federation of Labor, 1895–1903.

International Union of Textile Workers. *Proceedings of the Annual Convention, 1900–1901.*

Knights of Labor. *Records of the Proceedings of the General Assembly, 1883–1889.*

Southern Commercial Congress. *Proceedings, Third Annual Convention, 1911.*

Southern Cotton Spinners Association. *Certificate of Incorporation, By-Laws and Proceedings of the Seventh Annual Convention of the Southern Cotton Spinners Association, 1903.* Raleigh, N.C.: Edwards and Broughton, Printers and Binders, 1903.

United Textile Workers of America. *Proceedings of the Annual Convention, 1903–1905.*

NEWSPAPERS AND JOURNALS

Alabama Sentinel (Birmingham), 1887–1889.

American Federationist, 1894–1905.

Atlanta Constitution, 1886–1889, 1896–1903.

Augusta Chronicle, 1886–1903.

Carolina Spartan (Spartanburg, S.C.), 1885–1889, 1900–1905.

Charleston News and Courier, 1886–1889, 1890–1903.

Columbia (S.C.) *State,* 1891–1905.

Columbus (Ga.) *Enquirer-Sun,* 1886–1889, 1895–1903.

Columbus (Ga.) *Herald,* 1898–1899.

Fayetteville (N.C.) *Messenger,* 1887–1888.

Greenville (S.C.) *Enterprise and Mountaineer,* 1880–1889.

Greenville (S.C.) *Daily News,* 1898–1899.

Journal of United Labor, 1880–1889.

New York Times, 1896–1905.

Raleigh News and Observer, 1886–1905.

Rock Hill (S.C.) *Herald,* 1890–1902.

Published Secondary Sources

ARTICLES

DOUTY, HARRY M. "Early Labor Organization in North Carolina: 1880–1900." *South Atlantic Quarterly* 34 (July 1935), 260–68.

JOLLEY, HARLEY E. "The Labor Movement in North Carolina: 1880–1922." *North Carolina Historical Review* 30 (July 1953), 354–75.

MEYERS, FREDERICK. "The Knights of Labor in the South." *Southern Economic Journal* 6 (April 1940), 479–87.

MOGER, ALLEN WESLEY. "Industrial and Urban Progress in Virginia from 1880 to 1900." *Virginia Magazine of History and Biography* 46 (July 1958), 307–336.

SHAFFER, E. T. H. "Southern Mill People." *Yale Review* 19 (December 1929), 325–40.

SPILLANE, RICHARD. "Striking Facts about Southern Cotton Mills and Cotton Mill Employees." *Manufacturer's Record* 86 (December 11, 1924), 195–96.

THOMPSON, HOLLAND. "The Civil War and Social and Economic Changes." *Annals of the American Academy of Political and Social Science* 58 (January 1931), 11–20.

WILLIAMSON, GUSTAVUS G. "South Carolina Cotton Mills and the Tillman Movement." *Proceedings of the South Carolina Historical Association, 1949.* Columbia, S.C.: By the Association, 1949, 36–49.

BOOKS

ARNETT, ALEX MATHEWS. *The Populist Movement in Georgia.* Columbia University Studies in History, Economics, and Public Law, vol. 104, no. 1. New York: Longmans, Green and Company, 1922.

BONNER, JAMES C. "The Alliance Legislature of 1890." *Studies in Georgia History and Government.* Edited by James C. Bonner and Lucien E. Roberts. Athens, Ga.: University of Georgia Press, 1954, 510–28.

BRUCE, PHILIP ALEXANDER. *The Rise of the New South.* Vol. 17. *The History of North America.* Edited by Guy Carlton Lee. Philadelphia: Barrie and Sons, 1905.

CAMPBELL, CHARLES S. *Special Business Interests and the Open Door Policy.* Yale Historical Publications, vol. 53. New Haven, Conn.: Yale University Press, 1951.

CASH, WILBUR J. *The Mind of the South.* New York: Alfred A. Knopf, 1941.

COLEMAN, MCALISTER. *Eugene V. Debs: A Man Unafraid.* New York: Greenberg Publisher, 1930.

COMMONS, JOHN R., ed. *History of Labor in the United States.* Vol. 2. New York: Macmillan Company, 1921.

COPELAND, MELVIN T. *The Cotton Manufacturing Industry of the United States.* Harvard Economic Studies, vol. 8. Cambridge, Mass.: Harvard University Press, 1912.

DAVIDSON, ELIZABETH H. *Child Labor Legislation in the Southern Textile States.* Chapel Hill: University of North Carolina Press, 1939.

DUNN, ROBERT WARD AND HARDY, JACK. *Labor and Textiles.* New York: International Publishers, 1931.

FINE, NATHAN. *Labor and Farmer Parties in the United States: 1828–1928.* New York: Russell and Russell, 1961.

FONER, PHILIP S. *History of the Labor Movement in the United States.* Vol. 2. *From the Founding of the American Federation of Labor to the Emergence of American Imperialism.* New York: International Publishers, 1955.

————. *History of the Labor Movement in the United States.* Vol. 3. *The Policies and Practices of the American Federation of Labor: 1900–1909.* New York: International Publishers, 1964.

GILMAN, GLENN. *Human Relations in the Industrial Southeast.* Chapel Hill: University of North Carolina Press, 1956.

GINGER, RAY. *The Bending Cross: A Biography of Eugene Victor Debs.* New Brunswick, N.J.: Rutgers University Press, 1949.

GROB, GERALD N. *Workers and Utopia: a Study of Ideological Conflict in the American Labor Movement.* Evanston, Ill.: Northwestern University Press, 1961.

HERRING, HARRIET L. *Welfare Work in Mill Villages: The Story of Extra-Mill Activities in North Carolina.* Chapel Hill: University of North Carolina Press, 1929.

HOFSTADTER, RICHARD. *Social Darwinism In American Thought.* 2d rev. ed. Boston: Beacon Press, 1959.

JACOBS, WILLIAM PLUMER. *The Pioneer: Biographical Sketches of North and South Carolina Textile Manufacturers.* Clinton, S.C.: Jacobs and Company, 1935.

JENKINS, JOHN WILBUR. *James B. Duke, Master Builder.* New York: George H. Doran Company, 1927.

KENNEDY, STEPHEN J. *Profits and Losses in Textiles: Cotton Textile Financing Since the War.* New York: Harper and Brothers, Publishers, 1930.

LAHNE, HERBERT J. *The Cotton Mill Worker.* New York: Farrar and Rinehart, 1944.

LEFLER, HUGH T. AND NEWSOME, ALBERT R. *North Carolina: The History of a Southern State.* Chapel Hill: University of North Carolina Press, 1954.

LEMERT, BEN F. *The Cotton Textile Industry of the Southern Appalachian Piedmont.* Chapel Hill: University of North Carolina Press, 1933.

LINCOLN, SAMUEL B. *Lockwood Greene: The History of an Engineering Business, 1832–1958.* Brattleboro, Vt.: Stephen Greene Press, 1960.

MCILWAINE, SHIELDS. *The Southern Poor White from Lubberland to Tobacco Road.* Norman, Okla.: University of Oklahoma Press, 1939.

MARSHALL, F. RAY. *Labor in the South.* Cambridge: Harvard University Press, 1967.

———. *The Negro and Organized Labor.* New York: John Wiley and Sons, 1965.

MITCHELL, BROADUS. *The Rise of Cotton Mills in the South.* Johns Hopkins University Studies in Historical and Political Science, vol. 39, no. 2. Baltimore: Johns Hopkins University Press, 1921.

———. *William Gregg: Factory Master of the Old South.* Chapel Hill: University of North Carolina Press, 1928.

MITCHELL, BROADUS AND MITCHELL, GEORGE S. *The Industrial Revolution in the South.* Baltimore: Johns Hopkins University Press, 1930.

MITCHELL, GEORGE S. *Textile Unionism and the South.* Chapel Hill: University of North Carolina Press, 1931.

NOBLIN, STUART. *Leonidas LaFayette Polk, Agrarian Crusader.* Chapel Hill: University of North Carolina Press, 1949.

ODUM, HOWARD W. *Southern Regions of the United States.* Chapel Hill: University of North Carolina Press, 1936.

PERLMAN, SELIG AND TAFT, PHILIP. *Labor Movements.* Vol. 4. *History of Labor in the United States.* Edited by John R. Commons. New York: Macmillan Company, 1935.

POLLACK, NORMAN. *The Populist Response to Industrial America: Midwestern Populist Thought.* New York: W. W. Norton and Company, 1966.

POTWIN, MARJORIE ADELLA. *Cotton Mill People of the Piedmont: A Study in Social Change.* New York: Columbia University Press, 1927.

QUINT, HOWARD H. *The Forging of American Socialism: Origins of the Modern Movement.* Columbia: University of South Carolina Press, 1953.

Research and Education Department, The United Textile Workers of America. *The AFL Textile Workers: A History of the United Textile Workers of America.* Washington, D.C.: n.p., 1950.

REYNOLDS, LLOYD GEORGE AND KILLINGSWORTH, CHARLES C. *Trade Union Publications: The Official Journals, Convention Proceedings, and Constitutions of International Unions and Federations, 1850–1941.* 3 vols. Baltimore: Johns Hopkins University Press, 1944–1945.

ROBERTSON, BEN. *Red Hills and Cotton: An Upcountry Memory.* Columbia: University of South Carolina Press, 1960.

SIMPKINS, FRANCIS BUTLER. *Pitchfork Ben Tillman, South Carolinian.* Baton Rouge: Louisiana State University Press, 1944.

SIMPSON, WILLIAM HAYS. *Southern Textile Communities.* Charlotte, N.C.: Dowd Press, 1948.

SMITH, ROBERT SIDNEY. *Mill on the Dan.* Durham, N.C.: Duke University Press, 1960.

SMITH, THOMAS R. *The Cotton Textile Industry of Fall River, Massachusetts.* New York: King's Crown Press, 1944.

SPERO, STERLING D. AND HARRIS, ABRAM L. *The Black Worker: The Negro and the Labor Movement.* New York: Columbia University Press, 1931.

STARNES, GEORGE T. AND HAMM, JOHN. *Some Phases of Labor Relations in Virginia.* New York: D. Appleton-Century Company, 1934.

TAFT, PHILIP. *The A.F. of L. in the Time of Gompers.* New York: Harper and Brothers, Publishers, 1957.

THOMPSON, HOLLAND. *From the Cotton Field to the Cotton Mill: A Study of Industrial Transition in North Carolina.* New York: Macmillan Company, 1906.

TINDALL, GEORGE B. *South Carolina Negroes: 1877–1900.* Columbia: University of South Carolina Press, 1960.

VANCE, RUPERT B. *Human Geography of the South: A Study in Regional Resources and Human Adequacy.* Chapel Hill: University of North Carolina Press, 1932.

WARE, NORMAN J. *The Labor Movement in the United States: 1860–1895.* New York: D. Appleton and Company, 1929.

WESLEY, CHARLES H. *Negro Labor in the United States, 1850–1925: A Study in Economic History.* New York: Vanguard Press, 1927.

WINSTON, GEORGE T. *A Builder of the New South: Being the Story of the Life Work of Daniel A. Tompkins.* Garden City, N.Y.: Doubleday, Page and Co., 1920.

WOODWARD, C. VANN. *Origins of the New South: 1877–1913.* Vol. 9. *A History of the South.* Edited by Wendell H. Stephenson and E. Merton Coulter. Baton Rouge: Louisiana State University Press, 1951.

————. *Tom Watson, Agrarian Rebel.* New York: Oxford University Press, 1963.

WYLLIE, IRVIN G. *The Self-Made Man in America: The Myth of Rags to Riches.* New Brunswick, N.J.: Rutgers University Press, 1954.

YOUNG, MARJORIE, ed. *Textile Leaders of the South.* Columbia, S.C.: R. L. Bryan Company, 1963.

Unpublished Secondary Sources

BROOKS, ROBERT R. R. "The United Textile Workers of America." Ph.D. dissertation, Yale University, 1935.

CANNON, BERNARD M. "Social Deterrents to Unionization of Southern Cotton Textile Workers." Ph.D. dissertation, Harvard University, 1951.

CLAY, HOWARD B. "Daniel Augustus Tompkins, An American Bourbon." Ph.D. dissertation, University of North Carolina, 1950.

DAVIS, RICHARD H., JR. "The Role of South Carolina's Cotton Manufacturers on the United States' Far Eastern Policy: 1897–1902." Master's thesis, University of South Carolina, 1966.

DE LORME, CHARLES D. "Development of the Textile Industry in Spartanburg County from 1816 to 1900." Master's thesis, University of South Carolina, 1963.

DOUTY, HARRY M. "The North Carolina Industrial Worker: 1880–1930." Ph.D. dissertation, University of North Carolina, 1936.

EVANS, MERCER G. "The History of the Organized Labor Movement in Georgia." Ph.D. dissertation, University of Chicago, 1929.

GRAVES, LAWRENCE B. "The Beginning of the Cotton Textile Industry in Newberry County." Master's thesis, University of South Carolina, 1947.

LAHNE, HERBERT J. "Labor in the Cotton Mill: 1865–1900." Master's thesis, Columbia University, n.d.

MARSHALL, F. RAY. "History of Labor Organization in the South." Ph.D. dissertation, University of California, Berkeley, 1955.

PIERPONT, ANDREW W. "Development of the Textile Industry in Alamance County, North Carolina." Ph.D. dissertation, University of North Carolina, 1953.

SMITH, FENELON DE VERE. "The Economic Development of the Textile Industry in the Columbia, South Carolina, Area from 1790 Through 1916." Ph.D. dissertation, University of Kentucky, 1952.

STOKES, ALLEN. "John H. Montgomery: A Pioneer Southern Industrialist." Master's thesis, University of South Carolina, 1967.

THOMPSON, WILLIAM W., JR. "A Managerial History of a Cotton Textile Firm: Spartan Mills, 1888–1958." Ph.D. dissertation, University of Alabama, 1962.

WALLACE, DAVID DUNCAN. "One Hundred Years of Gregg and Graniteville." William Gregg Foundation, Graniteville, South Carolina, 1954.

WILLIAMSON, GUSTAVUS G., JR. "Cotton Manufacturing in South Carolina: 1865–1892." Ph.D. dissertation, Johns Hopkins University, 1954.

———. "Southern Cotton Manufacturers in a Year of Decision, 1886." (Unpublished MS in the possession of the author.)

Index

Paternalism and Protest was
composed in Linotype Times Roman
with Times Roman display type by
The Book Press, Brattleboro, Vermont.
The entire book was printed by
offset lithography.